Peace Through Media

This book is part of the Peter Lang Media and Communication list.
Every volume is peer reviewed and meets
the highest quality standards for content and production.

PETER LANG
New York • Bern • Frankfurt • Berlin
Brussels • Vienna • Oxford • Warsaw

Leara D. Rhodes

Peace Through Media

PETER LANG
New York • Bern • Frankfurt • Berlin
Brussels • Vienna • Oxford • Warsaw

Library of Congress Cataloging-in-Publication Data
Names: Rhodes, Leara.
Title: Peace through media / Leara D. Rhodes.
Description: New York: Peter Lang.
Includes bibliographical references.
Identifiers: LCCN 2015023826 | ISBN 978-1-4331-3024-3 (pbk.: alk. paper)
ISBN 978-1-4539-1685-8 (ebook pdf)
ISBN 978-1-4331-4096-9 (epub) | ISBN 978-1-4331-4097-6 (mobi)
Subjects: LCSH: War—Press coverage.
Social conflict—Press coverage.
Mass media and peace.
Journalistic ethics.
Journalism—Political aspects.
Classification: LCC PN4784.W37 R495 | DDC 070.4/333—dc23
LC record available at https://lccn.loc.gov/2015023826
DOI 10.3726/978-1-4539-1685-8

Bibliographic information published by **Die Deutsche Nationalbibliothek**.
Die Deutsche Nationalbibliothek lists this publication in the "Deutsche
Nationalbibliografie"; detailed bibliographic data are available
on the Internet at http://dnb.d-nb.de/.

The paper in this book meets the guidelines for permanence and durability
of the Committee on Production Guidelines for Book Longevity
of the Council of Library Resources.

Peter Lang Publishing, Inc., New York
29 Broadway, 18th floor, New York, NY 10006
www.peterlang.com

Printed in the United States of America

To my girls:
Jessica Ben Palumbo, Christiana Ben Palumbo,
and Viviana Donata Palumbo.

May they all live in peace.

CONTENTS

PREFACE

Why Peace and Why Media

Within these chapters, I hope to demonstrate that peace journalism can be taught and successfully implemented to keep the values that journalists have used for decades. Contorting these values currently are the stressors for journalists of adding new social media platforms, working with the fragmentation of traditional media, and including citizens, often activists who are not trained to use journalistic values of truth telling and transparency of information. With these stressors, journalists are trying to find ways to tell truthful stories that contribute to a continued democracy.

This book is a companion to standard journalism reporting texts; students need to know what it takes to work internationally especially with the global use of social media. The goal of this book is to argue that teaching peace journalism along with basic reporting skills is a way to facilitate peace, a basic human need. The people who play such a large role in creating how and what a community thinks about are journalists and they can help facilitate peace. In helping journalists understand how they are uniquely empowered to facilitate positive peace, this text defines *peace journalism* (Chapter 2); places the term in a theoretical concept (Chapter 3); introduces populations affected by conflict (Chapter 4); defines violence and introduces the nature of contemporary warfare and media's contribution to covering violence (Chapter 5); examines journalists' work environment and how they are working with citizen journalists (Chapter 6); identifies how to search for truth when lying, bias and propaganda are so prevalent (Chapter 7); explores how activists are using media to cover conflict (Chapter 8); identifies how governments and institutions are using media during conflict (Chapter 9); proposes an action plan with examples on how to implement peace journalism (Chapter 10); and facilitates a dialogue to motivate journalists and conflict-sensitive training professionals to work together (Chapter 11) to continue humankind's efforts to find a more peaceful world through the work of a perfectly placed legion of professionals.

ACKNOWLEDGMENTS

There are many people to thank, but two are special and I could not have done this without them. First, to Jessica Palumbo, who encouraged me to write the book, applauded my journey through the writing, and then read pages and offered wonderful comments that made the text much easier to read. Thank you. And to Sophie Barnes, who handled any request with professional care. Thank you.

I developed the concept for this book years ago through my work with media in Haiti, Trinidad, and Tanzania, but developed it further after meeting with the faculty members at the University of Ulster in Belfast and in Derry/Londonderry. The project would not have been possible without the faith of my editor, Mary Savigar, senior acquisitions editor at Lang. Thanks also to Dr. Janice Hume, chair of the Journalism Department at the Grady College of Journalism and Mass Communication at the University of Georgia, who gave me release time in the form of a Grady Fellowship so that the book could be written.

· 1 ·

SEARCH FOR PEACE

Why Peace Journalism Is Needed Today

Peace journalism is needed today because humans have been grappling with violence and the pursuit of peace since the beginning of time. Humans have been a violent species. In addition, while humankind has found a way to memorialize its triumphs and travails over the past few millennia, now is the time when modern journalists are uniquely positioned within our complex society to foster the development of peace by selecting frames to record our collective experience. This activity can be carried out only at the most intricate of crossroads because the definitions of peace shift across time and culture and because the cultures and groups on various sides of conflict shift as well; therefore, the pursuit of peace is more difficult. Before it is possible to fully explore the tools and techniques a journalist can use to achieve this end, it is important to investigate the shifting definitions of peace and why humanity will benefit if journalists are more invested in fostering a peaceful resolution to conflict.

The word *peace* in English originated in the eleventh century from the Anglo-French word *pes*, which evolved itself from the Latin *pax* and the Old French world *pais*. It is defined as reconciliation, silence, agreement (Peace, nd). The English word came into use in various personal greetings from c. 1300 as a result of Hebrew speakers substituting it for instances in which they would have used *shalom* (stemming from a verb meaning *to restore*).

There are various definitions of peace but two definitions occupy most of the discussions on peace: (1) peace as the absence of war or personal violence (so-called *negative* peace) and (2) positive peace, which is defined as the integration of human society or the absence of structural violence. The importance of positive peace over negative peace is underscored by the 2003 comments of David Adams, retired director of UNESCO, when he observed that a culture of peace needs more than the absence of war; it requires a profound cultural transformation.

Galtung (1990) suggested that, since there are many human cultures, there had to be other concepts of peace. This is underscored by the evolution of the word *peace* and its use in English. Therefore, any discussion of peace must be cognizant of any applicable cultural context. Nonetheless, in an apparent attempt to set a baseline for the international community to pursue, the United Nations has defined a *culture of peace* as:

> (…) values, attitudes, and behaviors that reflect and inspire social interaction and sharing based on the principles of freedom, justice, and democracy, all human rights, tolerance and solidarity, that reject violence and endeavor to prevent conflicts by tackling their root causes to solve problems through dialogue and negotiation and that guarantee the full exercise of all rights and the means to participate fully in the development process of their society. (United Nations, 1999)

Unsurprisingly, the United Nations (UN) has contributed significantly to the institutionalization of the word *peace*. The stated aims of the UN are to facilitate cooperation in international law, international security, economic development, social progress, human rights, and achievement of world peace. By institutionalizing peace, it was hoped that all-consuming conflict like the world wars could be avoided. This institutionalization also developed the academic study of international relations. Additionally, other groups and organizations within modern society, not national governments, began to specialize in the production of peace.

So Who Is in Charge of Making Peace Happen?

The first response to who is in charge of making peace happen is usually policy makers within national governments. The military, as controlled by those policy makers, is the next response. A third response, though, are journalists, who are finding that they are placed in the middle of conflict. Through their in-depth coverage, search for truth and ethical approaches, they know a lot about war; but, they do not know much about peace. In fact, conflict around the world is being covered in the same way since wars started: who wins, who loses and by how much.

The concept that journalists can help to facilitate peace is not a new idea. After World War II, journalists joined in to support the concept of peace journalism. This was a time when traditional journalists covering conflicts began to believe there had to be a better or at least a different way of writing about war rather than following a country's foreign policy or reinforcing the idea that the conflict was between *them* and *us*.

In the past, American correspondents followed military protocol for how to cover conflict and went along with American foreign policy until the Vietnam War. Reporters began to cover the conflict in Vietnam in ways that were not positive to the US government; therefore, the US government accused media of bringing the atrocities of the war into American homes and thus ending the war without the United States winning the war. Media were to blame.

To counteract what the military felt had been damaging reporting during the Vietnam War, media were blocked from entering Grenada in 1983 for three days during *Operation Urgent Fury*. President Ronald Reagan issued an Executive Order and the US military invaded Grenada supposedly to protect 1000 American medical students on the island but really to stop the Cubans from being more established in Grenada, deemed too close for comfort for communist proliferation. The Cubans had been brought in to assist the then-leftist government of Maurice Bishop to build a major airport and to provide security for the island nation. This procedure to delay media coverage of the invasion by the US military was considered a success. Through executive orders, US President Ronald Reagan created a press pool to formally organize media covering conflict involving the United States.

Initially the US Pentagon planned to create an 11-person contingency press pool that would include reporters for television, radio, the news agencies and magazines, but not newspapers. After protests from newspaper groups, the Pentagon altered the plan to include one newspaper reporter, bringing the number of positions in the pool to 12 (Halloran, 1984). The press pool members were to share their reports with other news organizations. In a capitalist society built on market competition, having professional journalists share information was not a good idea.

The press pool concept was first used in Panama as conflicts erupted through Central America. Members of the press pool were taken to the area of conflict after the battle. On-the-ground freelancers, other foreign correspondents, and locals got the story long before the members of the American press pool, an epic problem for producers of news. This press pool concept continued between the US military and media. Coverage was limited of conflict until the Gulf War, often referred to as the first video war. Though few members of the press were there to offer live coverage, the conflict was covered on televised video so much so that academic colleagues in Jamaica did not believe there even was a Gulf War because all they saw were images of the one reporter, Peter Arnett, standing on a rooftop with a background of missiles firing and air-raid sirens blaring. These images were seen to be contrived and not real. Arnett, however, became a household name worldwide providing live coverage from Baghdad. Working for CNN in 1991, Arnett was one of 40 foreign journalists in Baghdad but CNN had the technology to communicate outside of Iraq.

The press pool concept was used again to cover the conflict in the former Yugoslavia among the Muslims, Croats, and Serbs. Reporters from other countries were not included in the press pool and the American reporters were advised to cover the conflict from the US foreign policy point of view. There were no US ground troops initially in the conflict. The reporters, who were on the ground in the former Yugoslavia, heard that rapes within the refugee camps were being used as a war tactic. The journalists departed from US policy and began writing more investigative reports of what was happening. Amnesty International confirmed that all three warring sides in the conflict had committed widespread rape and human rights abuses (Poggioli, 1999). The conflict was difficult to cover. Sylvia Poggioli (1999) wrote:

> Covering the disintegration of Yugoslavia has often forced reporters to act as scouts without compasses in a completely unknown terrain. Reporters have had to wade through the complex cultural, historical and political geography of these conflicts. And very few had the necessary instruments. With the end of the Cold War, a whole set of principles of analysis had become useless, and reporters had to confront new problems that most of them had never explored before, such as ethnic self-assertion, tribalism, religious conflicts and the rights and limits to self-determination. (1999, para. 1)

Stressors on Journalists Covering Conflict

These conflicts and the use of a press pool created a dialogue among journalists, media professionals, audiences, and conflict-resolution experts to build a consensus and to reassess how to cover conflict. This dialogue initiated a unified belief that something was seriously wrong with contemporary media coverage of war and conflicts. Within this discussion was the additional problem of traditional media refocusing on industry economics during the 1980s. Media owners wanted to make money. Managements began adding MBAs in the newsroom to quantify news. Many of the *mom & pop* newspapers sold their family papers to the newspaper chains. Then, in the early part of the twenty-first century, there were major layoffs at media institutions, a decline in revenues, readjustments to the business models and a total rethinking of how to provide news. The industry has been in flux. However, as society has adjusted to the social media revolution and evidence is being produced to indicate that only entertainment and reality shows are viable to an audience who wants information simple, short and often, there is a reawakening of media professionals and academics that a change is needed if media are to provide information for audiences to make decisions related to a democratic society.

There are many stressors for working journalists such as time away from family and friends, pressures of deadlines and lack of funds and resources. Added to this list are the following stressors: fragmenting of media, adding social media platforms, learning new technologies, introducing citizen activists, using media to incite violence, changing the media business model, ongoing debate on truth seeking and objectivity, and romanticizing foreign correspondents in the academy and in the media institutions. It is the argument of this book that these stressors can be lessened with more training and sensitivity toward how conflicts are reported.

Fragmented Media Breaks Mirror Reflecting Society

Communication theorists suggest that media offer a view of the world and media can reflect society. If that is true, then our society is a reality show with games, dancing, and screaming news shows with people shouting over the top of each other. There is a crisis in journalism. A report, *The Reconstruction of American Journalism* (2009), verifies the problem. The report cites the following problems: decreasing circulations, shrinking profits, shortening television news, disappearing media outlets, reducing staff, and organizations with fewer correspondents, fewer foreign offices (Mancini, 2013, p. 44). In the Western world where there are lots of media choices with different channels, websites, radio stations, magazine and newspapers, there is a new problem of reaching target audiences. However, according to Martin Maximino (2014), a more fragmented media environment may prompt citizens to seek out more like-minded news sources, contributing to the reinforcement of prior beliefs and opinions and exacerbating polarization. Thus, an *echo chamber*, Fox News and MSNBC are often cited as examples, can make certain views even louder and more pronounced among a group of like-minded individuals. These media dynamics are thought to be at work as shifts in public opinion are viewed on topics such as climate change (Maximino, 2014, para. 2). Having a fragmented media means more work for the journalist in getting information to segmented often narrowcast audiences. The continued argument in this book is that the media mirror is broken and new processes must be developed to reach audiences with information deemed important, that is if one believes that the *public* needs to be informed in order to make democratic decisions.

Tweet: Social Media Platforms Increase Journalists' Work

Historically a journalist covered a major story in a conflict area with an entourage of people: photographer, fixer, driver, translator, and then videographer; each with equipment. The journalist was to tell a story. As to be demonstrated in the chapter on a journalist's work, that has changed. A journalist has to do it all, do it with small equipment, and do it fast. Additionally, journalists must create a variety of ways to tell the same story using different platforms. Journalists follow other tweets, create their own tweets, and move through many websites and blogs to locate sources, information, and facts. Tweets mean more work for the journalists but not necessarily more money. The Internet, Twitter, and blogs are dramatically changing the nature, procedures, and norms of traditional professional journalism (Mancini, 2013, p. 47).

New Technologies to Learn: They Never Stop

Added to a journalist's stressors is technological innovation. Though journalists and media scholars have debated if technology has changed the journalism landscape (Livingston & Bennett, 2003), change has happened and organizations have stepped in to assist journalists with methods of how to handle reporting using new technology. The European Union and the National Endowment for Democracy, a private, nonprofit foundation dedicated to the growth and strengthening of democratic institutions around the world, funded by the US Congress, created the Journalist Survival Guide (2012) that includes nine lessons in English and Arabic. These include how to defend against hacking and malware, how to permanently delete sensitive data, how to store, and share sensitive information and how to ensure mobile security. In addition, while new media technologies do not alter the fundamental tenets of journalism, they do change user behavior and hence news room paradigms, discussions, and decisions. The nature of information has also changed to be more entertaining, interactive, and instantaneous. Common today are the blogs, vlogs, YouTube, SMS (short message service), Twitter, Instagram, and chat apps. These technologies transcend the conventional nation state boundaries and have the capacity to absorb audiences at a global level (Aslam, 2011, p. 4). Additionally, with the Internet, the number of possible sources of information increases and, therefore, the number of consumers is distributed across a larger number of media outlets. This shapes new patterns of consumption that either give life to new consumers or move traditional consumers from old to new media. Mass media fragmentation generates audience segmentation. These new technologies are changing daily. A journalist has to learn the new technology and how to connect in order to work effectively.

Citizen Activists Change Sourcing for Journalists

As audience trust has declined for traditional media, citizen reporting has increased, particularly in areas of conflict where traditional journalists have been barred or the area is seen as too dangerous to enter or where journalists are not trusted to report all viewpoints. User generated content (UGC) has emerged as a result of losing trust in traditional media. Media houses have handled the new UGC in a variety of ways. One way is to subject the UGC to gate keeping practices used by traditional media, forcing the content into specific frames that preserve traditional news routines, thereby undercutting UGC's revolutionary purposes (Ali & Fahmy, 2013). Other media houses are creating their own social media sites, blogs, vlogs, and YouTube, to counter information contributed by UGCs. A journalist must now write a blog, post on websites, follow UGC blogs and postings for additional sources, run down these sources, verify information, and untangle rumors.

How Media May Be Used to Incite Violence: Makes Shouting Fire a Minor Offense

Media have been used to incite violence. Not a new tool, at all, but recognized globally as dangerous with the nationalistic wars of the 1990s of Rwanda, Bosnia and Sierra Leone. Within these countries, media disseminated hate messages resulting in killings (Bratić, 2008, p. 487). The Rwandan Radio-Télévision Libre des Milles Collines played a crucial role in initiating the slaughter of more than half a million people in less than 100 days. The broadcast messages explicitly called for the murder of the Tutsi population. In another part of the world, Bosnia, electronic and print media helped to promote ethnic conflict by promoting the ideology of nationalism with the cumulative impact of biased coverage fueling the hatred over a long period of time (Aslam, 2011). Taylor and Kent (2000) described the role of nationalist media in the Bosnian conflict as facilitators of war. Within Sierra Leone, an article in the *African Champion* accused the opposition Sierra Leone People's Party (SLPP) of using media to destabilize the ruling All People's Congress (APC) through dangerous propaganda. The report cited a meeting held at the residence of the SLPP Secretary-General, Jacob Jusu Saffa, where it was agreed to launch a propaganda campaign in the media to discredit the APC and cost them the confidence of the people. Pro-SLPP newspapers, radio, and the Internet were to be used to spread lies and hate messages that would give the APC a bad name. A source who attended the meeting reportedly said the SLPP members were determined that the APC did not have a smooth leadership during their tenure in office ("SLPP allegedly plots," 2007). Using media to incite violence places the journalist in unsafe positions and creates more distrust of media among the audiences.

Changing Media Business Model:
Does Not Increase a Reporter's Pay Check

Acknowledging that the media business model is changing contributes to the problem of how media may cover conflict. Media are businesses and must make a profit. Parry (2003) suggests that "media owners historically have enforced their political views and other preferences by installing senior editors whose careers depend on delivering a news product that fits with the owner's prejudices" (Parry, 2003, para. 13). Fiji journalism academic, Mosese Waqa, believes the mainstream media have been rejecting peace journalism for a decade simply because conflict sells (Aslam, 2011, p. 120). Chief among these reasons are that peace, unlike conflict, often does not serve the political interests of the influential actors around the media, and does not sell media content the way conflict does (Ishak & Ozohu-Sulaiman, 2012, p. 25). Journalism trainers and media developers in fragile or emerging nation states recognize traditional training is insufficient. These media workers must overcome the legacies of authoritarian government corruption, poverty, and absence of media diversity, editorial independence and a media-supportive legal infrastructure (Howard, 2015, para. 23). In addition, with the decline of paying for foreign correspondents in areas experiencing conflict, the journalists covering these conflicts are freelancers, stringers and local journalists, who must take the same risks of covering conflict but without the support of a media institution.

The Ongoing Debate on Truth Seeking
and Objectivity—or Not

Another stressor for journalists is based on the ideology attached to being a journalist in the first place and that is being objective. However, the dangers of objectivity, according to Lynch and McGoldrick (2005, p. 210), are that journalists can be biased, favor official sources, record events rather than the process, and encourage dualism: a winner and a loser. Though objectivity has been debated in journalism classrooms for decades, a more dangerous result of abandoning objectivity might mean that the audience loses all sense of who to believe and why. That loss of trust will have devastating results on how democracies may continue to exist. Qualified excellent journalists have placed themselves on war fronts for many reasons, none of which have to do with not telling the facts or attempting to find out what is true. However, journalists who believe in being objective may not be looking in the right places to reach such a judgment, especially if they take someone in power or position's word for it. The argument in this book is that audiences do not trust the media; therefore, another way must be sought to cover conflict.

Will Foreign Correspondents Please Take a Bow and Autograph Our Book

Foreign correspondents perform heroic work in the field. They put their lives on the line to provide information on conflict. In response to a social science colleague who thumbed his nose at media research in Haiti, I said, "I do not know of many sociologists who have died just doing their job. I personally know several journalists who were killed doing their job." Yes, foreign correspondents have a tough job, a stressful one, and a life-changing one. However, foreign correspondents often are seen as romanticized figures. Chris Hedges, an American war correspondent remembered his experiences in the Vietnam and the Gulf War: "I didn't go to the war to be objective; I wanted to be the champion of the weaker side" (Aslam, 2011, p. 3). The media industry makes heroes/heroines out of war correspondents. The glamour and romance which follows foreign correspondents on their return from war makes them the "role model" that all young journalists must aspire to (Aslam, 2011, p. 3), an unrealistic pose to hold for long periods of times as demonstrated with the firing of Peter Arnett, who accepted an interview on state-owned Iraq television. His celebrity status was cited as to why he did so (Cozens, 2003, para. 1).

With professional journalists advocating for change in covering conflicts, the fragmentation of traditional media and erosion of the business model, introduction of new technology, and the addition of citizen reporting, another paradigm shift in how conflicts are covered is needed. To make that shift, researchers like Galtung, Lynch, McGoldrick, and Keeble, have advocated peace journalism (Galtung, 1969; McGoldrick & Lynch, 2000; Keeble, Zollman & Tulloch, 2010). The overarching reason for retooling is, according to Mancini (2013) increased commercialization and Internet are dramatically changing the landscape of today's journalism along three main lines that imply important changes in relation to democracy. These are fragmentation, less clear identity of news organization and less defined professional identity (pp. 48–49).

What Peace Journalism Brings to the Negotiation Table

Conflict-sensitive journalism is a powerful tool for journalists seeking to facilitate peace and uses reporting that seeks international standards of media reliability such as accuracy, impartiality or fair balance and social responsibility (Howard, 2015). Media, as the reflection of a community's collective consciousness, can provide an emotional outlet. It can offer solutions and build confidence. Robert Karl Manoff of the Centre for War, Peace, and the Media at New York University, suggests that the regular journalistic activities are precisely the activities which professional conflict mediators conduct (Howard, 2015, para. 5).

Parallels between the roles of professional journalists and professional conflict resolvers, such as diplomats and truce facilitators, are that both journalists and mediators remain independent of the parties to a conflict, though they share similar positions, functions and even attitudes. The main difference between the journalists and mediators is the instinct journalists have for exposing anything secret (Howard, 2015, para. 5).

Peace journalism is considered to be a fringe movement, an incipient project on the periphery of the field of journalism, it is usually ignored outside its own relatively obscure realm of discourse. It attracts only occasional flak from traditional journalists who dismiss it for violating the professional canon of objectivity. At best, it is classified as a type of preventative journalism and a complement to investigative reporting focused on social problems. It is easily dismissed as a journalistic misnomer, a heartfelt complaint that conflates war reporting with peace advocacy (Ivie, 2009, p. 6). Peace journalism is perceived as falling outside the definitions of a journalist's responsibilities in aspiring toward objective reporting, or as being unrealistic (Fröhlich, 2005). However, despite all the criticism, peace journalism is worthy of consideration in the study and research of journalists, possibly as a prerequisite of good journalism and not its antipode.

Last Word: For peace journalism to be successful, journalists say that they, the journalists, need to develop strategies for maintaining quality in news reporting. Such efforts to maintain quality in journalism could be driven by institutions of self-regulation such as journalists' associations and press councils. On the other hand, communication, the discipline that deals with journalism from the viewpoint of a scientific observer, has been concerned with quality management (Hamdy & Gomaa, 2012, p. 491) and with creating audiences. Neither of these considers peace journalism to be important. The argument has shifted, though, to include citizens and governments along with journalists and academics through the introduction of social media. Contemporary warfare and media's contribution to covering violence: direct, structural, and cultural is significant to understanding peace journalism's role in conflict. By understanding how violence has been covered, peace journalism can possibly clarify the issues and lessen the impact of the violence. Jake Lynch, a former reporter for the BBC says, "Peace Journalism is that which abounds in cues and clues to prompt and equip us to 'negotiate' our own readings, to open up multiple meanings, to inspect propaganda and other self-serving representations on the outside" (Lynch, nd, p. 4).

Discussion: Identify military peace forces and the hierarchy of how decisions are being made around the world for peace.

References

Ali, S. R. & Fahmy, S. (2013). Gatekeeping and citizen journalism: The use of social media during the recent uprisings in Iran, Egypt, and Libya. *Media, War & Conflict*, 6(1), 55–69.

Aslam, R. (2011). From challenge to hope. *Media Development*, 58(2), 3–8.

Bratić, V. (2008). Examining peace-oriented media in areas of violent conflict. *International Communication Gazette*, 70, 487–503.

Cozens, C. (2003, March 31). Arnett fired by NBC after Iraqi TV outburst. *The Guardian*. Retrieved from http://www.theguardian.com/media/2003/mar/31/broadcasting.Iraqandthe media1.

Fröhlich, G. (2005). Emotional intelligence in peace journalism: A four-part paper. Section two: The evolution of peace journalism. *Global Media Journal American Edition*, 4(7). Retrieved from http://lass.purduecal.edu/cca/gmj/fa05/gmj-fa05-frohlich.htm.

Galtung, J. (1969). Violence, peace, and peace research. *Journal of Peace Research*, 6(3), 167–191.

Galtung, J. (1990). Cultural violence. *Journal of Peace Research*, 27(3), 291–305.

Hamdy, N. & Gomaa, E.H. (2012). Framing the Egyptian uprising in Arabic language newspapers and social media. *Journal of Communication*, 62, 195–211.

Howard, R. (2015). Global journalism ethics. Center for Journalism Ethics. School of Journalism and Mass Communication, University of Wisconsin-Madison. Retrieved from http://www.journalismethics.info/global_journalism_ethics/conflict_sensitivity_in_practice.htm.

Ishak, S. A. & Ozohu-Sulaiman, Y. (2012, Fall). War journalism and the Israel/Palestine zero-index shift hypothesis. *GmJ: Mediterranean Edition*, 8(1), 21–30. Retrieved from http://

www.academia.edu/2361329/War_Journalism_and_the_Israel_Palestine_Zero-Index_
Shift_Hypothesis.

Ivie, R. (2009). Breaking the spell of war: Peace journalism's democratic prospect. *Javnost-The Public*, 16(4), 5–21.

Journalists Survival Guide (2012). National Endowment for Democracy. Retrieved from www.
video.skeyesmedia.org.

Keeble, R. L., Zollman, F., & Tulloch, J. (2010). *Peace Journalism, War and Conflict Resolution*.
NY: Peter Lang Publishing.

Livingston, S. & Bennett, W. (2003). Gatekeeping, indexing, and live-event news: Is technology altering the construction of news? *Political Communication*, 20(4), 363–380.

Lynch, J. & McGoldrick, A. (2005). Peace journalism in the Holy Land. *Media Development*,
52(1), 47–49.

Lynch, S. (2014, April 22). Behind "students against the coup." *Al-Fanar Media. News & Opinion about Higher Education*. Retrieved from http://www.alfanarmedia.org/2014/04/behind-students-coup/.

Lynch, W. & Bravman, B. (2008). Modern warfare: An overview for world history teachers. *World History Connected*. Retrieved from http://worldhistoryconnected.press.illinois.edu/2.2/bravman.html.

Mancini, P. (2013). Media fragmentation, party system, & democracy. *The International Journal of Press/Politics*, 18(1), 43–60.

Maximino, M. (2014, August 22) Does media fragmentation contribute to polarization? Evidence from lab experiments. Journalist's Resource. Retrieved from http://journalistsresource.org/studies/society/news-media/media-fragmentation-political-polarization-labexperiments#sthash.m4RyMt64.dpuf.

McGoldrick, A. & Lynch, J. (2000). Peace journalism. What is it? How to do it? Reporting the world. Retrieved from https://www.transcend.org/tri/downloads/McGoldrick_Lynch_Peace-Journalism.pdf.

Parry, R. (2003). Price of the "liberal media" myth. *Consortium News*. Retrieved from https://consortiumnews.com/Print/123102a.html.

Peace (nd). Online Etymology Dictionary. Retrieved from www.etymonline.com.

Poggioli, S. (1999). An NPR reporter on the "disinformation trap" in former Yugoslavia. Retrieved from http://kosovo99.tripod.com/trap.htm.

"SLPP allegedly plots to destabilize APC through media" (2007, November 29). Review of Sierra Leone Media Reports, compiled by Public Information Office of UNIOSIL. Retrieved from https://appablog.wordpress.com/2007/11/29/review-of-sierra-leone-media-reports-16/.

Taylor, M. & Kent, M.L. (2000). Media transitions in Bosnia from propagandistic past to uncertain future. *Gazette*, 62(5), 355–378. DOI: 10.1177/0016549200062005002.

United Nations (1999). Declaration and programme of action on a culture of peace. Resolutions adopted by the General Assembly (Resolution 53/243), New York: Autor. UN Resolution, A/RES/52/13, A/RES/52/15, A/RES/53/25, A/RES/53/243, 1999.

· 2 ·

PEACE JOURNALISM

Definition and History

On September 21ˢᵗ, the International Day of Peace, the UN Secretary-General rings the *peace bell* cast from coins donated by 60 countries and placed at the UN headquarters in New York City by the UN Association of Japan in June 1954. Bells have been used as public announcements since the first Celtic bells rang in Ireland and historic bells rang in Russia. In 2012, Big Ben in London rang 40 times in 3 minutes while other church bells, doorbells and bicycle bells rang to welcome the Olympic Games to England. Weddings are ended with the ringing of the church bells. The New Year is welcomed with the ringing of the bells. Bells have become singing icons of news, good and bad, as in Hemingway's *For Whom the Bell Tolls*, and the disaster alerts of tolling the bells. Charles Dickens employed the word *tintinnabulation* in *Dombey and Sons* in 1847: "It was drowned in the tintinnabulation of the gong, which sounding again with great fury, there was a general move towards the dining-room." Tintinnabulation is the lingering sound of the bell that occurs after the bell is struck, a sound that can be linked to peace journalism: What is heard following conflict? Do the bells ring for victory, toll for loss, or linger in peace? In an effort to ring the bell for freedom, journalists must view the peace process differently. This chapter will define peace journalism through the words of scholars who helped to create the concept.

Peace Journalism Defined

Peace journalism is defined by Lynch and McGoldrick (2005) as when editors and reporters make choices of what to report and how to report it that create opportunities for society at large to consider and value non-violent responses to conflict. The Sydney University website defines peace journalism as: "Originally conceived by the eminent peace scholar, Johan Galtung, the peace journalism model is a source of practical options for journalists. Peace journalism shows backgrounds and contexts of conflicts; hears from all sides; explores hidden agendas; highlights peace ideas and initiatives from anywhere at any time" ("Peace Journalism: A Growing Global Debate," nd).

To further explain, like public journalism and development journalism, peace journalism is grounded in communitarian philosophy, namely, the commitment to the idea of civic participation, the understanding of social justice as a moral imperative, and the view that the value and sacredness of the individual are realized only in and through communities (Lee & Maslog, 2005, p. 312). Peace journalism is peace-oriented, looking at conflict formation, causes, and consequences. It avoids labeling good and bad, but has a multiparty orientation. It is also proactive, empathic, as it looks at the invisible effects of war (trauma, damage to society), as well as at the aftermath of the war. It is solution-oriented. This concept differs from how journalists have been covering conflict based on the war journalism concept that is violence-oriented, focusing on differences between the warring parties and showing the visible effects of war. War journalism focuses on elites and treats war as a zero-sum game. It stops reporting and leaves at the end of the war (Galtung, 2006, p. 1).

Galtung suggests that the peace journalism model can give journalists and their audiences a fuller understanding of conflict and alternatives to violence. In this way, journalists can avoid falling prey to political war rhetoric veiled in peace and humanitarian language or other military tactics. Philip Hammond suggests, "American military muscle was thus to be given new meaning in the post-Cold War era, no longer as a guarantor of the West's freedoms against the menace of communism but as the steel fist inside a humanitarian velvet glove" (2007, p. 38, cited in Perez de Fransius, 2014, p. 72). In coverage of the lead-up to the Iraq War, the *velvet glove* appeared in the form of American and British political leaders claiming that an invasion of Iraq was necessary to protect their populations from the threat of Saddam Hussein's weapons of mass destruction and to bring freedom and democracy to the people of Iraq; that argument was barely questioned by the mainstream media (Perez de Fransius,

2014, p. 72; and "Iraq and the Media," 2007). Essentially, peace journalism calls for journalists covering conflicts to use conflict analysis skills.

The Naysayers: Critics of Peace Journalism

To date, the discussion on whether or not peace journalism is a good idea has largely been bogged down in preliminary topics. Is peace journalism for activists or theorists? Can peace journalism prevent violence and war? Some critics argue that peace journalism could adopt the propaganda of the enemy or even become peace propaganda.

Peace journalism is not peace advocacy. Conflict analysis and peace research has shown why an explanation of violence is not the same thing as a justification for it (Yiping, 2011, p. 17). Proponents argue that journalists practicing peace journalism are meant to question war and the military logic, to respect the rights of the enemy and to be self-critical with realistic evaluations of their own rights and intentions (Hamdy and Gomaa, 2012, p. 10). Responsibility of preventing conflicts and making them constructive instead of destructive does not belong to journalists but to everyone. However, because of their profession, journalists are well placed to undertake this responsibility.

Another criticism is that the idea of a socially responsible peace journalism suggests that implementation of peace would be the task of the media when it should be the duty of the policy making class. Reporting on a foreign war or crisis is a challenging activity, a true professional test for a journalist. Media are often criticized for promoting violence by conflict reporting; peace journalism emphasizes the active role of journalists in de-escalation of conflict and encourages journalists to report on peaceful solutions (Oganjanyan, 2011).

Critics of peace research, like Schmidt, in his critical Marxist analysis, "Politics and Peace Research," (1968) argues that value positive concepts of peace were doomed to failure within peace research because it would not be possible for peace researchers to achieve a consensus on what constituted a positive view of peace. However, Schmidt's projections are proven null when *Reporting the World* codified the peace journalism model into a set of four ethical questions to ask of any conflict reporting in UK media (Reporting the World, nd). Scholars in the United Kingdom, Northern Ireland, and Australia have been leaders in researching peace journalism, taking these questions to an international level.

Ethical Questions to Ask of Any Conflict Reporting

- How is violence explained?
- What is the shape of the conflict?
- Is there any news of any efforts or ideas to resolve the conflict?
- What is the role of Britain; the West; the international community in this story?

History/Development from Pacifist to Peace

Where did peace journalism begin? Though part of its roots can be seen in the writings of Thomas Paine and also of Alexis de Tocqueville, peace journalism arguably evolved from the advocacy writings of European and American peace societies that began in the early nineteenth century. However, there is a distinction between pacifist writing, like the documents produced by the peace societies, and peace journalism. The only goal of pacifist writing is non-violence. The goal of peace journalism is to write about all sides of a conflict in an ethical way. The transition of pacifist writing to peace journalism can be understood through the history of peace advocacy, which has been central in US and UK political reform movements.

These political reform organizations recognized the potential power of the written word to sway public opinion on issues of war and peace, starting with the early nineteenth century periodicals such as the *American Peace Society's Advocate of Peace*. Churches became involved with many religious houses creating periodicals such as the *Catholic Worker*, founded in 1933 in New York City by Dorothy Day and Peter Maurin.

Then, Humphrey Moore in the United Kingdom created another pacifist periodical in 1936. Moore wanted his pacifist group to put their ideas and discussions into action by getting their message out to a wider audience. They published the first issue of *Peace News* on June 6, 1936, financed by donations from members of the study group and their friends (Rigby, 2011).

Peace societies were formed in the early nineteenth century in the United States to advocate peace and non-violence such as the American Peace Society (1828), the League of Universal Brotherhood (1846), the Women's International League for Peace and Freedom (U.S. branch, 1915), and the War Resisters League (1923). Central to the work of these organizations was advocacy writing. These groups wanted to get their messages out to audiences in a way that was protected by First Amendment guarantees of freedom of speech and press in the United States.

Following the formation of the US peace societies was the International Convention for the Use of Radio Broadcasting to promote peace, signed in 1936 in Geneva. This document specified that radios should commit and guarantee realistic broadcasting intended to provide peace and international compromise (Kearney, 2007). The UNESCO General Conference adopted the document, "The Declaration on Fundamental Principles Concerning the Contribution to the Mass Media to Strengthening Peace and International Understanding, to the Promotion of Human Rights and to Countering Racialism, Apartheid and Incitement to War," at its twentieth session, Paris, 22 November 1978. This document was viewed as an essential turning point in the process that evolved into peace journalism because this conference provided peace journalism to gain international backing and understanding as to its importance in promoting world peace.

Though the early periodicals described above distributed pacifist messages, each war has found many emerging publications that were antiwar. During the Vietnam War, an underground press emerged that included antiwar periodicals targeted to the drafted US military such as the *Ally* (1968–1974) published in Berkeley, California and directed toward US troops in South Vietnam. Another was *aboveground*, produced by soldiers at Fort Carson, Colorado (August 1969-May 1970). Some 227 underground antiwar newspapers were directed toward US military forces during the Vietnam War. Other influential anti-Vietnam War newspapers included *Ramparts* and *The Guardian* (Vaughn, 2007, p. 378).

Despite the intent, none of these periodicals truly met the need to cover conflict in an ethical way; they had a pacifist point of view. As these publications grew in number, peace journalism as a concept began to develop as participating journalists began to strive to cover all sides of conflict. Then institutions defined how they saw the role of the media in conflict such as the UNESCO Media Declaration from 1979, 102, Art. 3 (quoted by Kempf, 2007, p. 4): "the media have an important contribution to make to the strengthening of peace and international understanding and in countering racialism, apartheid, and incitement to war." The term *culture of peace* is increasingly popular among the leadership of UNESCO (Mandelzis, 2007, p. 2). Within UNESCO, a report, "Many Voices, One World," written by the Irish academic, Sean MacBride, addressed a new information order. "For many journalists, researchers and politicians, particularly in the developing countries....emphasis should be on the need to place events and issues in a broader context, thereby creating awareness and interest...they believe that news and messages essentially can never be neutral...in developing countries, the concept of news appears to need expansion to take in not only events but entire 'processes'" (MacBride, 1980, p. 157).

Then in the 1970s, Johan Galtung began using the term peace journalism. He was the Peace Professor and Director of the TRANSCEND Peace and Development Network. Galtung suggested that peace journalism would be more like health journalism where a good health correspondent would describe a patient's battle against cancerous cells eating away at the body (McGoldrick and Lynch, 2000, p. 10), rather than sports journalism of winners and losers. McGoldrick and Lynch (2000) also suggested alternative names for peace journalism: new journalism, post-realist journalism, solutions journalism, empowerment journalism, conflict analysis journalism, change journalism, holistic journalism, big picture journalism, journalists as mediators, open society journalism, development journalism, analytical journalism, reflective journalism and constructive journalism (p. 3).

Conflict and Peace Forums, a think-tank based in the United Kingdom in a series of international conferences and publications in the late 1990s, further developed the peace journalism model. These publications included *Peace Journalism Option* (1998); *What Are Journalists For?* (1999); and *Using Conflict Analysis in Reporting* (2000).

Another significant meeting pushed the concept of peace journalism further along in discussion within the Academy. During the Conflict and Peace Journalism summer school at Taplow Court in Buckinghamshire, UK (August 25–29, 1997), participants created the Peace Journalism Option. Participants, comprised of journalists, media academics and students from Europe, Africa, Asia, and the United States, divided their time between lectures, workshops, and debate on how to adequately define the role of journalists covering international conflicts. Additionally, significant books explaining peace journalism were released in the ensuing decade to include *Peace Journalism* (2005a) by Lynch and McGoldrick and *Reporting Conflict: New Directions in Peace Journalism* (2010) by Jake Lynch and Johan Galtung.

Many programs around the world now use peace journalism as a core to good journalism. These programs have already created curriculum and policies to further the peace journalism practice. Jeanette Patindol, national coordinator of The Peace and Conflict Journalism Network (PECOJON), offers a process of building a Peace Journalists' Network from the Ground by using a case study of the Philippines (Patindol, nd). For a sampling of programs proposing studies or information on peace journalism, see Exhibit I in the Appendix.

Last Word: Bells have been rung. Cultures have been brought together and conflict has happened. Should governments and institutions put together a culture of peace and identify how peace can be accomplished, then world peace might be realized. This chapter defined the term peace journalism and then using history, traced the development of peace journalism to indicate its differences from pacifist writing.

Discussion: Are there conflicts where peace journalism cannot be used effectively?

References

Galtung, J. (2006). Peace journalism as an ethical challenge. *Global Mediterranean Journal: Mediterranean Edition*, 1(2), 47–53.

Hamdy, N. & Gomaa, E.H. (2012). Framing the Egyptian uprising in Arabic language newspapers and social media. *Journal of Communication*, 62, 195–211.

Perez de Fransius, M. (2014, January). Peace journalism case study: US media coverage of the Iraq war. *Journalism*, 15(1), 72–88.

"Iraq and the Media: A critical timeline (2007, March 17). FAIR/Fairness and Accuracy in Reporting. Retrieved from http://fair.org/take-action/media-advisories/iraq-and-the-media/.

Kearney, M.G. (2007). *The prohibition of propaganda for war in international law* (pp. 28–33). Oxford: Oxford University Press.

Kempf, W. (2007). Peace journalism: A tightrope walk between advocacy journalism and constructive conflict coverage. *Conflict and Communication Online*, 4(4), 1–9.

Lee, S. T. & Maslog, C.C. (2005). War or peace journalism? Asian newspaper coverage of conflicts. *Journal of Communication*, 55(2), 311–329.

Lynch, J. (nd). (2) Peace journalism for journalists. Retrieved from https://www.transcend.org/tms/about-peace-journalism/2-peace-journalism-for-journalists/.

Lynch, J. & McGoldrick, A. (2005). Peace journalism in the Holy Land. *Media Development*, 52(1), 47–49.

MacBride, S. (1980). Many Voices, One World: Report of the International Commission for the Study of Communication Problems, Paris: UNESCO.

McGoldrick, A. & Lynch, J. (2000). Peace journalism. What is it? How to do it? Reporting the world. Retrieved from https://www.transcend.org/tri/downloads/McGoldrick_Lynch_Peace-Journalism.pdf.

Mandelzis, L. (2007). Representations of peace in news discourse: Viewpoint and opportunities for peace journalism. *Conflict and Communication*, 6(10), 1–10.

Oganjanyan, A. (2011). Western media on foreign crisis balance and conflict-sensitivity in foreign reporting with an example of the Russia-Georgia war of 08.08.2008. Master's Thesis. Hamburg. Retrieved from http://www.diplomica.de.

Patindol, J.C. (nd). PECOJON: Building a peace journalists' network from the ground—challenges and lessons learned. Retrieved from https://www.academia.edu/268614/PECOJON_ Building_A_Peace_Journalists_Network_from_the_Ground_Challenges_and_Lessons_ Learned.

"Peace Journalism: A Growing Global Debate" (nd). Centre for Peace and Conflict Studies, Sydney University. Retrieved from http://www.peacejournalism.org/Peace_Journalism/ Welcome.html.

"Reporting the world" (nd). Peacejournalism.org. Retrieved from http://reportingtheworld.net/ Homepage.html.

Rigby, A. (2011, June). Peace news: The early years. Peace News. Retrieved from http:// peacenews.info/node/6198/peace-news-early-year.

Schmidt, H. (1968). Politics and peace research. *Journal of Peace Research*, 5(3), 217–232.

Vaughn, S.L. (2007). Language arts & disciplines. *Encyclopedia of American Journalism*, p. 378.

Yiping, C. (2011). Revisiting peace journalism with a gender lens. Media Development. Toronto, Canada: WACC Publications. Retrieved from http://www.isiswomen.org/index.php? option=com_content&view=article&id=1505:revisiting-peace-journalism-with-a-gender-len&catid=22:movements-within&Itemid=229.

· 3 ·

PEACE JOURNALISM

Theoretical Approaches

Journalists constantly face the challenge of explaining why things happen. According to John Wihbey (2015), this is typically done through quoting relevant sources or officials and letting them do the explaining. If more rigorous thinking and methods are applied, great journalism can do much more than that. The core journalistic enterprise of verifying information and putting it in context has strong parallels with academic research methods: data are gathered through research and statistics, interviews and documents are reviewed, then tentative explanations are proposed and tested to arrive at final, defensible explanations of events (Wihbey, 2015). Being able to reason in this rigorous way about questions presented by current events can create deeper, more informed stories; thus, theory, a set of principles on which the practice of an activity is based, becomes relevant to a journalist.

While there are many definitions of theory, the one most germane to this discussion is as follows: a theory is a set of interrelated concepts, definitions, and propositions that explains or predicts events or situations by specifying relations among variables. Theories are used in social science research where researchers operate in two distinct but highly related worlds: the abstract (the world of concepts/ideas) and the concrete (the empirical/observable world). Theories link these two worlds and provide descriptions, summaries, integration and explanation about what is known from research as well as guidance for additional research and practice that will increase further understanding. Accordingly, through theoretical analysis and the embrace of theory, journalists and other media makers are better positioned to defuse frictions, to lessen violence or even to save lives through their work.

This chapter is a survey of literature using various theories in researching peace journalism. The research provided in this chapter will demonstrate that prior theories, including normative and framing theory, were used for reasons that may no longer apply to peace journalism research. This realization will set the stage introducing another philosophy that arguably, permits peace journalism to flourish. This philosophy includes the public sphere model, a model used to rethink what Hegel and Habermas suggest is the *public* in light of how the media landscape is changing and is affecting how democracies function.

Normative Theories Dominate Peace Journalism Research

The dominant theory discussed in most peace journalism studies is normative theory discussing what media are supposed to be doing. Historically, media were to be ever watchful over governments, institutions, and businesses as an eye for their audiences. Journalists were to be objective, neutral and search for the truth. However, critical theorists opposing the normative view argue that traditional media's claim to value neutrality and to reinforce the status quo simply serves the interest of the powerful (Nicholls, nd). The interests of the powerful are permitted to be served, if the critical theorists are correct, because media workers have traditionally followed a market model allowing ownership to set both the agenda and frames of information.

The market model for media is based on profits and like other industries media are conceptualized as primarily competitors in the marketplace. The market model suggests that society's needs are met through a relatively unregulated process of exchange based on supply and demand. This model calls for private, unregulated ownership of the media and suggests that consumers in the marketplace, not government regulators, will ultimately force companies to behave in a way that best serves the public (Croteau & Hoynes, 2006, p. 17).

This market model does not always work. Consider, for instance, some of the ways that governments and private industry use findings from psychology and sociology. Politicians, interest groups, and private corporations hire psychologists and run focus groups to find the best way to sell their policy initiatives to the public, rather than attempting to enhance public understanding of complex policy issues. Media are used as a tool to manipulate instead of enlighten. Critical theorists claim that knowledge produced this way fosters technocratic control within society and is thus ultimately corrosive to genuine democracy (Nicholls, nd).

The studies that have looked at peace journalism through the lens of normative theory identify expectations of what media and the journalists should be doing to cover conflicts. These studies have provided academics with directives to create curriculum and to perpetuate the idea that journalism ethics are all that are needed to cover conflict. A new paradigm of understanding is viewed as unnecessary. This normative view has been taught to generations of journalists and passed on within the editorial offices of media houses. However, given the introduction of both social media and UGC to cover conflicts, the traditional ethics are no longer common knowledge among all media makers and have been corrupted by using a market model for journalism. Moreover, these traditional ethics have been increasingly viewed as Eurocentric. As conflict seems to know no boundaries, maybe other philosophies and examination of other cultures by western journalists are needed.

If normative theory is the dominant theory used to evaluate peace journalism, then that means that peace journalism is seen as being a special mode of social responsible journalism (Hamdy & Gomaa, 2012, p. 484). Accordingly, journalists should cover conflict with all sides having a voice, being neutral in sourcing and gathering information and explaining the root causes of the conflict. This is when Galtung (1998, p. 7), who developed the term of peace journalism, began labeling the market approach to reporting on conflict as either *peace or conflict journalism* and *war or violence journalism*.

Galtung suggested that peace journalism was to encourage the exploration of what caused the conflict, to make these causes as transparent as possible, to give voice to the conflict parties, and to outline goals to promote a possible win-win situation (Neumann & Fahmy, 2012, p. 178). Peace journalism was to take a proactive stance and to enlarge the timeframe of the reporting to include before (the causes) and after (the healing and resolutions). Peace journalism was to include many people in the community who had a leadership role and who could promote peace initiatives to prevent future conflicts and to promote reconciliation. This was what Galtung expected.

However, the reality has been that coverage of conflict was reduced to a zero-sum game with only one winner in the end (Lynch & Galtung, 2010).

War coverage tended to be reactive with the acts of violence occurring before reporting started. War coverage often focused on elites, including evildoers and warmongers acting in self-interest and pursuing their own goals. War journalism using traditional news value logic and reporting ended once the conflict was over (Galtung & Ruge, 1965).

The research on peace journalism indicates that the normative discourse has shifted from a perspective that views peace journalism as a mere option, offering one of two options of approach (Galtung, 1998), to a more proactive view of peace journalism as a responsibility, contributing to the peacebuilding process (e.g., Iggers, 1998; Kempf, 2003; Shinar, 2007). This view is sometimes described as *conflict-sensitive journalism* (Howard, 2003) or simply *responsible reporting* (Ersoy, 2010; Kempf, 2008) in the literature. Although many Western media outlets still consider it an option, an alternative to conventional conflict reporting, independent journalists from conflict-ridden regions, interpret it as a responsibility (e.g., Nassanga, 2007; Obonyo & Fackler, 2010). Onduru (2008) stated that, "Peace journalism is not only a necessity, but is the responsible way to report in the midst of conflict" (para. 15). All of these arguments in favor of a responsible journalism, which can be traced to the work of Wilbur Schramm (1957), have at least one thing in common: they require journalists to keep an eye on the *public interest* or the *greater good* of society, whatever it may be.

Despite the plethora of normative studies on peace journalism, it has received little empirical attention (Neuman & Fahmy, 2012, p. 170). Part of the reason for this might be due to how the Internet is influencing journalism practices and how journalism is being redefined. Although online media are challenging this normative construct of journalism (Robinson, 2007), objectivity or at least the pursuit of objectivity remains one of the most salient features of journalism's professional character (Schudson & Anderson, 2008). The *objectivity* discussion is always present. Additionally, journalistic gate keeping (Shoemaker & Vos, 2009) has provided power and prestige to the press. Media gate keepers determine what information is *qualified* as news and therefore is worthy to fill a scarce *news hole*. In the theoretical discussions using objectivity, other theories beside normative began to emerge in the literature investigating peace journalism.

Frames Used in Communications Theories

Framing theory describes the process of organizing a news story to convey a particular interpretation of a news event to an audience (Entman, 1993; Scheufele, 1999). A story can be written with specific sources or data to give a point of view. In framing theory, visual frames are often used to analyze the frequency of visual coverage and variation over time since visual framing is seen to be less obtrusive than framing that occurs in writing. Photographs have the ability to imitate the appearance of the real world (Neumann & Fahmy, 2012, p. 178). Framing scholars argue that visuals have become effective tools for framing and articulating ideological messages (Fahmy, Bock, & Wanta, 2014, p. 55), thus suggesting that the photo-selection decisions by journalists and editors are important in framing a news story and possibly shaping public opinion. Different media houses have been identified as using visuals in framing. Reuters uses frames as war journalism and the Associated Press uses a peace journalism frame (Neumann & Fahmy, 2012, p. 194).

There are scholars who argue that reporters have a special duty to be aware of the frames they are using (Lakoff, 2005). To do this, there are three models for assessing structure and agency in journalism: Herman and Chomsky's Propaganda Model, Shoemaker and Reese's Hierarchy of Influences Model and Pierre Bourdieu's Fields Model (Hackett, 2006, pp. 2–10).

The propaganda model proposed by Herman and Chomsky, has five classes of filters in society that determine what *news* is; in other words, what gets printed in newspapers or broadcast by radio and television. This model also explains how dissent from the mainstream is given little or zero coverage while governments and big business gain easy access to the public in order to convey their state-corporate messages, or liberal frames such as free trade is beneficial, globalization is unstoppable and our policies are tackling poverty (Cromwell, 2002).

Shoemaker and Reese's Hierarchy of Influences Model has five levels of influence: individual, routines, organizational, extra media (institutional) and ideological (socio-cultural). Bias has been argued to be located with the individual journalist. Therefore, who is hired as a journalist is important and how broadcast journalists project the news is important. Other critics suggest that the organizational and institutional structures of the media industry are to blame for the bias. These critics argue for more public control of the media and more protection from big advertisers' control of the media (Reese, 2007).

Pierre Bourdieu's Fields Model suggests that a field is a social arena in which people maneuver and struggle in pursuit of desirable resources (Bourdieu, 1984). His theory focuses on the strategic conduct of social actors in relation to the social system. A field is developed and sustained by various kinds of players, not only individuals but also groups, organizations, and institutions. Players become involved in the game for various reasons, occupy different positions, and aim at different, often conflicting, but sometimes corresponding interests. The game metaphor gives a teleological connotation to the social construction of reality. The construction process is reduced to a set of intentions, calculations, and the pursuit of profit. Bourdieu's world is a dog-eat-dog world in which human beings engage in ploys, bluffs and disguises to increase their own capital to the disadvantage of others. Although party games are characterized by clear-cut endings with winners and losers, the social game is never ending, with only temporal winners. In order to maintain their status, winners must be able to attract less powerful players. This theory has been criticized with regard to questions of social change. It is a theory of reproduction but one that provides a framework for social change (Schedler, Glastra & Kats, 1998, p. 455).

Journalists who are aware of the frames capable of being used in portraying the news, like these three models suggest, can also be able to structure news to help limit bias in their own writing and producing stories. They can seek out additional sources, or ask different questions that may offer a deeper understanding of the issues surrounding conflict.

Suggestions for Additional Applicable Research Theories

Public relations have had a special role in building, sustaining and advancing democratic interests in society. As advocates, public relations should "provide a voice in the marketplace of ideas, facts, and viewpoints to aid informed public debate" (PRSA, 2012). Yet communication from activist groups using public relations may appear too one-sided or close-minded, reflecting a more propaganda approach than persuasive approach and thus hindering acceptance of new or different ideas (Freelon, 2012).

How people accept new ideas or change their opinions have been other ways of looking at the acceptance of peace journalism. One premise has been that people learn not only through their own experiences, but also by observing the actions of others and the results of those actions. This theory has been used to explain human behavior. The scholar who has articulated social cognitive theory, Bandura (1989), explains human behavior in terms of a three-way, dynamic, reciprocal model in which personal factors, environmental influences and behavior continually interact. This theory has been applied to counseling interventions for disease prevention and management.

Then scholars began trying to explain how the world was being shaped through the influence of globalization. Initially media industries were seen through the globalization lens as a capitalistic way of expanding and increasing profits. That view changed with the perception that media globalization was Western hegemony or cultural imperialism and that media were imposing Western messages across cultures. Although media globalization studies discuss how interconnected nation states and cultures have become, it is that very interconnectedness that creates a problem. There is no single dominant center of political power, communication, or intellectual production. This makes the reader's point of view dominant in the discourse and not objective knowledge from the journalist's point of view. Each reader sees his/her particular viewpoint as the universal hope viewpoint. Others should see life the way they see life, no matter what facts or evidence may prove otherwise. Thus, how information is distributed, who collects that information and the viewpoint of the information fundamentally alters the relationships between readers, information observed and those who consume and produce information. Globalization theories may be used in peace journalism research to compare media coverage within different nation states on particular issues and can isolate those media defined by peace journalism standards.

Other theories that could be used in peace journalism research would include theories related to the disciplines of international relations, social studies, economical studies, cultural studies, and religious studies. For example, conflict theory, used in international relations research is used in a study by Peleg (2006) who suggests that since peace journalism is a bold attempt to redefine and reconstruct the role of journalists who cover conflicts then academics should think about bolstering its analytical as well as its normative rigor by looking at it through conflict theory. Peleg posits that conflict theory can advance the lucidity of peace journalism and render it a powerful tool in the hands of reporters and their readers to realize the futility of conflict and to bring about its resolution. He suggests that media is a third party to a conflict as the facilitator of communication, the mediator or the arbitrator between the two rivaling sides. Peleg suggests that peace journalism as a third party can best enhance prospects for resolution and reconciliation by changing the norms and habits of reporting conflicts. Conventional journalism training and development generally contains little or no reference to the wisdom of five decades of academic and professional study of conflict (Howard, 2015, para. 8).

Galtung suggests that peace journalism would be more like health journalism (McGoldrick and Lynch, 2000, p. 10); therefore, specific theories used in the health and sciences field to explain behavior, like the change models, may be useful for peace journalism research. Building on the theoretical notion that research in peace journalism can be built by redefining who the public is, the following theoretical model is offered.

The Public and the Public Sphere Model

In the early formation of the peace journalism concept, the ideology was both philosophical and practical. Adam Curle, a sociologist and the first chair of the School of Peace Studies at the University of Bradford, UK in the 1970s, gave the concept of peace journalism a Quaker emphasis by stressing nonviolence and encouraged putting the concept into practice rather than developing a structured holistic approach, thus forgoing a theoretical development (Wadlow, 2014, p. 4). Curle also believed that there was a divine core within each person and in an effort to further explain how to view peace journalism, he used Buddha's *Dhammapada*: "We are what we think. All that we are arises with our thoughts. With our thoughts, we make the world" (Wadlow, 2014, p. 5). This Buddhist emphasis returned Curle's beliefs to the core of the person as to what they know and what they believe. Applied to the concept of peace journalism, the journalist should understand what is needed to think about in order to cover a conflict.

At this point in the development of the concept of peace journalism, the argument changes to include the philosophies of G.W.F. Hegel and Jüergen Habermas. By looking at these scholars' work, a rethinking of who is the *public*, especially in light of social media and the fragmentation of traditional media, must be made. The argument also comes from the point of view that information is power and essential for the *public* to make informed assessments of policies and societal influences and assumes that the *public* is in control. Habermas puts forth the notion that Enlightenment emphasized that truth can only emerge from unfettered rational dialog and even debate among equals (1991). However, Habermas also argued that these criteria for the *public* and for truth were no longer being met in twentieth-century democracy based on wide disparities in status among citizens, educational levels, access to information, and wealth. Media's role in creating and sustaining a broad, general sense of public have become more pronounced as new forms of media technology have become widespread (Self, 2010, p. 81). The argument could also include discussion on how social media have opened up to previously disenfranchised audiences and allowed a more public sphere through the Internet. Papaioannou & Olivos (2013) suggest that for those who are in the position and willing to take advantage of this networked public sphere, the Internet offers an increasingly useful and empowering platform for public deliberation and new possibilities for citizens to define their civic agency. There are other arguments that suggest that new audiences are issue focused, biased, and myopic in viewpoint.

New audiences created through social media may not be the best way of creating a public sphere. For example, in Egypt after the government blocked the Internet and phone service, when service resumed there was a flood of crude reportage and commentary on social media sites. This could be seen as a reaction to the inadequacy of traditional media coverage but can also be seen as a consequence of a development on the ground, where people have turned the public spaces of protest into sites of media, cultural, and artistic production, which then needed concomitant dissemination by the media (Aboubakr, 2013, p. 236).

Furthermore, the concept of the *public* has evolved and continues to change (Self, 2010, p. 86). In addition, with the changing situations, the idea of government, philosophical truth and the public right have also changed (Hegel, 1977). Enlightenment means that conflicting notions of truth among individuals and groups could exist in conflict at the same time and that Enlightenment societies could sustain ongoing debate. The nation state is not a fixed, static entity; it is a dynamic process of social relationships driven by the interplay of human freedom (Hegel, 1977). Hegel's argument is that human beings fight one another, not simply for change, but for recognition of their freedom to change, or, they want to project their particular values upon each other. He argues that it is this conflict that has produced the history of mankind. He suggests that history is the record of this conflict and believes that this conflict can only be finally resolved in the Enlightenment solution that conflicting ideas exist as the particular of freedom and struggle that empowers each group to actualize its own concepts, a freedom that manifests itself in conversation and conflict (Hegel, 2002, p. 150). Hegel's ideas were that truth could not exist outside of vocabulary for each group that shapes its view of the world; that is why dialog and conversation are critical in the struggle for universal recognition and for reducing conflicts.

By rethinking who the *public* is a reevaluation must be made of the role of media in communities, especially with the growth of social media (blogging, tweeting, chat apps and group communities). The twenty-first century seems to be about empowering virtual, guerilla and local communities to operate through media. These communities provide a voice to enable dialog and debate but with a twist, these communities view their particular situation as one that is universal (Self, 2010, p. 89). Self explains Hegel:

> He suggested that every individual and each community begins this journey anew, but that individuals and groups populate the landscape forever at different points in the journey. He said that conflict among these individuals and groups to assert universality of their particular projects constitutes much of the tension of human life. (Self, 2010, p. 89)

Now the discussion turns to the specifics of how a journalist may define the public. If the public is assumed to be out there more or less intact, then the job of a journalist is easy to state: to inform people about what goes on in their name and their midst. But if the public leads a more broken existence where money speaks louder than the public, problems overwhelm it, fatigue sets in, attention falters, cynicism swells. A public that leads this more fragile kind of existence suggests a different task for the press: not just to inform a public that may or may not emerge, but to improve the chances that it will emerge (Rosen, 2001). Some journalists have discovered what happens during the process of covering a conflict: a public may not always be there for them to inform, a troubling development that has caused journalists to think hard about what they were doing and why (Rosen, 2001, p. 2). "Millions of our fellow citizens have come to feel little interest in or responsibility for their communities and are choosing to avoid, not only the newspaper, but the whole sphere of politics and civic life" (Rosen, 2001, p. 5).

All of this is a new way of thinking about the role of media with the rethinking of what makes a public and in a time when social media, fragmentation, and citizen reporting are changing information production and distribution. "The emergence of new communication technologies, social networks of interactive media with murky sourcing, reveal the public to be a process, a flow, rather than an essence or group. To participate in that process, the twenty-first-century communicator will be required to join the conversation of particulars asserted and reasserted as constantly evolving visions and re-readings of universals" (Self, 2010, p. 90).

Turning Philosophy into Theory for Peace Journalism Research

Evaluating the concept of peace journalism through a theoretical lens has included the argument that peace journalism lacks a theoretical perspective. The concept has been evaluated through normative theories but lacks the core essence of peace journalism to expand coverage in dynamic ways to assist in the peace process. Media's role in contributing to cognitive, attitudinal, and behavioral change on a large scale is unique (Bratić & Schirch, 2008). Although conflict prevention and peace building professionals can use the media in harmony with their other programs, that is if they know when, why and how to use the media for the most strategic impact in lessoning the polarization between groups; media professionals still have much to learn about why and when their work can contribute to preventing violent conflict and building peace between groups. "The media and peace professionals both have their limitations and share an interest in the dynamics of conflict" (Bratić & Schirch, 2008, p. 26).

Despite an *optimistic shift* of media in conflict, the debate about the media's role in peace-making leaves many questions unanswered. The theoretical approach to the media's impact on peace is underdeveloped, the practical projects are vastly scattered and a systematic analysis of the practice is missing. To fill the gap, the Public Sphere Model is offered as a blend of journalism, conflict studies, and philosophy. The Public Sphere Model's basic principles are as follows (Croteau & Hoynes, 2006):

- Society's needs are not met entirely through the market system
- Consumer power is not democracy
- Media are not like other products
- Profitability is not the sole determinant of value
- Government has a necessary role

The vision of the Public Sphere Model is that media are a primary information source and storyteller. Media can be used as a forum for social dialogue, only if the media system is fully accessible. Ownership and control of media should be diverse and the people are citizens first and consumers second. As citizens, they need media to provide information about personal rights and about public political choices. They need media to voice criticism, to register alternatives, and to recognize themselves in media representations. These visions are built on the reality that markets are undemocratic, reproduce inequality, are amoral, do not meet all social needs, and do not meet all democratic needs (Croteau & Hoynes, 2006). This perspective, the Public Sphere Model, defines media as central elements of a healthy public sphere, the space within which ideas, opinions, and views freely circulate. Here, rather than profits, it is the more elusive *public interest* that serves as the yardstick against which media performance is measured (Croteau & Hoyes, 2006, p. 16).

Research Questions

Research questions asked within this theoretical discussion on peace journalism to be answered throughout this book are the following:

- Can journalists make sense of the issues surrounding conflict and help minimize harm through their reporting?
- Given that cultures vary, should media houses and/or journalists be regulated when covering conflict to adhere to international practices?
- How do governments and institutions impact how conflicts are covered?

To answer these questions, the book outlines the following: if a theory is a set of interrelated concepts, definitions and propositions that explains or predicts events or situations by specifying relations among variables, then by understanding what makes up those concepts (which are detailed in Chapters 4–9), how peace journalism is defined (Chapter 2) and what propositions exist to create action to incorporate those into covering conflicts (Chapters 10), then peace journalism can be explained through the relationships among these variables. The answers to these questions will be discussed in Chapter 11.

Last Word: The media's role in facilitating democracy and encouraging citizenship has always been in tension with its status as a profit-making industry. Mediating between these two has been the government, whose regulations (or lack thereof) have fundamentally shaped the environment within which the media operate (Croteau & Hoynes, 2006). For journalists to explain why things happen, especially during conflict, then communications have to be established among the media owners, governments, and audiences. This communication must begin with a rethinking of what it means to be a journalist in the twenty-first century and if there is a place for peace, love and understanding.

Discussion: Who is the Public? How can information be shared with these publics?

References

Aboubakr, R. (2013). New directions of internet activism in Egypt. *De Gruyter Mouton*, 38(3), 251–265.

Bandura, A. (1986). Social cognitive theory. In Vasta, R. (Ed.), *Annals of child development, Vol. 6. Six theories of child dDevelopment* (pp. 1–60). Greenwich, CT: JAI Press. Retrieved from http://www.uky.edu/~eushe2/Bandura/Bandura1989ACD.pdf.

Bourdieu, P. (1984). *Distinction: A social critique of the judgement of taste.* London: Routledge.

Bratić, V. & Schirch, L. (2008, June 3). The role of media in peace building: Theory and practice. Paper presented at symposium on journalistic training in conflict relation situations, DW-AKADEMIE, Bonn. Retrieved from http://www.kubatana.net/docs/media/dw_journalistic_training_symposium_2008.pdf.

Croteau, D. & Hoynes, W. (2006). Profits and the public interest: Theoretical and historical Context. In Croteau, D. & Hoynes, W. (Eds.), *The business of media: Corporate media and the public interest* (pp. 15–40). Pine Forge Press.

Cromwell, D. (2002). The propaganda model: An overview. Retrieved from http://web.archive.org/web/20030221041838/http://www.medialens.org/articles_2001/dc_propaganda_model.html

Entman, R. (1993). Framing: Toward clarification of a fractured paradigm. *Journal of Communication*, 43(4), 51–58.

Ersoy, M. (2010). Peace journalism and news coverage on the Cyprus conflict. *The Muslim World*, 100, 78–99. DOI: 10.1111/j.1478–1913.2009.01303.x.

Fahmy, S., Bock, M. A., & Wanta, W. (2014). Says what: Research on the content in visual communication. In Fahmy, S., Bock, M. A., & Wanta, W. (eds.), *Visual communication theory and research: A mass communication perspective* (pp. 51–68). Palgrave Macmillan.

Freelon, D. (2012). From the mailbag, 12/14/09. Retrieved from http://dfreelon.org/2009/12/14/from-the-mailbag-121409/.

Galtung, J. (1998). High road, low road: Changing the course for peace journalism. *Track-Two*, 7, 7–10.

Galtung, J. & Ruge, M. H. (1965). The structure of foreign news: The presentation of the Congo, Cuba and Cyprus crises in four Norwegian newspapers. *Journal of Peace Research*, 2(1), 64–91.

Habermas, J. (1991). *The structural transformation of the public sphere: An inquiry into a category of bourgeois society*. Translated by Thomas Burger. Cambridge, Mass.: The MIT Press. Retrieved from http://pages.uoregon.edu/koopman/courses_readings/phil123net/publicness/habermas_structural_trans_pub_sphere.pdf.

Hackett, R. A. (2006). Is peace journalism possible? *Conflict & Communication Online*, 5(2). 13 pages. Retrieved from http://www.cco.regener-online.de/2006_2/pdf/hackett.pdf.

Hamdy, N. & Gomaa, E. H. (2012). Framing the Egyptian uprising in Arabic language newspapers and social media. *Journal of Communication*, 62, 195–211.

Hegel, G. W. F. (1977). *Phenomenology of spirit* (Translated by A.V. Miller). New York: Oxford Press.

Hegel, G. W. F. (2002). *The philosophy of right* (Translated by A. White). Newburyport, MA: Focus Publishing.

Howard, R. (2003). Conflict-sensitive journalism. Copenhagen, Denmark: International Media Support & Institute for Media Policy & Civil Society.

Howard, R. (2015). Global journalism ethics. Center for Journalism Ethics. School of Journalism and Mass Communication, University of Wisconsin-Madison. Retrieved from http://www.journalismethics.info/global_journalism_ethics/conflict_sensitivity_in_practice.tm.

Iggers, J. (1998). *Good news, bad news: Journalism ethics and the public interest*. Boulder, CO: Westview.

Kempf, W. (2003). Constructive conflict coverage—A social-psychological research and development program. *Conflict & Communication Online*, 2(2). Retrieved from www.cco.regener-online.de.

Kempf, W. (2008). The impact of political news on German students' assessments of the Israeli-Palestine conflict. *Conflict & Communication Online*, 7(2). Retrieved from http://www.cco.regener-online.de/2008_2/pdf/kempf_2008.pdf.

Lakoff, G. (2005, September 2). Simple framing. Rockridge Institute, Berkeley, California. Retrieved from http://www.rockridgeinstitute.org/projects/strategic/simple_framing.

Lynch, J. & Galtung, J. (2010). *Reporting conflict: New directions in peace journalism*. Queensland, Australia: University of Queensland Press.

McGoldrick, A. & Lynch, J. (2000). Peace journalism. What is it? How to do it? Reporting the world. Retrieved from https://www.transcend.org/tri/downloads/McGoldrick_Lynch_Peace-Journalism.pdf.

Nassanga, L. G. (2007). Peace journalism applied: An assessment of media coverage of the conflict in northern Uganda. *Conflict and Communication*, 6(2). Retrieved from www.cco.regener-online.de.

Neumann, R. & Fahmy, S. (2012). Analyzing the spell of war: A war-peace framing analysis of the 2009 visual coverage of the Sri Lankan civil war in western newswires. *Mass Communication and Society*, 15, 169–200.

Nichols, T. (ed.) (nd). The Philosophy of Social Science. *Internet Encyclopedia of Philosophy, a Peer-Reviewed Academic Source*. Retrieved from http://www.iep.utm.edu/soc-sci/.

Obonyo, L. & Fackler, M. (2010, July 7). Peace journalism as a media education paradigm for East Africa. Paper presented at the World Journalism educators Congress, Grahamstown, South Africa. Retrieved from http://wjec.ru.ac.za/.

Onduru, L. (2008, March 25). Peace journalism in practice. European Journalism Centre. Retrieved from http://ejc.net/magazine/article/peace-journalism-inpractice#.VVc_8CmFaJU.

Peleg, S. (2006) Peace journalism through the lens of conflict theory: Analysis and practice. *Conflict & Communication Online*, 5(2). Retrieved from www.cco.regener-online.de.

Reese, S. (2007). Journalism research and the hierarchy of influences model: A global perspective. *Brazilian Journalism Research*, 3(2), 29–42.

Robinson, S. (2007). "Someone's gotta be in control here": The institutionalization of online news and the creation of a shared journalistic authority. *Journalism Practice*, 1(3), 305–321.

Rosen, J. (1999). What are journalists for? *The New York Times Review of Books*. Retrieved from http://www.nytimes.com/books/first/r/rosen-journalist.html.

Rosen, J. (2001). *What are journalists for?* Yale University Press.

Schedler, P. E., Glastra, F. F., & Kats, E. (1998, October-December). Public information and field theory. *Political Communication*, 15(4), 445–461.

Scheufele, D.A. (1999). Framing as a theory of media effects. *Journal of Communication*, 49(1), 101–120.

Schramm, W. (1957). *Responsibility in mass communication*. New York: Harper.

Schudson, M. & Anderson, C. (2008). Objectivity, professionalism, and truth seeking in journalism. In Wahl-Jorgensen, K. & Hanitzsch, T. (Eds.), *Handbook of journalism studies*, New York: Routledge, pp. 88–101.

Self, C. C. (2010). Hegel, Habermas, and community: The public in the new media era. *International Journal of Strategic Communication*, 4, 78–92.

Shinar, D. (2007). Epilogue: Peace journalism—The state of the art. *Conflict and Communication*, 6(1).

Shoemaker, P. J. & Vos, T. P. (2009). *Gatekeeping theory*. New York: Routledge.

Shukrallah, S. (2012, March 8). "Revolutionary" movements split over Egypt's looming presidential poll. Ahramonline. Retrieved from http://english.ahram.org.eg/NewsContent/1/64/36160/Egypt/Politics-/Revolutionarymovements-split-over-Egypts-looming-.aspx.

Wadlow, R. (2014, March 31). Adam Curle: Tools for transformation. Transcend Media Service. Retrieved from https://www.transcend.org/tms/2014/03/adam-curle-tools-fortransformation/.

Wihbey, J. (2015, March 8). Guide to critical thinking, research data and theory: Overview for journalists. Journalists' Resource.

· 4 ·

POPULATIONS AFFECTED BY CONFLICT

Calling Names

Hamwee Ibrahim Qashoosh sang a song during a demonstration in Homs, Syria. The song *Yalla irhal ya Bashar* (Get Out Bashar) became a hit and broke down the walls of fear and silence being felt in Syria (Sayfo, 2013). Words can be powerful tools. William Gay in his essay on The *Language of War and Peace* (1999) wrote: "If knowledge is power, language too is power; those who control the language of war and peace exercise an enormous influence on how we perceive war and peace and what behaviors we accept in relation to war and peace" (p. 303). Gay suggests that words chosen or not chosen provide meaning, for example the difference between referring to armed troops as *freedom fighters* and as *guerrilla terrorists*. These words can be interpreted by different audiences in different ways. Gay also suggests that word choices are shaped by social usage and that most nations reinforce politically preferred choices through institutions of socialization like the media where nations can be referred to as *rogue states* and leaders as *dangerous villains* (Gay, 1999).

Language can be twisted, masked, and distorted; used for manipulation to the point where the cruelty, inhumanity, and horror of war seem justifiable (Gay, 1999). Plato, in *The Republic*, cautioned that we should be careful about calling another people an *enemy*, since wars do not last forever and eventually they may again become our friends.

Language plays a role in peace journalism because war coverage is not just about the factions in conflict—the *us vs. them*, there are other people who are affected by conflict and how they are included or not included in the reporting. There are people who are invisible or referred to negatively or used as a stereotype. These populations include but are not limited to the following: women, children, elderly, disabled, individuals identifying as something other than strictly heterosexual, specific religious adherents, ethnic groups, and internally displaced persons. All of these populations are witnesses to conflict around the world and have suffered during the conflicts. Tactics used in war to conquer others include rape, sexual violence, isolation and torture, blockage of food, medicine, and potable water. What these populations have in common are their large numbers, their sufferings, and the limited coverage by traditional media or if covered, covered by the violence afflicted upon them. What these audiences need is to have their stories told through language that respects each. These populations offer different viewpoints from those who often initiated and participated in the conflict.

The goal of this chapter is to understand these audiences in light of what they have suffered, to identify who is supposed to protect them since they are vulnerable and to demonstrate how media have helped or hurt them. The point of view is that new technology, the use of social media, has not brought better understanding across humanity. It has, though, had the ability to coalesce groups of individuals around points of ideology, however extreme, because people seek others who agree with how they think. An example of how new technology in the form of social media has gathered individuals around points of ideology is when in 2015, a 22-year-old Egyptian man, middle-class, privately schooled, body builder, went from showing off and trying to attract women to watching videos and then joining ISIS and making body building videos for them. His father has disowned him (El-Naggar, 2015). The author in the *New York Times* video suggested that the lack of economic opportunity along with religion were causes for why the young man changed. The focus of the story was on the build-up to becoming a terrorist, not on the causes (El-Naggar, 2015) or on the other populations affected by his actions. He is still a body builder but has gone from good guy to bad guy in the media. Journalists need to know how to cover other populations affected by conflict.

Sins of Omission: Who Is Left Out?

If journalism is largely a practice of telling stories and constructing narratives, it follows that the challenge is to compose good stories—stories that are designed to be as honest, accurate, balanced, fair, complete, and critically aware as possible, but also timely, interesting, coherent, and credible within a prevailing socio-political framework of interpretation, including but not limited to cultural expectations, presumptions, value orientations, and assumptions about what counts as fact and appears to be reasonable (Ivie, 2009, p. 7). All of these factors can be summed up with the word *objectivity*. However, any journalistic claim to objectivity and truth has to be assessed against the how language is used, what audiences are being addressed and always during conflict, with limited resources and with limited perspectives.

By this reckoning—that is, by taking into account the filters of language, culture, and circumstance and the rhetorical dynamics of narrative form, all of which influence news production—the measure of a story is not whether it is true or objective in some narrow or isolated sense but instead how much and in what ways it is incomplete. What is overemphasized, underemphasized, missed, and otherwise distorted regardless of how compelling the story might be? What is the bias and limit of its perspective? What is ignored in order to make one party in a conflict appear legitimate and sympathetic and another party appear illegitimate and unsympathetic, one heroic and the other demonic, one present and another absent, one humanized and the other dehumanized? How would a shift in the story's focus alter what is seen and how it appears, who is victim and who is victimizer, where interests converge and diverge, etc.? What actual or potential interdependencies and complementarities between the opposed parties are missing from the story as it is spun? By this standard, news stories are assessed according to what is absent more than what is present.

Women

How has conflict affected women? Ninety percent of the current war casualties are civilians with the majority of those being women and children, whereas, a century ago, 90 percent of casualties were military personnel (UN Women Fact Sheet No. 5, nd). High proportions of stories on peace (64 percent), development (59 percent), war (56 percent), and gender-based violence

(56 percent) reinforce gender stereotypes ("Who Makes the News," 2010). These findings confirm the imperative need to include women and integrate gender perspectives in the news media and journalistic profession, including peace journalism (Yiping, 2011, p. 17).

Violence against women during conflict is often measured in statistics based on rape, despite not being the only population targeted for such violence. Trauma, loss of income, loss of family, insecurity, and limited resources are seldom measured nor or they recorded in traditional media. In Rwanda from April 1994 to April 1995, an estimated 500,000 women were raped, and every female over the age of 12 who survived the genocide was assaulted. In Bosnia from 1992 to 1995, an estimated 50,000 girls and women were sexually assaulted as part of the campaign of *ethnic cleansing*. In the Kashmir conflict in India, between 7,000 and 16,000 women have been sexually assaulted by militants/separatist groups and the security forces in the region ("Women's Political and Economic Leadership Statistics," 2000). Statistical examples can be quoted for Kosovo, Haiti and Somalia as well. Although these are alarming statistics, where are the numbers for trauma, loss of family, insecurity, and limited resources?

Who is supposed to protect women? Protection of women has been stated in the United Nations Security Council Resolution (UNSCR) 1325, unanimously adopted on October 31, 2000. The resolution addresses the impact of armed conflict on women, recognizes the under-valued and under-utilized contributions of women to conflict prevention, peacekeeping, conflict resolution and peace-building, and stresses the importance of their equal and full participation as active agents in peace and security. UNSCR 1820 passed in June 2008 established a strong link between sexual violence and sustainable peace and security. UNSCR 1888 (September 30, 2009) provided concrete building blocks to advance its implementation. These UN resolutions are binding on all UN member states (Yiping, 2011, p. 18), supposedly.

How have media helped or hurt women? Sexual assaults on women regularly *go viral* on social media platforms. A harrowing video of an attack in Tahrir Square, published on-line, was widely covered in both Egyptian media and the international press, prompting criticism of the *authorities'* inaction. The poor-quality video, apparently filmed on a mobile phone, showed a mob of men attacking a woman and stripping her of her clothes while a member of the security forces tries to intervene.

"A Dutch journalist....was gang raped in Tahrir Square. Hers was one of seven cases that human rights groups have noted all of them in or around

Tahrir, the site of the opposition protests. These criminal acts do not appear to be politically motivated or controlled. But unfortunately they do appear to be a sign that the crowds in Tahrir are out of control," according to the Facebook page of a presidential aide, Essam el-Haddad (Gabriel, 2013, para. 8). A television host, Maha Bahnasy of the Tahrir Channel, when the correspondent told her there had been isolated cases of harassment, Bahnasy, audibly laughing, replied the boys were "having a good time." Later Bahnasy said she was misunderstood (McCoy, 2014). The television host was suspended. Afterward an Egyptian actress, Ghada Abdul Razek, was quoted on social media as saying that "a visit from Sisi would be worth a sex attack ("Egyptian actress says," 2014).

The photos of the rape were distributed via cell phone, email, and Facebook, followed by tweets with photos. Operation Anti-Sexual Harassment/Assault, which patrols the square, said 46 group assaults were recorded in Tahrir on the first day of the protests alone ("Journalist gang raped," 2013). After the series of assaults in June–July of 2013 during protests by opponents of Mohamed Morsi, prominent members of the Muslim Brotherhood publicized the sexual assaults on social media (see, for example, tweet by Ikhwanweb on 29 June 2013, 2.54 AM: "Video of #Tahrir mobs and thugs aka 'revolutionaries' sexually assaulting [sic] young foreign woman, among many others"). Television channels known for supporting President Morsi leapt at the opportunity to claim that his opponents were nothing but *thugs* and *criminals* ("Circles of Hell, 2015, p. 42).

So is it just mobs of people out of control? Actually government officials, civilian authorities, peacekeepers and aid workers have been reported to demand sexual favors in exchange for necessities—safe passage, food, and shelter. Rape used as a war tactic is not new. It is often used to isolate and replace opposing populations. According to a worker in a Kenyan refugee camp, the camps are dangerous for women. Though the woman or girl may be raped, the harm is also to the children. In Kenya, as in many other African countries, lineage of the children goes with the father, so, if the woman is raped and has a child, then the child has no lineage, no tribe. The sense of fear, that sense of helplessness, has given rise to an unusual hash tag campaign called, *we will sexually harass men*. In tens of thousands of tweets, women condemn not just sexual harassment but a culture of tolerance that abets it. They want men to feel as victimized as they do (McCoy, 2014).

Traditional media limit coverage of gender-based violence and seldom report on how women are motivated to help themselves. Recognized by peace agencies and NGOs, women's dialogue initiatives are often the only channel of communication between hostile communities and nations (NGO Working Group on Women, 2005). In the context of the Israeli-Palestinian conflict, the Jerusalem Link and Women in Black served as two important examples of such a process. In the context of the conflict between Pakistan and India, groups such as WISCOMP (Women in Security, Conflict Management and Peace) and WIPSA (Women's Initiative for Peace in South Asia) have been facilitating communication between women's groups in the two countries. They have been consistent in facilitating such dialogue even when communication has been caught in war rhetoric and political jingoism and civil society dialogue has been irregular and limited (Schirch & Sewak, 2005, p. 7). An HBO documentary film, winner of a 2007 Peabody Award, *To Die in Jerusalem*, explores the anguish of two mothers whose daughters die in the same violent moment. Ayat al-Akhras was a suicide bomber in a Jerusalem supermarket. Rachel Levy died in the blast. Avigail Levy determines to meet Um Samir al-Akras but the barriers of politics, society, and culture, block the meeting for four years. Finally, through video they meet. The end is not happy and each woman's pain is revealed in words, charges and counter charges (Jensen, 2007).

Children

How has conflict affected children? There are 230 million children living in areas of violence around the world. During the last ten years, two million children have been killed in conflict, one million have been orphaned, six million have been seriously injured or permanently disabled and ten million have been left with serious psychological trauma ("Children in Conflict," nd). These statistics are from NGOs not media sites. These stories seldom make traditional media. Conflicts disproportionately affect children. Many are subject to abductions, military recruitment, killing, maiming, and numerous forms of exploitation of children.

Children are killed purposely as a technique of war. On December 17, 2014, members of the Pakistani Taliban killed at least 145 people, including 132 children. Scenes of bloodied students and mourning mothers sent shockwaves around the world, drawing condemnation from even the Afghan Taliban. The militant group's spokesman, Zabiullah Mujahid, said in a statement that "killing innocent children" goes against the group's principles (Khosla,

2014). According to *Save the Children*, Pakistan saw more than 800 attacks on schools between 2009 and 2012—some groups have counted more than 1000 attacks in the last five years (Khosla, 2014).

Children are also targeted culturally through marriage where there are *bride prices* and by marrying the girls off early may lower or increase the price thus helping the husband's family bring in a cheap set of extra hands or pays for the wife's family so they can eat. Huge percentages of girls are forced into child marriage, according to the International Center for Research on Women, more than 14 million girls are married each year before they are 18. In Iraq, there's a pending bill to allow girls as young as nine to marry. In Niger, 75 percent of girls are married off before they are 18 (McCoy, 2014).

Young women also are targeted through religious ideology. Websites like Twitter, Ask.fm, and Facebook have been used by ISIS to groom young women into believing they have a moral duty and obligation to join the militant group. For girls from conservative Muslim families in Britain, who may be denied the same opportunities as their brothers and male peers, messages offering the chance to "do something with your life" can prove tempting, said managing director Haras Rafiq of the Quilliam Foundation (Guilbert, 2015). Female supporters promised the girls an Islamist utopia.

In addition to the deaths, disabilities, and trauma of the children in conflict, since 1998 there have been armed conflicts involving child soldiers in at least 36 countries. Children are easier to intimidate and will do as they are told. They are less likely than adults to run away and they do not demand salaries. Sometimes the military unit is a refuge serving as a surrogate family. Joining an army may be the only way to survive to secure food and protection. In Myanmar, parents volunteer their children for the rebel army because the guerrillas provide clothes and two meals a day. Some join to fight for social justice, for their religious belief or cultural identity and sometimes to seek revenge for the deaths of family members (Unicef, 1995a).

Armed groups aim propaganda specifically at young people. In Sri Lanka, the Liberation Tigers of Tamil Eelam (LTTE) have been active in the school system, indoctrinating children. Government forces in El Salvador, Ethiopia, Guatemala, and Myanmar have all conscripted children. Opposition groups in Angola, Mozambique, Sri Lanka, and the Sudan have seized children. Some of these children have been brutalized, given drugs, and forced to witness or take part in the torture and execution of their own relatives. They are used to cook or to carry water, as messengers or spies and during the Iran–Iraq war, child soldiers were sent out ahead in waves over minefields (Unicef, 1995a).

Children are used as suicide bombers, including children with disabilities or who were sold to armed groups by their families, according to the United Nations Committee on the Rights of the Child (CRC). Children are also used as human shields to protect ISIS facilities from airstrikes, to work at checkpoints or to build bombs for the jihadists. A bomb strapped to a girl exploded in a busy market place in the Nigerian city of Maiduguri on January 10, 2015, killing at least 16 people and injuring more than 20, security sources said. "The explosive devices were wrapped around her body and the girl looked no more than 10 years old," a police source said (Ola & Abrak, 2015, para. 2).

Who is supposed to protect the children? Protection for children is offered through the 1989 Convention on the Rights of the Child introduced through the UN to define standards of how children should and should not be treated such as protection against exploitation and violence; protection against torture, or any other cruel, inhuman, or degrading treatment or punishment; avenues for family reunification; and to obtain a name and nationality. What is missing are the mechanisms and the will for enforcement. Attempts at this are often found in immigration law. Conscription of children is a bar to entry into the United States, for example. In today's armed conflicts, many of the offenders are not nation states but rather a loose collection of sub-national groups, civilian and military, that argue they are not bound by the provisions of such conventions.

Children are inside the arena of war, either physically or via the media; they witness conflict and are impacted accordingly in ways that are not automatically noticeable. One study that addressed these impacts analyzed the dreams of 114 children from the West Bank, aged 9 and 10. Two-thirds of the dreams were political, one-third nightmares, and three-quarters had a bad ending with only one-quarter with a good ending. In 85 percent of the dreams, there were physical confrontations, while 15 percent contained verbal confrontations. None of the dreams included friendly contact with Israelis (Masalha, 2003).

How have media helped or hurt the children? The children who are victims of war or armed conflict suffer limited opportunities. In conflict, they cannot go to school. If they are forced to flee and live in a refugee camp, they do have school but the schools are not respected. The quality is frequently subpar and resources are minimal. With no money, no structure, no hope, what is being done to help the children who cannot help themselves? There are a lot of organizations reaching out to help the children because they are the easiest group to fund. With the help of numerous NGOs and other organizations, children are being offered hope. Examples relevant to the use of discourse to facilitate peace include Balanda, MEND, and Crossing Borders. All three are using forms of media and communication to increase youth activism for peace and coexistence. Balanda, an Arab youth nonprofit organization, attempts to strengthen Arab youth's understanding of democracy and gender equality, to foster pluralism and tolerance, and to enable a discussion and debate about Arab Palestinian history, grievances and culture ("Youth Activism for Peace," nd).

Another group, MEND, is a Palestinian institution addressing issues related to nonviolence and democracy through a variety of projects focused on training and utilizing innovative media techniques. The younger generation is reached by a new set of Sesame materials, *Sesame Stories*, which include public service announcements and teachers' training in the use of the materials. The series was given a successful high-profile launch in early November 2005. The radio soap opera, *Home is our Home*, reaches the youth and now has a curriculum for use by teachers and by Mend's ANV centers ("Youth Activism for Peace," nd).

Crossing Borders is a newspaper written by young Israelis, Arab-Israelis, Palestinians, and Jordanians. It is published in English every two months. While it does focus on the conflict, its main aim is to produce a newspaper covering everything teenagers are interested in: poetry, sports, politics, society, culture, and opinion ("Youth Activism for Peace," nd).

Additionally, some governments, like the Lebanese government, have included peace education in the national curriculum. In Liberia, a Children's Peace Theatre has been touring since 1992, promoting unity and reconciliation. In Mozambique, a Peace Circus uses art, dance, and theatre to demonstrate that differences do not have to be settled at the point of a gun (Unicef, 1995b). These efforts are seldom covered in traditional media.

An example of how media have influenced specific cultures would be Disney's television program for Israeli-Palestinian children—*Rechov SumSum/ Shara'a SimSim*, which has had significant effect in fostering cross-cultural understanding between Israeli and Palestinian children (Warshel, 2007). The results of Warshel's study indicate the effectiveness of media-based interventions such as *Rechov Sumsum/Shara'a Simsim* on countering negative stereotypes by building a peer-oriented context that introduces children to the everyday lives of people from different cultures (Cole *et al.*, 2003).

Elderly

How has conflict affected the elderly? An estimated 10 percent of refugees are over age 60, according to the UNHCR. Elderly are marginalized in conflict for a variety of reasons. Sometimes, in a conflict situation, the younger generations see the elderly as responsible for the current crisis. The elderly not only lose their respectability but also their self-esteem. They are left to suffer, particularly if dependent on the young for mobility and safety or if the supportive infrastructure falls to conflict. During war, many older persons are abandoned by their fleeing relatives who might view them as a burden. Many never make it to the refugee camps and, though elders tend to be respected in the camps; few are there.

Who is supposed to protect the elderly? Though entitled to equal protection under international human rights and humanitarian law as members of the general population, the elderly often are denied or lack access to humanitarian resources, lose their livelihoods, suffer from isolation, and are discriminated against based on age. The elderly often are targeted in conflict. For example, very old women were abducted from their village in the Pujehun district, in eastern Sierra Leone and gang-raped by rebel fighters from Liberia. The rebels' reason for molesting the elderly women was because, unlike younger women, the elderly were regarded as *virgins* since they might have refrained for a long time from sexual activities (Deen, 2004).

During wartime, when traditional social-support networks break down, women of all ages are especially vulnerable to sexual assault. Anecdotal evidence from clinics and community groups that deal with sexual violence in war zones indicates that many older women have been raped in the DRC, Liberia, Sierra Leone, and Rwanda (Cranston, nd).

During times of conflict, the elderly also have been made prisoners. In January 2015, ISIS (Islamic State) jihadists freed 200 elderly Yazidis in northern Iraq (Mojon, 2015). "Some were wounded, some have disabilities and many are suffering from mental and psychological problems," according to Khodr Domli, a leading Yazidi rights activist (Mojon, 2015, para. 4). Some elderly have been made prisoners in their own homes because of conflict not allowing them opportunities to leave. In the Ukraine, 80,000 elderly and infirm Jews lived in an area where there was violence and could not leave home. They were pensioners, often poor, some were living alone. Though these elderly were imprisoned, they were not alone. Newspapers reported that the old and infirm in the area of Independence Square, in the heart of the Ukraine uprising, were receiving visits and care packages to the sound of sniper fire. An emergency network of volunteers and professionals ensured the supply of food and medical care (Borschel-Dan, 2014, para. 3).

How have media helped or hurt the elderly? Besides the brief reports of the help in the Ukraine, another example is Munesuke Yamamoto, a freelance photo journalist, who has witnessed numerous deaths in war zones around the world and is now focusing on the living, specifically elderly people in Japan. "I have realized I cannot depict a death without knowing about how he or she lived and how precious a life is," Yamamoto, 53, said, referring to his new photo collection, *See You Tomorrow—Scenes of Old Age in the Japanese Archipelago.* The collection has about 80 photos of people aged between 70 and 100. "It is important to be aware of the delight, anger, sorrow and pleasure of elderly people and how they are leading active lives prior to their deaths," he said. Yamamoto is known for his coverage mainly of Asia, including Myanmar and the Philippines. He conducted four interviews with Myanmar democracy leader Aung San Suu Kyi (Hirano, 2006, para. 22).

Disabled

How has conflict affected the disabled? There are few statistics on the disabled in conflict. There are many statistics of how men, women, and children have become disabled due to conflict: shootings, bombs, and land mines. What happens to those who are disabled prior to the conflict or even during the conflict?

In the stressed context of a war, communities develop different coping mechanisms out of necessity. An aid worker shared his horror of seeing people tied or chained to a tree in a refugee camp. What the aid worker finally realized was the community in the camp used the method to keep the person safe. People who had to be looked after in the camps needed to be safe and since everyone had to work to survive, securing the person to a tree was the only recourse they had. Inventive uses of tools also had the people in the refugee camps create wheeled carts to get people about.

Mental illness in many cultures means pushing these people out of sight. In Lebanon, it is predicted that 25 percent of the total Lebanese population must cope with mental illness at some point in their lifetime, according to Georges Karam, psychiatrist and senior director at Lebanon's Institute for Development, Research, Advocacy and Applied Care (Weatherbee, 2015).

People in Lebanon are not secure and there is a significant association between exposure to war-related trauma and mental health conditions related to mood, anxiety, and impulse control. The compound effects of political insecurity and high poverty rates also exacerbate disorders like depression and anxiety. Suicide attempts are widespread, according to data from the World Health Organization and the Lebanese Health Ministry, but remain underreported. Community pressure often causes those suffering to stay silent, for fear of discrimination (Zawya, 2015).

Who is supposed to protect the disabled? The Convention on the Rights of Persons with Disability approved by the UN General Assembly on December 13, 2006, is the first treaty of the twenty-first century and incorporates eight guiding principles: (1) respect for inherent dignity and individual autonomy (including personal freedom of choice); (2) nondiscrimination; (3) full and effective participation and inclusion in society; (4) respect for difference and acceptance of persons with disabilities as part of human diversity and humanity; (5) equality of opportunity; (6) accessibility; (7) equality between men and women; and (8) respect for the evolving capacity of children with disabilities and respect for the right of children with disability to preserve their identities (Forsythe, 2009, p. 45).

How have media helped or hurt the disabled? Scant reporting on the disabled is in traditional media. One source, though, that is offering hope to the disabled is a web site called *Created It Gets Brighter*, where individual testimonials across the world are placed into a virtual space and encouragement is shared (Weatherbee, 2015) with the belief that ostracized groups often find comfort and increased ability to cope when organized and in communication with one another. Campaign organizers say that there is courage in the vulnerability of sharing a personal story, and there is power in collective storytelling to address misconceptions and stereotypes of mental illness (Weatherbee, 2015). The project began with a group of University of Oxford students in March 2013.

Persons Identifying as Something Other Than Strictly Heterosexual

How has conflict affected the gay community? Individuals who are thought of as being anything other than strictly heterosexual—whether they are or not—are some of the most vulnerable populations in armed conflict. A series of images show two masked men in Syria throwing the victim—charged with having a *homosexual affair* from a seven-story building. After surviving the fall, the man was stoned to death by locals in the ISIS stronghold of Raqqa (Saul, 2015a & 2015b). Photos posted on LiveLeak show the man being checked after the fall and finally being circled by a waiting crowd. Discussants say that ISIS may label someone as gay when they are actually perceived to be a dissident. IGLHRC (International Gay and Lesbian Human Rights Commission) and MADRE (global women's rights group) caution media not to assume the man was gay or was involved in homosexual acts. Media should be cautious and consult those this person loved as widespread publicity potentially exposes their families, loved ones and intimate partners to harm (IGLHRC, 2015).

Who is supposed to protect the gay community? Amnesty International interprets the Universal Declaration of Human Rights to include the rights and the protection of the rights of LGBT people around the world. The Yogyakarta Principles on the Application of International Human Rights Law in Relation to Sexual Orientation and Gender Identity, developed in 2006 by a group of LGBT experts in Yogyakarta, Indonesia in response to well-known examples of abuse, provides a universal guide to applying international human rights law to violations experienced by lesbians, gay men, bisexual and transgender people to ensure the universal reach of human rights protections (Amnesty International, nd).

How have media helped or hurt the gay community? Homophobic speech and laws can be political tools to justify, on *moral* grounds, human and civil rights abuses. Yelena Klimova, moderator of an Internet portal that has published more than 1000 confessions of Russian LGBT teenagers, has been charged with providing *homosexual propaganda* to minors and faces a fine of 100,000 rubles ($1500) (Mirovalev, 2015). Prime-time shows on Russian television feature politicians and public figures whose vitriolic speeches fuel homophobia. An anchor with a government-funded television network said in a 2013 talk show that gays should be prohibited from donating blood and organs for transplants, and their hearts "should be burned and buried" (Mirovalev, 2015).

A Russian based Neo-Nazi gang uses social networking and dating websites to identify gay teenagers, to beat and humiliate them in front of a video camera, and then the gang posts the videos online. The gang's leader, Maxim Martsinkevich, has been sentenced to five years in jail for *inciting hatred*, but his followers are still active (Mirovalev, 2015). Although Uganda has a thriving press and media infrastructure, according to Heaf, one of the most controversial topics is the role that national newspapers have had in the persecution of gay people. In 2010, the names of 100 men and women were published in a small circulation newspaper as being gay. The article in the newspaper called for the execution of all homosexuals. Besides the names, other details were published to include professions, social hangouts and home addresses (Heaf, 2014).

The organization, This World: The Values Network and Stand with Us placed an ad in *The New York Times* the last week of 2014. The ad featured a man proclaiming in a bold headline: "My name is Rennick Remley. I'm a gay American. And I support Israel" (Boteach, 2014). The article was how gays in Israel are treated versus the beliefs of Hamas. Boteach used descriptors of Hamas as "gay-hating, radically homophobic, murderous and barbarous death cult" (2014, para. 5). *Newsweek* and *The Washington Post* have called Rabbi Shmuley Boteach "the most famous Rabbi in America." His network, This World: The Values Network defends Israel in the media (Boorstein, 2012).

Religious Affiliation

How has conflict affected the religious? In the discussion about whether or not the Muhammad cartoons should be published in text books, Mai Mercado, a spokesman for the right-wing Conservative Party in Denmark, said that children needed to learn about the cartoons to receive a key message about Danish society, "No matter how strong one's religious feelings are, or how much one cultivates their religion, you do not earn the right to violence or threats" (Taylor, 2015, para. 7). Religion is covered in traditional media when it is in conflict but seldom when it supports or is positive. Often religious conflict and ethnic conflict are so intertwined as to be inseparable. A study on Chin refugees living in New Delhi, India found that persecution due to ethnicity, religion and politics was the main reason for seeking asylum in India from Burma (Bosco, 2015).

In a conference held in Switzerland in 1999, delegates from Buddhist, Protestant, Catholic and Orthodox Christian, Jewish, Muslim, and other religious affiliations, believed that 56 conflicts around the world had religious elements. The conflict in Northern Ireland—*the troubles* between the Roman Catholic nationalist community who sought union with Ireland and the Protestant unionist community who wanted to remain with the United Kingdom—arguably has roots in religious differences. However, many other conflicts between groups of different religions as in the former Yugoslavia or in

Sudan have actually stemmed from land or other resource issues and religious beliefs have simply provided convenient fault lines along which borders could be drawn and people could be *othered*. The war in Bosnia-Herzegovina was among the Muslim, Roman Catholic, and Serbian Orthodox Christian. The civil war in Sudan (Republic of South Sudan) was among Muslims, Christians, and Animists ("Religiously-based civil unrest," 2014, paras. 8 and 9) though initially the conflict grew from the need to share water.

A Jewish man was killed outside Copenhagen's main synagogue, which prompted Israeli Prime Minister Benjamin Netanyahu to urge European Jews to return to Israel in the face of increasing attacks, not only in Denmark but in France, Germany, and the United States. Jewish-owned or run schools, temples, and supermarkets globally have requested round-the-clock security (Kamya, 2015, para. 5). ISIS released a video of 21 Coptic Christians who were beheaded at a beach in Libya (Kamya, 2015, para. 7).

Who is supposed to protect the religious? Though there are 19 major religious groups in the world, according to David Barrett *et al.* of the World Christian Encyclopedia (with those subdivided into 270 additional groups) (Barrett, Kurian & Johnson, 2001), three religious groups stand out as advocates to the peace process: Buddhists, liberation theologians and the Quakers. Buddhism of Thich Quang Duc, since 1963, includes socially and politically engaged versions of Buddhism in India, Sri Lanka, Thailand, Tibet, Taiwan, Vietnam, and Japan. These movements have reinterpreted traditional Buddhist discourse to emphasize the practice of nonviolence and quest for global peace. Liberation theology in Latin America performs a similar function among Roman Catholics, advancing the idea that God speaks through the poor and that the church should be actively engaged in improving the lives of the poor. To build the church, libertarian theologians established base communities of 10–30 church members. These communities study together and attempt to meet each other's immediate needs for food, water, sewage disposal, and electricity. The movement gained strength in Latin America during the 1970s. Because the movement insisted that the church be included in the political struggle of the poor against wealthy elites, they were considered to be more Marxist than Roman Catholic (Rhodes, 1991). Bertrand Aristide in an interview with Peter Hallward with the *London Review of Books*, described how liberation theology worked in Haiti:

> The emergence of the people as an organised public force was already taking place in Haiti in the 1980s, and by 1986 this force was strong enough to push the Duvalier dictatorship from power. It was a grass-roots movement, not a top-down project driv-

en by a single leader or a single organisation. It wasn't exclusively political, either. It took shape above all through the constitution, all over the country, of many small church communities or *ti legliz*. When I was elected president it wasn't the election of a politician, or a conventional political party; it was an expression of the mobilisation of the people as a whole. For the first time, the national palace became a place not just for professional politicians but for the people. Welcoming people from the poorest sections of Haitian society within the centre of traditional power—this was a profoundly transformative gesture. (Hallward, 2007, para. 8)

The Quaker's *Alternatives to Violence* project teaches linguistic tactics to facilitate nonviolent resolution of conflict. Nelson (2006) describes the concept:

At its heart, it is the effort to maintain unity among men. It seeks to knit the break in the sense of community whose fracture is both a cause and a result of human conflict. It relies upon love rather than hate, and though it involves a willingness to accept rather than inflict suffering, it is neither passive nor cowardly. It offers a way of meeting evil without relying on the ability to cause pain to the human being through whom evil is expressed. It seeks to change the attitude of the opponent rather than to force his submission through violence. It is, in short, the practical effort to overcome evil with good. (Nelson, 2006, para. 1)

How have media helped or hurt the religious? Media have not covered religion in ways that make sense to those who are not of those specific faiths. However, several stories have been distributed widely through social media that reinforces how media may be helping the global community make positive strides toward peace. The movement, *I will ride with you*, spread on social media in Australia when anti-Muslim sentiment was fueled after a self-styled sheikh killed two of his hostages in a gun battle in a Sydney café (Wardell, 2014, paras. 1–2). After this incident, a woman called Rachael posted on social media about an experience she'd had on a Sydney train. Sitting beside her was a Muslim woman, who was silently removing her hijab. She didn't want outward signs of her religion to show for fear of misplaced retaliation from commuters about the hostage situation in Martin Place, Sydney. Rachael ran after the woman at the next stop and said reassuringly, "Put it back on, I will walk with you." The Muslim woman instantly burst into tears, hugged Rachael and then walked off alone (Rizvi, 2015).

Other support for religious groups came from a group of Muslims in Norway who formed a *ring of peace* around a synagogue in Oslo on February 21, 2015. The group explained their motivations for promoting the event on their Facebook page. This was their invite:

Islam is about protecting our brothers and sisters, regardless of which religion they belong to. Islam is about rising above hate and never sinking to the same level as the haters. Islam is about defending each other. Muslims want to show that we deeply deplore all types of hatred of Jews, and that we are there to support them. We will therefore create a human ring around the synagogue on Saturday 21 February. Encourage everyone to come! (Tharoor, 2015, para. 4)

"We think that after the terrorist attacks in Copenhagen, it is the perfect time for us Muslims to distance ourselves from the harassment of Jews that is happening," 17-year-old event organizer Hajrad Arshad said in an interview with Norwegian television. "If someone wants to attack the synagogue, they need to step over us first," posted another of the event's organizers on Facebook. More than 1,000 people formed a ring around the synagogue (Tharoor, 2015, para. 6).

Ethnic Groups

How has conflict affected ethnic groups? There are more than 5000 ethnic groups in the world. This is according to a report entitled *By the Numbers: Ethnic Groups in the World* published in *Scientific American* (Doyle, 1998). Estimates vary, and the classification of ethnic groups remains vague and debatable. Yet the fact that there are 6909 living languages worldwide substantiates the thousands of distinct ethnic groups throughout the world (Lewis, Simons & Fennig, 2015). Many groups live in harmony; Trinidad and Tobago pride themselves in calling their society the Rainbow Society embracing descendants of people from Africa, India, China, Europe, the Mediterranean, the Middle East, and South America. However, language differences, politics, resource scarcity, and disenfranchisement of certain groups frequently cause conflict that breaks down upon ethnic lines. In Myanmar, the government began a peace initiative with eleven major rebel forces in 2013. Little headway has been made as distrust of the government army runs deep among ethnic minorities (Matsui, 2015). Many contemporary struggles are between different ethnic groups in the same country or geographical area. When ethnic loyalties prevail, a perilous logic clicks in. The escalation goes from ethnic superiority to ethnic cleansing to genocide.

There are countless examples of how ethnicity is seen in conflict given the genocides of the twentieth century. At this point, it is important to recognize how Western media have created the central nature of ethnicity in conflict.

In regard to Rwanda, Western media have been alleged to have colluded with the US Clinton administration to construct the narrative of the genocide as a *tribal war* so as to not create concern, and then pressure, to do anything (Baldauf, 2009). Contrast this with coverage of Darfur, which tended to talk more about the religious identity of the involved groups to force pressure on the US Bush administration to do something, much Bush's support came from mega churches, the members of which did not like to hear about the persecution of Christians by Muslims (Power, 2004).

Who is supposed to protect ethnic groups? Legislative measures by nation states include launching and implementing public awareness campaigns intended to prevent racial discrimination and increase tolerance. When nation states lack the foundation for protecting minority rights or governments actively encourage intolerance for minority groups then conflict-ridden environments ensue. As tensions involving national minority issues are enflamed, disenchantment with one's government can evolve into conflict situations. In the past ten years alone, ethnic conflicts have plagued a hand full of countries such as Rwanda and Burundi, the former Republic of Yugoslavia and more recently, Indonesia, East Timor, and Fiji ("Multi-ethnic states and the protection of minority rights," 2000).

In 1992, the General Assembly adopted the Declaration on the Rights of Persons Belonging to National or Ethnic, Religious and Linguistic Minorities. It includes a list of rights that minorities are entitled to, including the right to enjoy their own culture without interference, and the right to participate effectively in decisions at the national level, among others ("Multi-ethnic states and the protection of minority rights," 2000).

Multilateral monitoring of the compliance of nation states to their international commitments with regard to protecting minority rights has increased transparency. Within the United Nations system, this responsibility is shared by the Commission on Human Rights, the Sub-Commission on the Prevention of Discrimination and Protection of Minorities, the Committee on Economic, Social and Cultural Rights, and the Committee on the Elimination of Racial Discrimination. A Working Group on Minorities has also been established in order to review the promotion and practical realization of the Declaration. It serves as the focal point of the United Nations in the field of minority protection and is the main forum for constructive dialogue on the treatment of minorities by governments ("Multi-ethnic states and the protection of minority rights," 2000).

How have media helped or hurt ethnic groups? In Nigeria in November 2008, newspapers were accused of allowing their ethnic and/or religious interests dictate the prism through which journalists viewed and reported the crisis.

> What we have been witnessing in the reportage of the ethno-religious conflict in northern Nigeria is a form of journalistic recklessness that reflects total disregard for the truth or the continuing survival of Nigeria as a corporate and sovereign entity. These included the Northern newspapers of the *New Nigerian* and *Daily Trust* as well as broadcast media like the Federal Radio Corporation of Nigeria (FRCN), Kaduna, the Hausa versions of international broadcast organizations like the BBC, VOA, Radio France International (RFI) and Deutsch Welle (DW) as pro-Islamic North. (Musa & Ferguson, 2013, p. 8)

Another example of how media can influence specific cultures is the Studio-Ijambo project in Burundi. This project was found to have had positive impact on inter-ethnic relations, social and political mobilization, political elite negotiations, public institutions, and mass or elite conflict behavior in post-conflict peace building in Rwanda but also in neighboring Burundi (Hagos, 2001, cited in Bratić, 2008). Studio Ijambo (*wise words* in Kirundi) is an independent radio production studio in Burundi that produces radio programs to promote dialogue, peace, and reconciliation. Studio Ijambo was formed in the aftermath of the Rwandan genocide of 1994, during which the *hate* radio broadcasts of Radio Mille Collines fomented ethnic violence. In neighboring Burundi, many feared a similar outbreak of genocide. Ethnic tensions were high, Hutu-Tutsi relations were polarized, and violence was a daily occurrence. Rumors and lies fuelled the environment of hatred and mistrust. Created in 1995, Studio Ijambo was a direct response to this climate of fear and recognized the power of radio to affect hearts and minds, as in Rwanda, but this time toward peace and reconciliation. Paluck (2007) similarly reported that radio had positive impact in communicating social norms and influencing behaviors that contributed to intergroup tolerance and reconciliation in post-conflict Rwanda. Since 1993, at least 200,000 Burundians have been killed in the civil war. In reporting on this violence, Studio Ijambo's mixed Hutu and Tutsi team of journalists work to present a face of ethnic unity otherwise absent in the society. Rather than a Hutu journalist reporting on killings by Tutsis, or vice versa, journalists report on violence committed by their own ethnic group (Helmann, 2002).

During the war, at a time when Tutsis were afraid to enter Hutu neighborhoods and vice versa, radio stations deployed teams of mixed ethnicity. They gave airtime to Hutu rebel leaders and civil-society activists and told stories of Burundians who had risked their lives to save people of different ethnicities. Journalists were trained in conflict resolution, says Floride Ahitungiye, the Burundi director of Search for Common Ground, an American non-profit that broadcasted the first independent reports during the civil war. Call-in political talk shows and soap operas promoting peace and democracy were hugely popular, despite their pedagogical themes (Currier, 2014). The programs, in Kirundi and French, included current events, public affairs, and cultural programming. Messages about social and political change were integrated into the development of characters and story lines. For example, one radio drama featured a Hutu family and a Tutsi family who lived next door to each other. Entitled *Umubanyi Niwe Muryango* (Our Neighbors, Ourselves), this drama aimed to help listeners identify with problems faced by others and to devise positive, nonviolent ways of resolving conflicts. For additional programs offered by Studio Ijambo see Exhibit II in the Appendix (Studio Ijambo, nd).

Unlike Rwanda, where the response to genocide was to ban all mention of ethnicity and to clamp down on the press, Burundi saw "this remarkable opening," says Marie-Soleil Frère, a Belgian researcher specializing in Central African media, "where the national radio became much more pluralist and the private radios became very popular and powerful" (Currier, 2014, para. 13).

With 85 percent of the population in Burundi having access to radios; Studio Ijambo has reached an estimated 12 million people throughout the Great Lakes region. A 1999 evaluation revealed that over 90 percent of Burundian radio listeners described the radio dramas as dealing with true-to-life issues in a way that brings Burundians together. In 2000, 82 percent of those surveyed said that Studio Ijambo's programmes help reconciliation *a lot* (Helmann, 2014). The recipient of several awards, Studio Ijambo was the subject of a story by the United States ABC-TV news program Nightline. Its broadcasts are used regularly by other news organizations such as Reuters, the BBC, and Voice of America (Helmann, 2014).

Internally Displaced Persons

How has conflict affected Internally Displaced Persons (IDPs)? In 2013, the number of IDPs was at 33.3 million worldwide, according to data from the UNHCR, the UN Refugee Agency (Annual Report, 2014). Sixty-three percent were in five conflict and violence-ridden countries: Syria, Colombia, Nigeria, Democratic Republic of Congo and Sudan. Colombia's civil war has been going on for half a century with government security forces and paramilitary units combating insurgent forces within the country, particularly the Revolutionary Armed Forces of Colombia (FARC) and the National Liberation Army (ELN). Add in the United States-funded death squads and the powerful Colombian drug industry and the conflict has significantly damaged the people of Colombia (Højen, 2015).

Within Colombia, people have been displaced by the drug industry to expand coca cultivation in areas formerly inhabited by local farmers. Most displacements take place in the remote rural areas where armed conflicts are common. Most of the IDPs in Colombia are indigenous people and Afro-Colombians. The result has been an increased economic and social inequality as the poor become poorer and specific ethnic groups suffer more than others do with a flow from rural to urban (Højen, 2015, para. 3).

Who is supposed to protect the IDPs? The difference between displaced and refugee status is that both have fled their homes often as a result of conflict but people become refugees when they cross over into another country. A United Nations report *Guiding Principles on Internal Displacemen* defines IDPs as "persons or groups of persons who have been forced or obliged to flee or to leave their homes or places of habitual residence, in particular as a result of or in order to avoid the effects of armed conflict, situations of generalized violence, violations of human rights or natural or human-made disasters, and who have not crossed an internationally recognized state border" (Lam, 2013, para. 5).

How have media helped or hurt IDPs? In the Ukraine during the conflict in 2014, the Crimea SOS initiative is an example of how social media provided help to displaced people on a daily basis. The help did not come from the government but from ordinary people. Media in the Ukraine portray IDPs as arrogant and lazy people who live at someone's expenses and who are somehow always dirty with negative descriptions of their political views and behavior. In monitoring how media covered IDPs' issues, Crimea SOS reported that coverage was limited to publicity of private funds and not on IDPs' problems or how to help the IDPs. Ukrainian television provided coverage of how volunteers were helping the army, but no stories on initiatives to help IDPs with food and clothes ("UNHCR invites media," 2014).

In Syria, IDPs remain invisible and live in constant fear instead of receiving international protection and media coverage. As in the case of Syria, with the State's restrictions on international media coverage and public assistance, very little protection for displaced persons can be had (Lam, 2013).

In Pakistan during the early days of the conflict, the Pakistani news media's coverage of the IDPs' plight was intense, with regular news and special features coverage, along with fundraising drives for charities and government relief efforts. IDPs now say, however, that as the media's gaze has been drawn toward antigovernment protests in Islamabad and elsewhere, the attention being paid to the humanitarian catastrophe unfolding around them has began to dry up (Hashim, 2014).

Last Word: The research on these populations affected by conflict suggests that a majority of negative coverage, if any coverage, is often through traditional media and that positive media products are being produced by NGOs and private institutions. Giving voice to the voiceless is the goal of peace journalism. This can be accomplished by illustrating the nature of people's problems and concerns and by fostering a realization that people are the true peacemakers, not elites or their treaties or institutions, and that language matters. When cultures have different words to communicate, journalists need to understand there are differences and to ask more questions. For example, how are statistics to be used in the small Amazon community in their language, Pirahã, which has no words for numbers (Hartshorne, 2009)? Journalists need to think in the language of the conflict they are covering. A University of Chicago study showed that thinking in a foreign language actually reduces deep-seated, misleading biases and prevents emotional, unconscious thinking from interfering with systematic, analytical thinking (Harms, 2012).

Discussion: Choose an audience affected by violence, argue how media may strengthen or weaken this audience.

References

Amnesty International (n.d.). *Amnesty international USA LGBT pride tool kit*. Retrieved from http://www.amnestyusa.org/pdfs/YogyakartaPrinciples.pdf?_sm_au_=iVV5402rZ6PZQ066.

Annual Report (2014). Annual report shows a record 33.3 million were internally displaced in 2013. UNHCR. The UN Refugee Agency. Retrieved from http://www.unhcr.org/537334 d0427.html.

Baldauf, S. (2009, April 7). Why the US didn't intervene in the Rwandan genocide. *The Christian Science Monitor*. Retrieved from http://www.csmonitor.com/World/Africa/2009/0407/p06s14-woaf.html.

Barrett, D., Kurian, G. T., & Johnson, T. M. (2001). *World Christian Encyclopedia*. Oxford University Press. Retrieved from http://www.worldchristiandatabase.org/wcd/doc/WCE_Northern_Cyprus.pdf.

Boorstein, M. (2012, October 31). Rabbi and pop-culture star Shmuley Boteach adds political candidate to résumé. *The Washington Post*. Retrieved from http://www.washingtonpost.com/local/rabbi-and-pop-culture-star-shmuley-boteach-adds-political-candidate-toresume/2012/10/31/8d6ef540-2303-11e2-ac85-e669876c6a24_story.html.

Borschel-Dan, A. (2014, February 24). Volunteers brave 'war zone' to aid elderly Jews in Kiev. *The Times of Israel*. Retrieved from http://www.timesofisrael.com/volunteers-brave-war-zone-to-aid-elderly-jews-in-kiev/.

Boteach, S. (2014, December 22). The story behind an ad condemning the treatment by Hamas and Iran of the LGBT community. *The Jerusalem Post*. Retrieved from http://www.jpost.com/landedpages/printarticle.aspx?ld=385442.

Children in conflict (nd). SOS Children's Villages. Retrieved from http://www.child-soldier.org/.

"Circles of Hell: Domestic, public and state violence against women in Egypt" (2015). Amnesty International. Retrieved from http://www.amnestyusa.org/sites/default/files/mde_120042015.pdf.

Cole, C. F., Arafat, C., Tidhar, C., Tafesh, W. Z., Fox, N. A., Killen, M., Ardila-Rey, A., Leavitt, L. S., Lesser, G., Richman, B. A., & Yung, F. (2003). The educational impact of Rechov Sumsum/Shara'a Simsim: A Sesame Street television series to promote respect and understanding among children living in Israel, the West Bank, and Gaza. *The International Society for the Study of Behavioral Development*, 27(5), 409–422. Retrieved from http://jbd.sagepub.com/content/27/5/409.full.pdf+html.

Cranston, G. (nd'). Abuse of elderly woman. *IrinNews*. Retrieved from http://www.irinnews.org/pdf/bb/12irin_duo-elderly-abuse.pdf.

Currier, C. (2014, April 19). Snap, crackle, hiss: The sound of democracy in Burundi. *Aljazeera America*. Retrieved from https://www.sfcg.org/snap-crackle-hiss-the-sound-of-democracy-in-burundi/.

Deen, A. R. (2004, August 11). Aged in Africa. Global Action on Aging. Retrieved from http://globalaging.org/armedconflict/countryreports/africa/aroun.htm.

Doyle, R. (1998, September). Ethnic groups in the world. *Scientific American*, 279(3), 30. Retrieved from http://www.nature.com/scientificamerican/journal/v279/n3/pdf/scientificamerican0998-30.pdf.

"Egyptian actress says a visit from Sisi 'worth sex attack' (2014, June 14). *Al Arabiya News*. Retrieved from http://english.alarabiya.net/en/variety/2014/06/14/Egyptian-actress-says-a-visit-from-Sisi-worth-sex-attack-.html.

El-Naggar, M. (2015, February 18). From a private school in Cairo to ISIS killing fields in Syria. *The New York Times*. Retrieved from http://www.nytimes.com/2015/02/19/world/middleeast/from-a-private-school-in-cairo-to-isis-killing-fields-in-syria-video.html?_r=0.

Forsythe, D. P. (Ed.) (2009). Convention on the rights of persons with disabilities. *Encyclopedia of Human Rights*, Oxford University Press, p. 45.

Gabriel, T. G. (2013, July 1). New wave of sexual assaults reported in Egypt. *Big Story AP*. Retrieved from http://bigstory.ap.org/article/new-wave-sexual-assaults-reported-egypt.

Gay, W. C. (1999). The language of war and peace. In Kurtz, L. (Ed.), *Encyclopedia of Violence, Peace and Conflict*. San Diego: Academic Press, 2, 303–312.

Guilbert, K. (2015, February 23). Islamic State uses social media to groom British Muslim girls—think tank. *Thomson Reuters Foundation*. Retrieved from http://www.trust.org/item/20150223182031-io9hj/?source=fiOtherNews3.

Hagos, A. (2001). Media intervention in peace building in Burundi: The studio Ijambo experience and impact. Retrieved from http://pdf.usaid.gov/pdf_docs/PNACY570.pdf.

Hallward, P. (2007, February 27). An interview with Jean Bertrand Aristide. *London Review of Books*. Retrieved from http://www.lrb.co.uk/v29/n04/peter-hallward/an-interview-with-jean-bertrand-aristide.

Harms, W. (2012, April 25). Thinking in a foreign language helps economic decision-making. *UChicago News*. Retrieved from http://news.uchicago.edu/article/2012/04/25/thinking-foreign-language-helps-economic-decision-making.

Hartshorne, J. (2009, August 18). Does language shape what we think. *Scientific American*. Retrieved from http://www.scientificamerican.com/article/does-language-shape-what/.

Hashim, A. (2014, October 23). North Waziristan's forgotten, desperate displaced people. *Beacon Reader*. Retrieved from https://www.beaconreader.com/asadhashim/northwaziristans-forgotten-desperate-displaced-people.

Helmann, D. (2002, February 15). Studio Ijambo. *Media Development*. Retrieved from http://www.comminit.com/media-development/content/studio-ijambo.

Hirano, K. (2006, July 31). Photographer captures essence of elderly full of life, near death. *The Japan Times*. Retrieved from http://www.globalaging.org/elderrights/world/2006/japanphoto.htm.

Højen, L. (2015, February 2). Colombia's "invisible crisis": Internally displaced persons. Council on Hemispheric Affairs. Retrieved from http://www.coha.org/colombiasinvisiblecrisisinternally-displaced-persons/.

"IGLHRC, MADRE on alleged executions for sodomy by ISIS in Iraq" (2015, January 21). Windy City Media Group. Retrieved from http://www.windycitymediagroup.com/lgbt/IGLHRC-MADRE-on-alleged-executions-for-sodomy-by-ISIS-in-Iraq/50286.html.

Ivie, R. (2009). Breaking the spell of war: Peace journalism's democratic prospect. *Javnost-The Public*, 16(4), 5–21.

Jensen, E. (2007, October 24). Grieving mothers on 2 sides of a suicide bombing. *The New York Times*. Retrieved from http://www.nytimes.com/2007/10/24/arts/television/24die.html?_r=0.

"Journalist gang raped in Tahrir Square during Egypt protests" (2013, July 4). *The Clarion Project*. Retrieved from http://www.clarionproject.org/news/journalist-gang-raped-tahrir-square-during-egypt-protests.

Kamya, S. (2015, February 22). Rwanda: Why can't we all just get along? *AllAfrica*. Retrieved from http://allafrica.com/stories/201502230361.html.

Khosla, S. (2014, December 17). This graphic shows how dangerous it is for children to go to school in Pakistan. *Globalpost*. Retrieved from http://www.globalpost.com/dispatch/news/regions/asia-pacific/pakistan/141216/chart-pakistan-education-under-attack.

Lam, A. (2013, November 13). The invisible refugees—internally displaced people. *New America Media*. Retrieved from http://newamericamedia.org/2013/11/the-invisible-refugees---internally-displaced-people.php.

Lewis, M. P., Simons, G. F., & Fennig, C. D. (eds.) (2015). Ethnologue: Languages of the world. Eighteenth edition. Dallas, Texas: SIL International. Online version: http://www.ethnologue.com.

Masalha, S. (2003). Children and violent conflict: Disturbing findings from a study of Palestinian children's dreams in the second Intifada. *Palestine-Israel Journal of Politics, Economic and Culture*, 10(1), 6 pages. Retrieved from http://www.pij.org/details.php?id=82.

Matsui, M. (2015, February 26). Deadly fighting looms over general election campaign. *Nikkei Asian Review*. Retrieved from http://asia.nikkei.com/print/article/77851.

McCoy, T. (2014, June 18). Egypt's sexual harassment pandemic—and the powerlessness of hashtags. *The Washington Post*. Retrieved from http://www.washingtonpost.com/news/morning-mix/wp/2014/06/18/egypts-sexual-harassment-pandemic-and-the-powerlessness-of-hashtags/.

Mirovalev, M. (2015, January 21). Russia's rising anti-gay hysteria. *Al Jazeera*. Retrieved from http://www.aljazeera.com/indepth/features/2015/01/russia-rising-anti-gay-hysteria-2015 11992033980189.html.

Mojon, J. M. (2015, January 17). IS jihadists free 200 elderly Yazidis in north Iraq. *Business Insider*. Retrieved from http://www.businessinsider.com/afp-is-jihadists-free-200-elderly-yazidis-in-north-iraq-2015-1.

"Multi-ethnic states and the protection of minority rights" (2000, July). World Conference against racism. *Press Kit Issues*. Retrieved from http://www.un.org/WCAR/ekit/minority.htm.

Musa, A. O. & Ferguson, N. (2013, April). Enemy framing and the politics of reporting religious conflicts in the Nigerian press. *Media, War & Conflict*, 6(1), 7–20.

Nelson, R. (2006). Alternative to violence. Speak truth to power, a Quaker search for an alternative to violence, a study of international conflict, prepared for the American Friends Service Committee. Retrieved from http://www.quaker.org/sttp-4.html.

NGO Working Group on Women, Peace and Security (2005). Retrieved from http://www.womenpeacesecurity.org/publications.

Ola, L. & Abrak, I. (2015, January 10). Child suicide bomber kills at least 16 in Nigeria. Reuters. Retrieved from http://www.reuters.com/article/2015/01/10/us-nigeria-violence-potiskum-idUSKBN0KJ0HH20150110 accessed January 27, 2015.

Paluck, E. L. (2007). Reducing intergroup prejudice and conflict with the mass media: A field experiment in Rwanda. A PhD Dissertation. Connecticut: Yale University.

Power, S. (2004, August 30). Dying in Darfur: Can the ethnic cleansing in Sudan be stopped? *The New Yorker*. Retrieved from http://www.newyorker.com/magazine/2004/08/30/dying-in-darfur.

"Religiously-based civil unrest and warfare" (2014, August 10). Ontario Consultants on Religious Tolerance. Retrieved from http://www.religioustolerance.org/curr_war.htm.

Reporters without borders (nd). http://en.rsf.org/.

Rhodes, R. (1991, Winter). Christian revolution in Latin America: The changing face of liberation theology. *Christian Research Journal*. Retrieved from http://home.earthlink.net/~ronrhodes/Liberation.html.

Rizvi, J. (2015, January 13). Dear Australian Muslims: We will ride with you. Mamamia Woman's Network. Retrieved from http://www.mamamia.com.au/social/dear-australian-muslims-will-ride/#jtcT1fDeFvgDRtG3.99.

Saul, H. (2015, April 9). ISIS 'throw man off a building for homosexual affair' and beat him to death when he survives. *The Independent*. Retrieved from http://www.independent.co.uk/news/world/middle-east/isis-throw-man-off-a-building-for-homosexual-affair-and-beat-him-to-death-when-he-survives-10012709.html.

Sayfo, O. A. (2013, May 6). Syria's music wars. *Al-Monitor: the Pulse of the Middle East*. Retrieved from http://www.al-monitor.com/pulse/originals/2013/05/music-syria-war-pop-rap-dabke-regime-rebels.html#.

Schirch, L. & Sewak, M. (2005). The role of women in peace building. Paper issued by European Centre for Conflict Prevention. Retrieved from http://www.google.com/url?sa=t&rct=j&q=&esrc=s&source=web&cd=1&ved=0CB8QFjAA&url=http%3A%2F%2Fwww.conflictrecovery.org%2Fbin%2FIssue_paper_on_the_Role_of_Women_in_Peacebuilding_Jan2005.doc&ei=IyQoVfGRM8P4gwSF1YKwDw&usg=AFQjCNGzaAgpv_ESncIxgMycjdwUTu1PAQ&bvm=bv.90491159,d.eXY.

Studio Ijambo (nd). Programs. Retrieved from http://www.studioijambo.org.

Taylor, A. (2015, March 6). Denmark debates putting Muhammad cartoons in school text books. *The Washington Post*. Retrieved from http://www.washingtonpost.com/local/rabbi-and-pop-culture-star-shmuley-boteach-adds-political-candidate-to-resume/2012/10/31/8d6ef540-2303-11e2-ac85-e669876c6a24_story.html.

Tharoor, I. (2015, February 18). Norwegian Muslims will form a human shield around an Oslo synagogue. *The Washington Post*. Retrieved from https://www.washingtonpost.com/news/worldviews/wp/2015/02/18/norwegian-muslims-will-form-a-human-shield-around-an-oslo-synagogue/?utm_term=.85290655ac6d.

Unicef (1995a, December 11). State of the World's Children. Cited Hammarberg, Thomas, presentation to the Regional Consultation on the Impact of Armed Conflict on Children in the Arab Region, in Cairo, 1995. Retrieved from http://www.unicef.org/sowc96/2csoldrs.htm.

Unicef (1995b, December 11). War Relief for Children. Retrieved from http://www.unicef.org/sowc96/16relief.htm.

"UNHCR invites media to discuss how to improve media coverage about displaced persons" (2014, September 19). UNHCR The UN Refugee Agency. Retrieved from http://unhcr.org.ua/en/2011-08-26-06-58-56/news-archive/1339-unhcr-invites-media-to-discuss-how-to-improve-media-coverage-about-displaced-persons.

Wardell, J. (2014, December 15). Sydney siege sparks 'I'll ride with you' campaign for worried Muslims. Reuters. Retrieved from http://www.reuters.com/article/2014/12/16/us-australia-security-solidarity-idUSKBN0JU01120141216.

Warshel, Y. (2007, August 29). "As though there is peace": Opinions of Jewish-Israel children about watching Rechov Sumsum/Shara'a Simsim amidst armed political conflict. *Democracy and Governance*. Retrieved from http://www.comminit.com/democracy-governance/content/though-there-peace-opinions-jewish-israeli-children-about-watching-rechovsumsumsharaa-s.

Who Makes the News? Global Media Monitoring Project (2010). Published by the World Association for Christian Communication (WACC). Retrieved from http://www.whomakesthenews.org/.

Women's Political and Economic Leadership Statistics (2000, May). Women's Learning Partnership, National Council of Women's Organizations. The United Nations High Commissioner for Refugees. Report of the International Panel of Eminent Personalities to Investigate the 1994 Genocide in Rwanda and Surrounding Events, May 2000, Women's E-News, United States Department of Education.

Yiping, C. (2011). Revisiting peace journalism with a gender lens. Media Development. Toronto, Canada: WACC Publications. Retrieved from http://www.isiswomen.org/index.php?option=com_content&view=article&id=1505:revisiting-peace-journalism-with-a-gender-len&catid=22:movements-within&Itemid=229.

Youth activism for peace and co-existence in Palestine and Israel (nd). The Free Child Project. Retrieved from http://www.freechild.org/PromotingCoexistence.htm.

Zawya (2015, February 5). It Gets Brighter offers hope for the mentally ill. *The Daily Star*. Retrieved from https://www.zawya.com/story/It_Gets_Brighter_offers_hope_for_the_mentally-ill-DS05022015_dsart*286430/.

Zwi, A. B., Garfield, R., & Loretti, A. (2002). Collective violence, In Krug, E. G., Dahlberg, L. L., Mercy, J. A., Zwi, A. B., & Lozano, R. (Eds.), *World Report on Violence and Health* (pp. 213–239). Geneva: World Health Organization.

· 5 ·

VIOLENCE

Nature of Contemporary Warfare and Media's Contribution to Covering Violence

Uriel Henao is a balladeer in Colombia who is called the king of the prohib-
ited ballads, a musical genre that describes the exploits of guerrilla commanders, paramilitary warlords, lowly coca growers, and cocaine kingpins. Simon
Romero in a *New York Times* article (2010, para. 1) describes Henao's en-
trance into El Retorno, Colombia: "He arrived at this town on the edge of
guerrilla territory with his entourage. They included a producer, a sound man,
two scantily clad dancers and a harried servant, who carried his cowboy hat,
his snakeskin boots, his tequila and, of course, his bling: a bulky gold necklace
emblazoned with the name of Uriel Henao."

Romero (2010) writes that the ballads give graphic descriptions of the
drug trade, descending from Mexico's narcocorridos, and are not played on
the radio but sung by 600 bands around the country. The genre, according to
Romero (2010), has developed into a form of oral history of Colombia's long
internal war involving guerrilla groups, paramilitary factions, and government
forces. Romero suggests that the ballads provide an outlet for Colombia's folk
culture, especially in urban slums and remote rural areas. At the end of the
concert, Henao says: "Colombia needs people like me to tell it the truth about
what takes place in this country. The truth sells" (Romero, 2010). The bal-

ladeers tell stories about the war within their countries. They tell the stories left out of traditional media.

Globally, violence takes the lives of more than 1.6 million people annually; 12 percent of that is through war. The World Health Organization defines violence in this context as "the intentional use of physical force or power, threatened or actual, against oneself, another person, or against a group or community, which either results in or has a high likelihood of resulting in injury, death, psychological harm, maldevelopment, or deprivation," but acknowledges that the inclusion of "the use of power" in its definition expands on the conventional meaning of the word ("Definition of Violence," nd).

Media's coverage of violence appears to be a priority when the number of stories are tallied that are delivered to audiences who appear eager to know the horrors and statistics. If there is a different way of reporting on violence, then both the journalists and communication academics need to understand the nature of contemporary warfare so that they can cover the conflict in a different way, a more peaceful way. The chapter is divided into two parts. The first goal is to describe contemporary warfare and how it is changing so as to better prepare future journalists for covering conflict. A secondary goal is to describe how media may have fostered violence and how media can encourage peace.

Part 1: Nature of Contemporary Warfare

Interconnectedness of people around the world brought about by the advent of technology and social media has changed how wars are and will be conducted (Metz, 2000, p. vii). The information revolution has increased accumulation of information but has slowed the pace of decision-making. Put another way, Metz suggests, "that interconnectedness undercuts the viability of authoritarianism by allowing repressed citizens to communicate, organize and mobilize; it also places handcuffs on elected governments" (2000, p. viii). Thus, this pull-push effect of interconnectedness through use of technology also has created warfare only imagined in movies.

At the beginning of the twenty-first century, there were three modes of warfare: formal war, informal war and gray area war. Formal war is between state militaries. Informal war is armed conflict between a state military and an insurgent army or ethnic militia. These wars are based on some combination of ethnicity, race, regionalism, economics, personality, and economics and often use refugee disasters to attract outside attention and intervention. Gray area wars combine elements of traditional war fighting with those of organized crime (Metz, 2000).

Future wars are forecasted to be attacks via computer viruses, worms, logic bombs and Trojan horses rather than bullets, bombs and missiles. Those future wars are here with examples taken from North Korea, China, and Russia. Information technology provides a way to damage an enemy's national or commercial infrastructure badly enough to attain *victory* without having to first defeat fielded military forces (Metz, 2000, p. xiii). Additionally, other emerging technologies could prove equally revolutionary, such as psycho technology where military commanders might have the technology to alter the beliefs, perceptions, and feelings of enemies. In addition, whereas democracies may be bound by duty, honor, sacrifice, and the highest ethical standards, the world is changing and information technologies will be used to fight wars. It is hard enough for democracies to follow ethical standards but not all parties involved in conflict will do the same. There is concern that the number of democratic states may decline and along with the erosion of using media as the public sphere and therefore promote democracies, the problem of how a journalist can effectively cover conflict is accentuated.

Histories of modern warfare indicate that there has been a decline in traditional warfare since the end of World War II. This decline in traditional warfare suggests that there has been a long span of world peace, but the conflicts in Iraq, Afghanistan, the former Yugoslavia, the Great Lakes region of Africa, Ukraine, Central America, and Sudan prove otherwise. Arguments for new forms of warfare use examples of war as international policing (Bosnia), the increasing privatization of military functions (US operations in Somalia and Iraq), new forms of combat based on space-based reconnaissance and unmanned aerial vehicles, increasingly technical *information war*, and the changing world political order (no longer bipolar, but an almost medieval collection of states, substates, and suprastate entities rubbing against each other) (Lynch & Bravman, 2008, p. 14). One thing is certain; information and how it is used and developed will be used in modern and future warfare.

War Makes Money

War is big business. As of 2015, the United States spent two billion dollars fighting ISIS, eight hundred billion in Iraq with an equal amount in Afghanistan, to total spending one trillion dollars in conflict since 2001 ("Cost of

National Security," 2015). To evaluate the actual size of business costs of warfare, the desire of a government or organization wanting to control natural resources must also be calculated in. For example, in the Middle East there have been constant invasions to control natural resources and trade routes, according to Ivana Peric, a Croatian blogger living in the Middle East. "There can be no social, political or economic stability while neocolonialism and conflicts are continuing, ever-present, with profound consequences, and with no real efforts from the international society to stop them. International society, particularly USA and NATO countries, have had their share in stirring up the conflicts. When it was necessary for resources and power, they helped the dictators, supported the bad regimes, and when it was necessary, again for resources, they took it upon themselves to 'rid the countries of the dictators,' delivering democracy with no real exit strategy, without examining the consequences wars have on societies" (Peric, 2015). The cost of warfare may be big business for some, but for others it is a catastrophe where everything is lost: life, limbs, family, home, employment, and quality of life.

Effects of Violence

Media portrayals of conflict show violence. The devastation is obvious in the photos of entire neighborhoods bombed and images of people dead in the streets. Media have not adequately reported the extenuating damage violence has had on the infrastructures within nation states, specifically the environment. In Nigeria, 162 editions of three national dailies: *The Punch*, the *Vanguard* and the *Daily Sun*, were examined on the effect of Boko Haram violence on the environment (Nwabueze & Ekwughe, 2014). The authors found that the Nigerian dailies gave prominence to the Boko Haram ("Western education is forbidden") and their killing of 13,000 civilians in northeast Nigeria but little attention was paid to the environmental implications of the violence. Lewis (2014) suggests that there have been several attempts made to explain the extreme violence of Boko Haram to focus on resource scarcity, overpopulation, environmental degradation, and especially climate change (para. 1).

Other examples of how the environment has been affected by conflict can be seen with Libya's struggle to supply power and gas. Lack of electricity has caused ten-hour shortages and has affected mobile phone coverage. Power plants have been hit by insurgents or made inaccessible due to nearby clashes. Departure of foreign partners worsened the situation ("Libya struggles to keep electricity on," 2015). In Kenya, the armed conflict over resources between the Pokot and Turkana communities exacerbated the drought conditions along with the discovery that the water in the regional aquifer was too salty to drink. Limited resources affected the traditional nomadic herders in the area, who make up 60 percent of the population. Malnutrition rates have been above the emergency level of 15 percent. The herding communities have become heavily armed with weapons from the Sudanese and Ugandan wars (Ruvaga, 2015). In Iraq, more than five million people need medical service. In the northern region of Kurdistan, there are 2.5 million people displaced by conflict since last year ("5 million people need health service in Iraq: UN," 2015).

Can Violence Be Understood?

Violence can be described, but journalists must also understand violence. Learning from people who have experienced violence is one way to begin understanding violence. Galtung, who developed the concept of peace journalism, used his experiences to cement his ideas. At 12 years old, his country, Norway, was occupied by Germany during World War II. The Nazis arrested his father. This experience caused Galtung, as he became older, to become a peace mediator; thus, he chose to perform 18 months of social service in place of his obligatory military service. After 12 months, he insisted that the remainder of his service be spent in activities relevant to peace, but instead, the Norwegian authorities sent him to prison for six months. Through these experiences, Galtung began developing peace journalism. He defined violence as three types: direct, structural and cultural (Galtung, 1969).

Direct violence is physically manifested, it is related to a discernible event, and it has to involve a perpetrator and a purpose (Kaufman, 2014). An example of direct violence is murder.

Structural violence refers to a form of violence where some social structure or social institution may harm people by preventing them from meeting their basic needs. Institutionalized elitism, ethnocentrism, classism, racism, sexism, nationalism, and ageism are some examples of structural violence. Structural violence and direct violence are said to be highly interdependent, including family violence, racial violence, hate crimes, terrorism, genocide, and war. Other related types of violence emerging from structural violence include self-destruction (alcohol abuse, drug abuse, suicide, depression, and internalized oppression), community destruction (crime, interpersonal violence, domestic violence, and rape), and national and international destruction (rebel move-ments, terrorism, civil wars, revolutions, coups, and war) (Schirch and Sewak, 2005).

Structural violence issues have been reported through global telecommu-nications. Not only wars, but also major tragedies—such as famines, home-lessness, and the plight of refugees and human rights abuses—are graphically portrayed on our television screens. Structural violence in South Africa was how apartheid separated and gave unearned privileges to white Afrikaners while disadvantaging black and colored South Africans. In India, the caste system has continued to perpetuate intercaste violence and social ostracism. A final example of structural violence was in the forced movement of people by Pol Pot during the rule of the Khmer Rouge in Cambodia resulting in the deaths of 25 percent of the Cambodian population.

Cultural violence refers to aspects of culture that can be used to justify or legitimize direct or structural violence, and may be exemplified by religion and ideology, language and art, empirical science, and formal science. Cultur-al violence makes direct and structural violence look or feel right, or at least not wrong, according to Galtung (1990). The study of cultural violence high-lights the way in which the act of direct violence and the fact of structural violence are legitimized and thus made acceptable in society. This is relevant because of the growing way in which communicative processes are linked to cultural processes. Cultural violence is defined as when any aspect of culture such as language, religion, ideology, art, or cosmology is used to legitimize direct or structural violence (Hyndman, 2009).

An example of cultural violence can be seen in the February 2015 video of ISIS extremists demolishing statues and artefacts in the Mosul Museum and at the Nergal Gate to the ancient Assyrian city of Ninevah. Reports from Bagh-dad told of further iconoclastic crimes in the north of the country, including the obliteration of more Assyrian monuments at Nimrud and the razing of the Parthian ruins of Hatra. Irina Bokova, the director-general of UNESCO, described these acts as an attempt at *cultural cleansing*: devastating a people by annihilating that which roots them to the past (Marks, 2015, para. 1).

Part 2: How Media Have Covered Violence: The Good, Bad, and Ugly

To understand violence and how media may have covered violence, a review of the *Journal of Peace Research* has been made with some comparisons with the *Journal of Conflict Resolution* to better understand trends in peace research over the past 50 years. The results indicate that negative peace, essentially the absence of war, was the main focus in peace research from the start. Positive peace, in the sense of cooperation or integration, has emerged on the peace research agenda. Despite this shift in focus, many articles continue to have violence or related terms in the title (Gleditsch *et al.*, 2014), which brings to the forefront that violence, as a term, can be discussed separately from other dimensions of peace journalism.

The Good Media Coverage

Media have helped change how people react to acts of violence. For example, Neda Agha Soltan, a 26-year-old woman, was shot and killed in Iran's postelection protests of 2009. This story was used in social media to define the significance of political violence. Cell phone footage of Neda dying was posted online by an anonymous citizen-journalist. Immediately, media users began juxtaposing images sampled from the footage with words, texts, photographs, drawings, and music (Gyori, 2013), transforming her into a symbol of the antigovernment movement. There were 6,860 hits for her name on the Persian-language Google website. Some of the comments suggested changing the name of Kargar Street, where she died, to Neda Street. As a result of all the media coverage, the Iranian government ordered the family to bury her immediately and barred family members from holding a memorial service (Fathi, 2009). This story illustrates how the users of media transformed a death into a symbol. However, one must ask, what caused the reaction to be so widespread? There were many other deaths, why Neda? The answers must include timing of the event, using social media and frustration of the people involved. Traditional media came into the story after it went viral.

The Bad Media Coverage

Media can be negative when the journalistic process shapes attitudes and stokes hatred thus fueling or amplifying violence. An example is in northern Nigeria city of Jos, a 2008 study of 160 newspaper articles from *THISDAY* and *Daily Trust*, reported that enemy images and stereotypes were used to demonize part of the population, reinforce intolerance and spread hate and amplify conflicts (Musa & Ferguson, 2013).

Media's spread of hate is definitely negative but so is maintaining a system or a government that is negative by keeping the status quo. Used as a tool for social control and maintenance of the status quo, media can be manipulated. Strenuous media routines can cause journalists, wittingly or unwittingly, to construct and to use culturally based narratives and frames that may resonate with their audiences (Taha, 2012, p. 148). Why the media in South Africa maintained the status quo of apartheid cannot be fully explained; however, it was the international media that finally helped to bring the atrocities happening in South Africa to light (Kasaval, 2012, p. 14). What could journalists have asked in these stories to understand why the media reported negatively? What was going on in the society that polarized the groups? Did particular sectors of the society control the media?

The Ugly Media Coverage

Ugly media examples are easy to find. Media were thought to have provoked violence when Maluku plunged into so much conflict that the Indonesian journalists became so preoccupied with the conflict that their preoccupation became a story in itself. In February 2000, the *Jakarta Post* article, "Islamic media defy taboos on sensitive reporting," examined claims that reporting, particularly in the Islamic press, provoked violence. One paper baldly declared: "The war in Maluku is not one of social or economic groups; it is clearly among Christians and Muslims, and what is happening is a genocide against Muslims" (Lynch, 2000, para. 15).

Social media have been used to provoke violence or to show violence so graphically that many Western media houses have refused to show the videos. An example is when ISIS released a video in February 2015 showing men and young boys gathering to watch the burning to death of a Jordanian pilot captured by ISIS when his F-16 crashed over Syria on Christmas Eve during a US-led coalition bombing raid near Raqqa, the group's Syrian stronghold. The video, entitled "Muslims' joy at burning of Jordanian Pilot," showed crowds cheering and chanting what appears to be Allahu Akbar (god is great) as First Lieutenant Muath al-Kasaesbeh is set on fire in a cage. It is believed that he was actually killed on January 3 (Saul, 2015b). How could these stories have been reported to understand why the extreme violence was used? Specifically, why was the Jordanian pilot used to send a message?

How Can Violence Be Lessened Using Media?

Media can be used to show all sides of a conflict. Reporting on violence is only one story. There are many other stories remaining to be told to put the entire picture of violence into perspective. In an article entitled, "The History of Violence" in *The New Republic*, Steven Pinker offers evidence that, on average, the amount, and cruelty of violence to humans and animals has decreased over the last few centuries (2007). This is good news. Scientific research shows that a strategy addressing the underlying causes of violence can be effective in preventing violence ("3rd milestones," 2007). This too is good news. However, scientific evidence about the effectiveness of interventions to prevent collective violence is lacking. Policies that facilitate reductions in poverty, that make decision-making more accountable, that reduce inequalities between groups, as well as policies that reduce access to biological, chemical, nuclear, and other weapons have been recommended. Additionally, approaches to planning responses to violent conflicts have been recommended. These include assessing as early as possible when people are the most vulnerable and what their needs are, then coordinating activities among the various players and finally working toward global, national, and local capabilities to deliver effective services during the various stages of an emergency (Zwi, Garfield & Loretti, 2002). The question remains: how have journalists covered modern warfare? Historically, journalists have covered modern warfare through fragmentation of content (bits of news trickling in), use of questionable sources such as unknown or anonymous sources (risks are too high to go on record), unreliable expert sources (who may have agendas), official sources (who offer political party jargon), and sources who take great risks in being quoted. Through the action plan offered in Chapter 10 of this book, journalists can begin to cover future conflicts with the emphasis on peace through media.

Last Word. To cover violence a journalist must also understand the causes of violence. Though the lyrics from the "Ballad of the Coca Grower" blame the *gringo* for creating the problem, the causes of violence are many: lack of resources, culture—to include ethnicity and religion, money and power. If peace through media is to be realized, these causes must be reported.

Discussion: Identify an area experiencing violence that is being covered by media. Search for stories that cover the three types of violence.

References

"Cost of National Security" (2015). National Priorities Project. Retrieved from https://www.nationalpriorities.org/cost-of/.

"Definition of Violence" (nd). World Health Organization. Retrieved from http://www.who.int/violenceprevention/approach/definition/en/.

Fathi, N. (2009, June 22). In a death seen around the world, a symbol of Iranian protests. *The New York Times*.

"5 million people need health service in Iraq: UN" (2015, March 16). Agence France Presse. Retrieved from http://dailystar.com.lb/News/Middle-East/2015/Mar-16/290981-5-million-people-need-health-services-in-iraq-un.ashx.

Galtung, J. (1969). Violence, peace, and peace research. *Journal of Peace Research*, 6(3), 167–191.

Galtung, J. (1990). Cultural violence. *Journal of Peace Research*, 27(3), 291–305.

Gleditsch, N., Nordkvelle, J., Strand, H., Buhaug, H., & Levy, J. (2014, March). Peace research—Just the study of war? *Journal of Peace Research*, 51(2), 145–158.

Gyori, B. (2013, December). Naming Neda: Digital discourse and the rhetoric of association. Journal of Broadcasting & Electronic Media, 57(4), 482–503.

Hyndman, J. (2009). Violence. In Gregory, D., Johnston, R., Pratt, G., Watts, M., & Whatmore, S. (Eds.), *Dictionary of Human Geography*, (pp. 798–799). NJ: Wiley-Blackwell.

Kasaval, R. (2012). *Touching the rainbow: Tribute to Nelson Mandela's leadership*. Author House. Retrieved from http://stakerope.sprinterweb.net/touching-the-rainbow-tribute-to-nelson-mandelas-leadership-book/?i=1.

Kaufman, A. (2014, May). Thinking beyond direct violence. *International Journal of Middle East Studies*, 46(2), 441–444.

Lewis, M.W. (2014, June 5). Does the Boko Haram insurgency stem from environmental degradation and climate change? Geo Currents: The People, Places & Languages Shaping Current Events. Retrieved from http://www.geocurrents.info/geopolitics/insurgencies/boko-haram-insurgency-stem-environmental-degradation-climate-change.

"Libya struggles to keep electricity on" (2015, February 11). Reuters. Retrieved from http://af.reuters.com/articlePrint?articleid=AFL5NOVL2VP20150211.

Lynch, J. (2000). Using conflict analysis in reporting. The peace option 3. Part 2. Retrieved from http://www.oldsite.transnational.org/SAJT/features/2000/LynchPart2.html.

Lynch, W. & Bravman, B. (2008). Modern warfare: An overview for world history teachers. *World History Connected*. Retrieved from http://worldhistoryconnected.press.illinois.edu/2.2/bravman.html.

Marks, T. (2015, March 29). Editor's letter: The cultural desecration of Iraq. *Apollo Magazine*. Retrieved from http://www.apollo-magazine.com/editors-letter-the-cultural-desecration-of-iraq/.

Metz, S. (2000, April). Armed conflict in the 21st century: The information revolution and post-modern warfare. Report of the Strategic Studies Institute, U.S. Army War College, Carlisle, PA. Retrieved from http://www.au.af.mil/au/awc/awcgate/ssi/metz_info_rev.pdf.

Musa, A. O. & Ferguson, N. (2013, April). Enemy framing and the politics of reporting religious conflicts in the Nigerian press. *Media, War & Conflict*, 6(1), 7–20.

Nwabueze, C. & Ekwughe, V. (2014, March). Nigerian newspapers' coverage of the effect of Boko Haram activities on the environment. *Journal of African Media Studies*, 6(1), 71–89.

Peric, I. (2015). Personal correspondence. Ina.maliprinc@googlemail.com.

Pinker, S. (2007, March 19). The history of violence. *The New Republic*. Retrieved from http://www.newrepublic.com/article/77728/history-violence.

Romero, S. (2010, September 4). Ballads born of conflict still thrive in Colombia. *The New York Times*. Retrieved from http://www.nytimes.com/2010/09/05/world/americas/05colombia.html?pagewanted=print.

Ruvaga, L. (2015, March 10). Tests show Kenya's Turkana water unfit for consumption. *VOA News*. Retrieved from http://www.voanews.com/content/kenya-turkana-water-unfit-for-consumption/2674350.html.

Saul, H. (2015, April 9). ISIS 'throw man off a building for homosexual affair' and beat him to death when he survives. *The Independent*. Retrieved from http://www.independent.co.uk/news/world/middle-east/isis-throw-man-off-a-building-for-homosexual-affair-and-beat-him-to-death-when-he-survives-10012709.html.

Schirch, L. & Sewak, M. (2005). The role of women in peace building. Paper issued by European Centre for Conflict Prevention. Retrieved from http://www.google.com/url?sa=t&rct=j&q=&esrc=s&source=web&cd=1&ved=0CB8QFjAA&url=http%3A%2F%2Fwww.conflictrecovery.org%2Fbin%2FIssue_paper_on_the_Role_of_Women_in_Peacebuilding_Jan2005.doc&ei=IyQoVfGRM8P4gwSF1YKwDw&usg=AFQjCNGzaAgpv_ESncIxgMycjdwUTu1PAQ&bvm=bv.90491159,d.eXY.

Taha, M. (2012). Decoding the Darfur conflict: Media framing of a complex humanitarian crisis. *Journal of Arab & Muslim Media Research*, 5(2), 147–166.

"3rd milestones of a global campaign for violence prevention" (2007, July 17–19). Violence Prevention Alliance, World Health Organization. Retrieved from http://www.who.int/violenceprevention/events/17_07_2007/en/.

Zwi, A. B., Garfield, R., & Loretti, A. (2002). Collective violence, In Krug, E. G., Dahlberg, L. L., Mercy, J. A., Zwi, A. B., & Lozano, R. (Eds.), *World report on violence and health* (pp. 213–239). Geneva: World Health Organization.

JOURNALISTS LEARN TO WORK
WITH CITIZEN JOURNALISTS

Bob Marley may have insisted that the people stand up for their rights, but when it comes to the working journalists, the rules are based on who wants to make the rules. Sometimes the foreign correspondents create such an aura around their work and lives that other journalists find the routine day-to-day coverage of news unexciting. These foreign correspondents have been immortalized in films, books, and dramas. They have found a way to work within the culture, in the time, with the money, or no money. Some become romanticized. For example, Graham Greene, after serving in Indo-China as a war correspondent for *The Times* and *LeFigaro*, began to write *The Quiet American* (1956) in room 214 of the Grand Hotel Continental in Saigon, Vietnam. Seen as an antiwar book by Americans, it was only after the remake of the film with Michael Caine playing the role of the war correspondent, Fowler, that an American audience accepted the movie, though not a big audience. The movie has conflict, sex, triangular love affair, war images, espionage, CIA, dictators, and an exotic location. It was based on a novel, but Greene's experiences played a large role in how he wrote the story. The work of a war correspondent is multifaceted and includes all the components to create a best-selling novel. Green's fame resulted in yet another door with his name on it. He stayed in

Hotel Oloffson in Port-au-Prince, Haiti. It was in this room he conceived the idea for his book, *The Comedians* (1966), and his name is on the door.

The goal of this chapter is to describe the working environment of a foreign correspondent to include how to work with new technology and with citizen journalists. By understanding the issues these journalists face every day in their jobs, preparation, and guidance to use peace journalism principles may be better accepted by both the journalists and the media owners.

Limited Journalism Training

Journalists have learned to cover stories by experience. They have depended on the traditional *shoe leather style* of getting out in public and finding the stories. As government and social issues have become more complex, journalism programs were created in colleges and universities to train journalists how to interpret the information gathered. Seldom have journalists been taught how to cover conflict. They learn to record who, what, when, where, how and why. These elements have been the mantra taught in journalism programs to be able to cover any event. Pause the frame...this is not always the way the system works, other factors come into play like culture, nation states laws, government systems, who owns the media, etc. Journalists interested in covering foreign conflicts often must learn on the job or sometimes a media house may offer briefings before the assignment. Some media houses like *The Guardian* in the United Kingdom have offered online sources for how to use new technology in the field.

In communications programs, students often learn from visiting foreign correspondents invited into the classroom to answer questions. Inevitably, the conversation resorts to war stories and how the journalist survived. Personally, students always have wanted to know about the coup in Haiti that ousted Aristide. These stories romanticize foreign correspondents in the classroom as they sit on the edge of a desk, in jeans with their mobile phone vibrating in their hand. The students sit in awe and absorb every detail. The guests do mention some of their challenges of being a foreign correspondent: safety, sources, language, technology, economies, stress, pressure to cover fast moving stories, jockeying for stories; but the romantic idea lingers. No mention is made of the number of journalists killed or imprisoned, kidnapped or wounded, suffering from posttraumatic syndrome, or divorce. Being a foreign correspondent comes with a price. The isolation, separation from family and friends, and the struggle to cover conflict under fire with bombs and land-mines and shootings definitely has a price. Embedding the journalists in the military has lessened danger but has been argued that it does not provide a broad perspective of the conflict.

A foreign correspondent for *The New York Times*, Lynsey Addario, wrote about her experiences covering conflict. "As a photojournalist documenting conflict zones in the post-9/11 wars, I had been in dozens of risky situations. I was kidnapped by Sunni insurgents near Fallujah, in Iraq, ambushed by the Taliban in the Korengal Valley in Afghanistan and injured in a car accident that killed my driver while covering the Taliban occupation of the Swat Valley in Pakistan" (Addario, 2015, para. 2). With so much danger, why do journalists want to do this type of work? Addario has an answer. "Each one of us knew that this work was an intrinsic part of who we were: it was what we believed in; it governed our lives" (Addario, 2015, para. 19). She had been asked many times why she was a photojournalist and explained that leaving at the last minute, jumping on planes, feeling a responsibility to cover wars and famines and human rights crises was her job. To stop doing those things would be like firing herself. She described a night in Baghdad when someone asked a group of foreign correspondents attending a party, who had gotten separated since the start of the war in Iraq. Most of the people in the room raised their hands. "Work," she wrote, "remained my priority, keeping me on the road 280 days a year" (Addario, 2015, para. 22).

The Office

Work environments for foreign correspondents are unique. Often they work out of their suitcases with a fist full of visas. Costs of placing a foreign correspondent in the field have gotten too expensive for most media houses. A foreign correspondent now flies into areas, covers the story, and flies back out again, referred to as parachute journalism. Why? Reasons offered are costs and lack of audience interest. Alisa Miller, CEO of Public Radio International, noted in a 2008 TED talk, that news networks have drastically scaled back their foreign bureaus in recent years. "Aside from one-person ABC mini-bureaus in Nairobi, New Delhi, and Mumbai, there are no network news bureaus in all of Africa, India, or South America, places that are home to more than 2 billion people" (Friedman, 2013, para. 9).

Costs of live coverage of wars like the Gulf War broke the budgets of most media houses as they tried to compete with the 24-hour CNN coverage. Staff was cut and local *stringers* began to cover the stories. In areas of conflict, the foreign correspondent would work with the stringers and a fixer, someone who worked out the logistics of travel and bridged language gaps. These fixers were the drivers as well. Some foreign correspondents would supplement the drivers' pay to assure loyalty.

Costs also enter into the argument as to why international coverage is reduced and the media owners' answer is that their audiences do not want international news. The media owners feel that the audiences who are interested in international news tend to be an older demographic that many advertisers do not care to reach; therefore, with less money to be made in international news coverage, foreign news gathering had to be cut (Brooks, 2006, p. 29).

The foreign journalist must work with reduced costs, a perceived lack of audience interest by media owners, and within a fixed structure. This structure is based on institutional, technical, political, and economic constraints imposed on a journalist's work, especially during a crisis. This fixed structure varies from country to country to include how that particular government system operates and how the media system operates. Government systems include the following: authoritarianism (autocracy, despotism, dictatorship, totalitarianism); democracy (direct, representative); monarchy (absolute, constitutional); oligarchy (aristocracy, military junta, plutocracy, stratocracy, timocracy); and others (anarchy, anocracy, kritarchy, republic, theocracy, caliphate). Media systems can be authoritarian, Western, libertarian/social responsibility, Marxist/communist, revolutionary and developmental (Hachten & Scotton, 2007). The government system and the media system are not always the same system. For example, in Dominica, an island in the Caribbean, the newspaper was privately owned as a Western market model and the radio was a developmental model under government control. These two models worked together until the newspaper, *The New Chronicle*, was sold to an organization sponsored by the government. A former editor, Julius B. Samson, wrote an editorial in an online publication lamenting the sale to someone who he felt was turning the 100-year-old newspaper into a propaganda organ for the regime in power. Samson wrote: "Along the way I renamed the venerable publication the 'Conscience of the Nation' to emphasize its role in being the moral arbiter and the voice of reason and moderation in a nation that was transitioning into the independence era" (Samson, 2014, para. 2).

To work within these various government and media systems is how news is prepared in each nation state. In addition, news preparation cannot be considered simple. There are many direct and indirect factors that affect news preparation. These include the media type or platform being used and the legal and ethical values relating to the media, which vary from country to country. Who owns the media must be considered. Communication between management and the journalist as a worker definitely affects news preparation as do security issues, access to resources, journalism practices and understanding of the country's culture and systems, all can affect news preparation. A journalist must learn the systems of each country to be effective and to be safe.

Waving a White Flag Does Not Work

Security is a major part of the working environment for a foreign correspondent. Special attention must be paid to the safety of journalists covering conflict situations who face a real danger of physical injury and emotional stress (Yiping, 2011). This includes stringers, local people hired by international media to report stories. Although local journalists may be the only source of independent information, journalists not only face death every day, they also are looked upon with mistrust by many of the governments (Aslam, 2011). For example, in Myanmar, during a conflict in 2015, reporters fled the scene as it became apparent that they were also unsafe from police attacks. Police had beaten Maung Maung Myo, a *Union Daily* reporter, and two other foreign journalists were harassed ("Scenes of indiscriminate," 2015, para. 13). A statement issued by the Myanmar Press Council condemned the arrest of the reporters who had been covering the conflict. The statement said that the journalists neither supported, nor condemned, nor participated in the protest; they were reporting what they saw ("Scenes of indiscriminate," 2015, para. 15).

Another example on insecurity for media personnel is how the Taliban has been hostile to the presence of any outside media person, considering them all Western spies. A media-related international NGO, *Internews Pakistan,* reported in June 2006:

> The chronicles of violations against media freedoms in Pakistan this year make for grim reading: at least three journalists killed; two abducted; 206 attacked, beaten, tortured and shot at; 65 arrested; four jailed; five threatened; 19 publications, 32 TV channels and 16 websites banned; 13 newspaper presses raided; one FM station

sealed; 12 journalists and media organizations slapped with court cases; 21 prevented from covering official functions and seven newspapers denied state-sponsored advertising from public funds for being critical of government policies—making all this one of the worst years of journalism in Pakistan in recent years. (Rehmat & Jan, 2006, para. 3)

The Pakistan Press Freedom Report concluded that reporters in the Sindh province faced threats and attacks from local authorities and political or tribal figures during the year. In total, more than 100 such instances were reported throughout 2006. Conditions for reporters covering the ongoing unrest in the tribal areas bordering Afghanistan were particularly difficult, with a number of local and foreign correspondents detained, threatened, or otherwise prevented from covering events there, either by the Taliban and local tribal groups or by the army and intelligence services (Pakistan, 2007, para. 17).

Journalists are neither invisible nor immortal. Missiles targeted at the "enemy" can hurt journalists who happen to be covering the conflict. In Iraq, among other incidents, were the deaths of two Reuters journalists ("Leaked US videos", 2010); the 2003 US air-to-surface missile attack on the offices of Al Jazeera in Baghdad that left three journalists dead and four wounded; and the US firing on Baghdad's Hotel Palestine the same year that killed two foreign cameramen. On October 8, 2001, the second day of the US bombing of Afghanistan, the transmitters for the Taliban government's Radio Shari were bombed and shortly after, the US military bombed some 20 regional radio sites. US Defense Secretary Donald Rumsfeld defended the targeting of these facilities, saying: "Naturally, they cannot be considered to be free media outlets. They are mouthpieces of the Taliban and those harboring terrorists" (Blum, 2015, para. 13).

Safety issues for journalists include being in an environment deemed to be too dangerous to cover without protection from an army. Foreign correspondents like to believe that they travel with an implicit *white flag*—a pledge of independence and neutrality that will be respected by everyone; but that is not the world of a journalist today. A *Washington Post* journalist, David Ignatius, said being embedded means observing from just one perspective, not seeing the whole. Journalists gain access to information and to talkative sources, but also inherit the distortions and biases that come with being *on the bus* or *on the plane* (Ignatius, 2010, para. 4). "We can't understand what we don't see; we can't explain a conflict if we hear from only one side" (Ignatius, 2010, para. 5). In an embedded world, journalists are often required to take sides, or to see things from only one side, as a condition of doing their job. In this world, it is hard to blame an *Al-Jazeera* viewer for thinking that Fox News cares about only one side of a war, or a Fox viewer for feeling the same way about *Al-Jazeera* (Ignatius, 2010, para. 13).

Journalists have been kidnapped as a weapon of war so that it has become all but impossible for Westerners to travel freely in Iraq. The Committee to Protect Journalists reported that government officials and their allies were responsible for killing a third of the journalists, a higher proportion than killings attributed to terrorist groups or criminal enterprises (Carr, 2012). Journalists killed included Mahmoud al-Kumi and Hussam Salama, who worked as cameramen for Al-Aqsa TV, which is run by Hamas. They were covering events in central Gaza when a missile struck their car, which, according to Al-Aqsa, was clearly marked with the letters *TV* (Carr, 2012).

Israeli officials have said Hamas was using journalists and their operations as human shields, and a press officer for the Israeli Defense Force warned in a Twitter post that reporters should be wary of the company they keep: "For your own safety, stay away from #Hamas positions and operatives" (Carr, 2012, para. 10).

Tweeting While You Work

A foreign correspondent has to keep up with new technology. However, journalists often must learn how to use new technology on their own, which by the way undermines the traditional basis of journalism and that is of the collective, organized, and institutional character of news work. This process can actually subordinate the individual journalist to the collective, a strategy that may well serve to limit journalistic freedom rather than to increase it (Ornebring, 2013, p. 49).

Social media brings to the journalist a new set of problems. By using social media, the line between the professional and personal is often blurred in the interest of audience engagement. Putting out a daily broadsheet is hard enough, now with tweets, the media houses have new concerns on legalities. Twitter, as a publishing service, is subject to the same laws as other media. The case that brought this to most people's attention was #twitdef, Australia's first Twitter defamation suit (Dawson, 2011). The case was not about a leading news organization being sued for something one of its journalists had tweeted. It was about a leading news organization that was suing for something a citizen journalist had tweeted (Clayfield, 2012, p. 96).

It's All in Who You Know

The nature of the job, being a foreign correspondent, means many reporters are natural loners, individualists who display the most remarkable resourcefulness to ferret out information which others would rather they did not have. They are instinctive non-joiners of things but they do come into their careers impressed by the need to network—it's not what you know, but whom you know.

Sources for information are the building blocks of news stories. Sources are fundamental to the agenda and framing of a story as it unfolds (Knight, 2012, p. 62). The traditional and often easiest way of getting information is to rely on institutional sources, which can be viewed as a mechanism by which the public discourse is controlled by the power elites within a society. The practices of sourcing are therefore a key measure of shifting discourse and power within the media. However, when a journalist is called upon to turn around some material, which has just arrived, for the top of the next hour's program, the time available to check the sources and content against previous claims is heavily circumscribed (Phillips, 2010).

The need to network sometimes means bouncing ideas off others and sharing a viewpoint with friends. As a journalist, that can backfire. A reporter sent an email to friends; she found that her viewpoint went viral on the web. As an Iranian-American, Farnaz Fassihi's email that expressed her views about the deteriorating situation in Iraq circled the globe when it was to only be for a few friends' eyes. As a reporter for *The Wall Street Journal* her viewpoint was provocative, incisive and to some, shocking (Sullivan, 2013, para. 1). What her email did was to open the debate about whether reporters should expose their personal views. Some journalists believe that their thoughts and beliefs matter; that objectivity is a myth. If the argument is made that trust in media is declining due to the middle ground or biases not expressed, then should a journalist state where he or she is coming from, that journalist may more likely be trusted. The other side of the argument is that as professionals, journalists need to put aside personal opinions or to keep them to themselves; just as other professionals are expected. Sullivan, in her essay, continues the arguments by saying both sides are gray and not black and white. She suggests that a bureau chief might not want to have a Web page summarizing whom he voted for, whether he believes in abortion rights, and with what political party he is registered; nor are reporters and editors expected to be faceless, impersonal entities. Being transparent is the new objective (Sullivan, 2013).

Citizen Journalists Enter the Journalists' Work Place

Working with citizen journalists has become part of a foreign correspondent's job. Technology driven changes have reshaped how international news flows by lowering the economic barriers of entry to publishing and broadcasting and encouraging the proliferation of nontraditional international news sources. Citizens, for a variety of reasons, began covering conflict due to losing trust in traditional media, to having new opportunities for expressing a viewpoint and to living in an area not safe for foreign correspondents. These citizen journalists are providing images and stories that are changing how news is produced. A group of disconnected digital activists in Iran realized they had the technical ability to get textual and visual information out to the public. These individuals or citizen journalists began distributing content to members of the international press and general public via social networking sites. Specifically, Twitter was heavily used. It gave protestors the opportunity to reach audiences beyond Iran ("Editorial: Iran's Twitter," 2009). As a result, Western media such as *Newsweek* magazine suggested that the 2009 post-Iranian election was the "true birthplace of citizen journalism" (Human Rights Watch, 2010). The Iranian government, however, quickly unleashed a widespread crackdown and the revolution eventually failed.

Citizens report through blogs, Facebook, and tweets. A blogger became a major news source for BBC during the early days of the conflict unfolding in Baghdad. Salam Pax's blog, "Where is Raed?" (Dear-raed.blogspot.com) became internationally popular. That popularity, however, became a problem with traditional journalists who have expressed the difficulty of sorting out the authentic and factual from the errors, rumors, and misinformation. Traditional journalists mistrust participatory journalism and believe that it "threatens to undermine what they consider core values" such as editorial control and objectivity (Gillmor, 2004, p. 114). At BBC, journalists saw blogs as "an extension of, rather than a departure from, traditional journalistic norms and practices (Hermida, 2009, p. 269). For example, though Salam Pax's blog was popular, initially there was no way of knowing if he was who he said he was or even if he (or she) was in Baghdad. Yet, Salam Pax, whose authenticity has since been validated by an American newsperson, also shows the virtues of amateur reporting. His web accounts offered a valuable perspective at considerable personal risk. This still-anonymous blogger has been celebrated with Salam Pax T-shirts and coffee mugs. Additionally, citizens like Salam Pax may be especially important as long as traditional foreign correspondents remain scarce with reduced budgets for international news coverage. The flip side of the coin is that with the public having other sources of getting international news, traditional media may continue to reduce coverage of international events (Hamilton & Jenner, 2003).

Though *Newsweek* may have named the birth of citizen journalism, the major crisis within the industry is that the public is losing trust in media and is able to get information without traditional media (Turner, 2010). Whereas professional journalism has been seen by many scholars to be the guardian of democracy (Papacharissi, 2009), this guardianship is increasingly perceived as a failure, suggesting the need for what the more optimistic proponents of citizen journalism identify as media witnessing (Frosh and Pinchevski, 2009; Gillmor, 2004). Internationally, this problem has not been addressed within communications programs. For example, Sami Ghaleb, editor of the weekly newspaper *Al Nidaa*, said that journalists in Yemen operate unprofessionally but that they come with a shortage of resources and below-par university curricula based mostly on theoretical journalism courses. Raddad Mohamed Al-Salami, editor at Al Taghyiir.net website, said that what he learned in his four years at Yemen University's School of Communication was that the minds of most faculty members stopped with journalism practices of the 1980s and 1970s (Abu-Fadil, 2009). Traditional journalism has not always kept up with the times.

Social media fills a gap for many nonjournalists to communicate. The people on the street are learning how to use technology as it emerges in new forms as one way of communicating with the public. Users who are generating content see social media as a tool. Wael Ghonim, a Google executive in Egypt who launched his Facebook group, called *Kullena Khaled Said* (We Are All Khaled Said), told NPR on Fresh Air that sites like Facebook are tools that can help connect people and disseminate information to the masses, but cannot create social changes on their own. Arguably, the death of Saeed, a young Egyptian businessman who was beaten to death by police outside a cybercafé in the Sidi Gaber area outside Alexandria on June 6, 2010 (Bradley, 2010), was a major icon for the revolution that prompted an unprecedented solidarity among Egyptians and eventually became a catalyst that brought the regime to its knees (Ali and Fahmy, 2012). Ghonim thought Saeed was killed because he had posted video footage of police corruption. After viewing graphic photos of Saeed at the morgue, Ghonim created the Facebook group. The site caught on and in the weeks before the revolution, the site had more than

350,000 followers who were invited to protest against the regime on January 25, 2011 (Heaven, 2011). Many of the followers replaced their personal pictures on Facebook with images of Saeed's face (pre- and/or postdeath). Similar to Iran, the influence of the social media was exaggerated, giving Facebook credit for starting the revolution.

Another social media phenomenon was built around Esraa Abdel Fattah, a leading member of the April 6 Strike Group in Egypt and known as *the Facebook girl*. She was known for her role using social media during the movements of 2008 and 2011. She, too, said that the social media in 2008 and 2011 was a tool, a tool for change (Disler, 2014, para. 3). Her role in using social media during the Egyptian movements had her nominated for the 2011 Nobel Peace prize (Chick, 2011).

Citizens reporting conflict appear to be gaining acceptance as journalists adjust to the changes within their industry. The inclusion of citizen journalists in the work of traditional journalists is less a story of exploitation and more a story of negotiation (Palmer, 2013). Journalists are using citizen journalists' information to then check out the sources and verify the content. To work closer with these citizen journalists, media houses are creating new services and apps. Blottr is a UK-based user-generated news service where anyone can capture and report news. BBC has developed a *news gatherer* app for citizen journalists to send stories directly to the BBC's content-management system (EJC, 2011). CNN, the Associated Press, Al Jazeera, NBC, and UK broadcaster Sky News, all have mobile apps linking citizens to newsrooms (Mills et al., 2012). Meporter offers a journalism app for citizen journalists linked to multiple news outlets. Scoopshot acts as an intermediary between media organizations and freelancers or citizen photojournalists enabling access to news content. Meporter and Scoopshot pay for the content by licensing and syndicating it to news organizations. MS (multimedia) messages have been the most widely promoted way to send mobile news content to the news media (Mills et al., 2012, p. 670).

How to Play Well Together

Despite their differences, citizen journalists and traditional journalists share many things—the most obvious being their desire to communicate about topics that they both feel worthy of the public's attention. Both care whether their words are being read or heard; otherwise, they would be no different than private diarists. They both benefit from and presumably endorse a culture of free speech, including the right to criticize government and its office holders without fear of punishment or retaliation. In addition, both can influence the way people think, feel and behave by exposing the public to stories that move or impact them in one way or another (Kawamoto, 2013, p. 3).

Citizen journalists can serve as a vital complement to mainstream journalism, however not as its substitute (Reich, 2008, p. 739). Citizen journalists are hindered by not having access to major news sources unlike traditional journalists who may use major news sources extensively and thus favor them with coverage (Reich, 2008). Citizen journalists use human, man-on-the-street sources and report stories using one source. Often these citizens are reluctant to interact with their sources and the information they gain is more ad hoc exchanges than long-term role relationships. On the other hand, citizen journalists have adopted several mechanisms that help them make up for their comparably limited access. They are much more likely to pursue stories at their own initiative. They tend to predicate their stories on firsthand witnessing, technical sources (mainly Internet), personal acquaintances and their own experience (Reich, 2008).

Conversely, citizen journalists are well equipped to cover the following types of stories (Reich, 2008, p. 751):

- Stories that are not dependent on human agents, especially the regular suppliers of mainstream content and situations in which the sources are expected to make the first move.
- Stories that can be obtained from technical or textual sources (e.g. the World Wide Web), personal experience (e.g., as citizens or activists), and personal acquaintances.
- Straightforward issues, such as stories that do not require the following activities: negotiating with and interrogating several sources; juxtaposing disparate versions and voices; or elaborate processing.
- Occurrences that can be observed on a firsthand basis, instead of relying on the testimony of others.

By stepping forward and reporting on conflict, citizen journalists have become targets in authoritative regimes. They may be subjected to harassment, intimidation, and even death. Regardless, some individuals still find ways to circumvent their respective governments and bring first-hand breaking news to audiences, mainly Western ones (Ali & Fahmy, 2013). Although technological advances have allowed citizen journalists to disseminate information beyond government control, the political elite also have become savvy to these advances and have found ways to largely keep these citizens' influences within boundaries set by the political elite (Nguyen, 2009). An example of how citizen journalists disseminated information beyond government control was in Vietnam in the early 2000s. The government allowed chat rooms and forum discussions; however, in 2006, bloggers announced when former Vietnamese Prime Minister Vo Van Kiet died unexpectedly in a Singapore hospital nearly two days before the mainstream media were allowed to report on the story. Thus, 88 million people were informed of his death back home before the story actually broke (Ali and Fahmy, 2013).

Citizen journalists are being used by traditional journalists who understand that to do their job well, they must find the necessary resources and sources to tell their stories. Some foreign correspondents seek out Twitter users and follow the ones who seemed reliable and immersed in what was happening. Journalists work off tips gotten from sources and then if they would see breaking news on Twitter they would scramble to find witnesses (Clayfield, 2012, p. 94).

By liberally retweeting others' comments and links, and becoming a kind of human content aggregator in the process, these journalists fall not only into the category of a crowd sourcer but also into that of what *The Guardian's* Paul Lewis has called the anchor journalist, who function like Twitter conductors—digesting, sorting, corroborating, debunking, and disseminating snippets of citizen journalism in an attempt to sort the chaos during big news events. Some have described the process as Twitter curation, an essential new skill journalists must develop in their management of audience engagement (Clayfield, 2012, p. 96). Communication is no longer a one-way practice and is becoming more collaborative and consensual. To use a common metaphor, traditional journalism was like a lecture, but working with today's citizen journalism is more like a conversation (Gillmor, 2004; Kunelius, 2001).

However, traditional journalists might not buy into this notion of collaboration. In a study on journalists' work with letters to the editor, newsrooms were abuzz with the *idiom of insanity*, which assumes that most of those who contribute their views as citizens are crazy or extreme (Wahl-Jorgensen, 2007). Additionally traditional media owners argue that participatory media formats have been around for decades in the letters to the editor, radio phone-ins, television talk shows and vox pop interviews. However true, with the influx of social media, some traditional media have created a space to incorporate user-generated content (UGC). One newspaper that has done this is *The Guardian* in the United Kingdom. This shared space has raised issues regarding credibility, accountability, and newsworthiness. The researchers found that, despite the growing amount of UGC, journalists interviewed were cautious of the contributing public and only incorporated those comments that shared the normative framework created by institutional routines and values. Core journalistic values of a particular news organization thus remained unchanged as traditional media professionals continued to maintain control over every stage of the news production process (Singer & Ashman, 2009; see also Domingo *et al.*, 2008). In a series of interviews with reporters and editors, gate-keeping practices in organizations like *The Times* were keen to use a lot of UGC but only select those comments that *fit their brand* (Hermida and Thurman, 2008, p. 350). Information that deviated from the story or did not meet the standards of audience expectations, as deemed by editors, were filtered out. Similar to text, television stations have been large consumers of UGC, especially in the form of videos, photographs, and interviews with individuals who have provided first-hand accounts. Television stations also have filtered UGC based on gate keeping processes that they considered valuable to their audiences. Television editors and managers have used UGC as just another source for news stories (Williams *et al.*, 2011).

This gate keeping practice did not change even when media were located in geographical areas where traditional media have been generally subjected to strict government control. Studies have shown that UGC had been allowed and made available to the public such as the ethnographic study examining the official website of Al-Arabiya during the 2003 Iraq War. Despite the perceived freedom afforded by UGC, its content is still subjected to gate keeping processes that fall within the routines of a news organization. Although users had the freedom to add comments to stories uploaded by Al-Arabiya, the comments lacked the authority of rational debate. Rather, most users added their opinions to stories, as well as links to other news sites such as Al-Jazeera. In addition, because the station is owned and managed by the Saudi government, some of the selected UCG "is intended to serve the interests of the (Saudi) government" (Al-Saggaf, 2006, p. 330).

Checking validity of information has become more complex with content produced by citizen journalists using social media. *The Wall Street Journal* reported that many people using cell phones to send informational texts and images to second-party distributors outside Iran were being tracked by the Iranian government via technology purchased from Nokia Siemens (Rhoads &

Chao, 2009). The situation was so prevalent that even the iReporters had to provide written permission from CNN to repost. Nonetheless, the images circulated around the world from various computers and cell phones in and outside of Iran were difficult to trace back to specific owners, largely because these people did not at all wish to be traced. The individualistic Western rhetoric of ownership held no value to the people who simply wanted the information copied and distributed on multiple platforms; such recognition could place these individuals in grave danger. Many of the iReporters were not based in Iran and one told a reporter that he could not even engage in correspondence with the reporter as he had discontinued all political activity for the safety of his family. Thus, the Western understanding of ownership was quite beside the point (Palmer, 2013).

Citizen journalists not only reported, they linked the content to major news sources. Many bloggers had ties to traditional media as former or current journalists; thus, they maintained the traditional media hegemony by being a major source of information for citizens. To illustrate this point more clearly in this context, it was Ghonim's appearance on Dream TV that led to the increased publicity of his Facebook page (Heaven, 2011). The Facebook page "We are all Khaled Saeed" [sic] gained a stronger following once Al-Jazeera picked up the coverage of Saeed's visuals and the related protests. This event created a symbiotic relationship between traditional media and social media (Ali & Fahmy, 2013, p. 63).

Reporting from the streets with cell phones created raw coverage of the conflicts. This unfiltered journalism was difficult or impossible to verify. In the Arab uprisings, since journalists were not allowed, the only images and proof that came out of the uprisings were those found on the Internet and social networks, obtained and distributed by anonymous citizens who, lacking the appropriate knowledge of professional journalism standards, were unable to verify their data nor were they able to offer objective and verified information (Soengas, 2013, p. 149). Media literacy is not part of many societies that find themselves in conflict, therefore citizens attribute similar levels of credibility to all media formats because they do not differentiate between the specific roles that each one should have. For these people, the images that circulate on the Internet are documents whose very existence supports the veracity of the events they are supposedly documenting and they do not question other details that a professional would in a similar situation (Soengas, 2013, p. 149).

Future for Foreign Correspondents

What must a journalist do to prepare to cover conflict? Future foreign correspondents must be a portable media shop. They must find other platforms and new ways to tell stories. They must cultivate and write to specific audiences and also must find ways to regain the trust of these audiences. Finally, they must continue to learn and to practice ethical reporting and writing. Then they, the media houses and journalists, must figure out how to pay for telling truthful stories.

As portable media shops, journalists of the future must be able to do it all: report, edit, shoot, film and tell compelling stories. They must have a sense of curiosity and a passion for reporting on events and people in another country. These future foreign correspondents must be willing to exit their comfort zone. They must be willing to be flexible especially in regions full of uncertainty with insecurity, and in areas where social media and new technologies are blurring the boundaries between intellectual and physical labor. These journalists will be more mobile with careers that are constantly shifting (Orenbring, 2013). These future foreign correspondents will need to have a firm foundation in journalism. To be successful they should be fluent in the language of the region they cover, know the region's history, current events, and culture. They may even specialize in international reporting or foreign affairs.

Beth Dickinson, an Ebyline freelancer, suggests that a foreign correspondent should obtain a non-US passport if possible. She also suggests that young reporters who want to be foreign correspondents should network locally to develop sensitivity to who are the good guys and the bad guys. Young reporters need to hang out with older, more experienced correspondents to soak up knowledge (Ebyline Staff, 2011). Beth Dickinson might know what she is talking about. She is based in the Arabian Peninsula with clips in *The New Yorker, Foreign Policy, The Economist, Politico Magazine*, the *Christian Science Monitor*, the *Wall Street Journal*, the *New York Times*, and *The Financial Times*, among others, according to her web site (http://www.elizabeth-dickinson. com/). She has reported from five continents and speaks French, Spanish, and Krio (Sierra Leone), as well as basic Yoruba and Arabic.

To work in hostile environments and under repressive regimes, journalists need training, insurance, and protection. *The Guardian* offered a class on "How to be a Foreign Correspondent" curated by John Hooper. A foreign journalist is described: "Nothing beats feet on the ground, eyes to observe and record, ears to distinguish variations in tone, human contact, and inter-action with different players in a story" (Abu-Fadil, 2014, para. 12). In an article published by the Oxford-Reuters Institute for the Study of Journalism, Richard Sambrook asks if foreign correspondents are redundant. He points out that this may be true with the transformation of foreign reporting, the role of social media in supplementing and complementing traditional news organizations' output, and how outside actors like NGAs and governments are circumventing correspondents by going directly to the public with content (Abu-Fadil, 2014, para. 25). However, other studies indicate the bloggers and citizen journalists must use traditional media sites for information to share and a place for distribution.

Future foreign journalists must find other platforms and new ways to tell their stories. The web blog, www.LiveJournal.com, is one of many services that allow anyone to create a journal on line. The site is an important source of information for people living in remote parts of Russia and other places where news agencies seldom send reporters (Ornebring, 2013, p. 37). The mobile phone technology equipped with high-resolution, videocapture, 3G or greater network connection, GPS functionality, Wi-Fi, and web browsing, is fast becoming a legitimate media collection and dissemination tool (Mills et al., 2012, p. 669).

Learning all the technology and processes of being a foreign correspond-ent is not enough for some journalists do their job. One mainstream jour-nalist, Kunda Dixit, realized that, "the problem in war reporting in Nepal was that journalists were not involved enough; that there was no space for in-depth stories." So Dixit and his two friends decided to turn to other means. "I chose photojournalism to tell the Nepal story through pictures while one of my friends wrote a novel and the other has made a documentary," he said. Finding alternate mediums was not only another way for them to put across their message for peace; it also became their salvation (Dixit, 2010, cited in Aslam, 2011, p. 7).

Future foreign correspondents must cultivate and write to specific audi-ences. Observing events from inside a community is becoming more preva-lent, partly as a result of technologies and platforms (the Web, social media networks) that have carved mass audiences into particular niches. When three networks and a few major newspapers dominated the information landscape, journalists were trained to report for everyone. Now, niche audiences want more intimacy and connection—even if that means less old-school independ-ence and objectivity (Ignatius, 2010).

Trust Us: Cross Our Hearts

These niche sites attract audiences because these sites rarely challenge audiences' ideas and beliefs—these sites reinforce ideas and beliefs. The message is: you and your values are right, and those who disagree are wrong. In such a situation, the facts can also be up for grabs. The new consumer of news seems to trust the new ideologically embedded media over the traditional independent media. These consumers think *The Washington Post* has an agenda; and that the mainstream media as a whole are tainted and biased (Ignatius, 2010, para. 18).

To regain the trust of these audiences, there must be a shift in the culture of the newsroom, putting an end to relentless negativity, abandoning "the false premise that attack is the best way to flush out the truth, more tolerance of the frailty of human institutions and their leaders, greater care in the treatment of public officials, a deeper aversion to hype, and an openness of mind that encourages both self-criticism and outside criticism. Most of journalism needs a generous spirit, infused with human warmth, as ready to see good as to suspect wrong, to find hope as well as cynicism—journalism concerned that society has a chance to solve its problems" (Rosen, 1999, para. 62).

Robert Karl Manoff, director of the Centre for War, Peace and the News Media at New York University, argues that once it is established that journalism cannot be objective, it assumes an extra responsibility:

> Nevertheless, it is of critical importance that the international community explore the potential of the media to prevent conflict precisely because, taken together, the diverse mass media technologies, institutions, professionals, norms, and practices constitute one of the most powerful forces now shaping the lives of individuals and the fate of peoples and nations. To be sure, media influence is not evenly distributed in space or time and varies with circumstance. But, overall, media influence is significant, and increasingly so, and as a result the media constitute a major human resource whose potential to help prevent and moderate social violence begs to be discussed, evaluated, and, where appropriate, mobilized. (Manoff, 1998, para. 8)

What Ethics?

And finally, academic journalists must do a better job of teaching ethics in the classroom so that regardless of the pressures in the field, the work of the journalist will be reliable. An example of why this is important comes from Moscow State University's Department of Journalism. A dozen soon-to-be-journalists created a calendar and posed in sexy lingerie. The calendar was to be a Happy Birthday to the Russian President, Vladimir Putin. Next to their smiling photos were slogans, *About a Third Time?*, *Who Else if not you?*, and *You are only getting better with years*. Names of the girls and their department were mentioned on every page. The blogger, Oleg Kozlovsky (2010), offered the information that was first published in another blog by Nashi spokesperson Kristing Potupchik. She, Kozlovsky, explained that the people who organized the whole thing, Vladimir Tabak and Maksim Perlin, were connected with the government. The former one was an employee at the Federal Agency for Youth Policy (whose head, the infamous Vasily Yakemenko, was a long-time leader of the same Nashi); the latter one worked for Russia.ru government-controlled Website. According to Potupchik, 50,000 copies of the calendar were already on sale in Moscow malls. What made this story even more controversial was that the girls were proud students or would-be students at the well-respected Department of Journalism of Moscow State University, or Zhurfak. Many prominent journalists were Zhurfak alumni including Anna Politkovskaya, who was assassinated on October 7, 2006. Her murderers have not been convicted—just like the killers of another Zhurfak student, Anastasia Baburova, who was shot dead on January 19, 2009. Kozlovsky asked, "Who will replace Politkovskaya, Baburova and the others if Zhurfak students pose semi-naked for public servants instead of investigating their misconduct?" (2010).

The answer soon followed. In 24 hours, another calendar was published on the Web. Six different Zhurfak girls posed for it in black business suits, their faces thoughtful and serious, and their mouths shut and covered with tape, symbolizing the lack of freedom of speech in Russia. They ask Putin uncomfortable questions. "When Will [Former Oil Tycoon Turned Political Prisoner Mikhail] Khodorkovsky Be Released?," "Is Freedom of Assembly Always and Everywhere?", "Who Killed Anna Politkovskaya?," "How Will Inflation Influence Corruption?," and "When Is The Next Terrorist Attack?" With so many journalists killed, forced into exile or left jobless and even more turned to self-censorship, Russian political media was seen to be in crisis. The Zhurfak controversy shows that the question at stake is the mission of journalism: Is it about getting naked before public officials or is it about discovering and making public naked truth? (Kozlovsky, 2010, para. 5).

The future for foreign correspondents, according to Richard Sambrook, Cardiff School of Journalism professor, will be as much about verification, interpretation, and explanation as revelation. They will need social and collaborative skills. They will need to take steps to ensure the way they work is as transparent as possible in order to win the trust of editors and the public (Abu-Fadil, 2014, para. 30).

Then they, the media houses and journalists, must figure out how to pay for telling truthful stories. Suggestions have been offered. Obtain more grants. The former *Washington Post* editor Leonard Downie and Michael Schudson recommended a mix of private donations, foundation support and a national Fund for Local News, with fees collected by the Federal Communications Commission. These suggestions come with the counter argument that direct government support would undermine claims of independence and integrity. "We need to restore the white flag; we need to reassure people everywhere that we have checked our baggage—national, ideological, cultural, political and religious—at the door when we become journalists" (Ignatius, 2010, para. 24).

Last Word: To be a journalist many feel it is more of *a calling* than a job. There is a passion to be a *watchdog* for the people. There is pride in being able to forge through information, sources, interviews, data, and contradictions to find some sort of truth in what the story is about. The work of a journalist is never done and can run the gamut from routine and boring to risk taking and life changing. Additionally, there is always criticism of any job a journalist may do from someone. David Ignatius remembered Katharine Graham, former publisher of the *Washington Post*, who once chided them, "Just because you are getting attacked from both the left and right doesn't mean you're doing a good job" (Ignatius, 2010, para. 26).

Discussion: Choose a country. Research the media and government systems of that country. How do they work together, how are they different from the US system?

References

Abu-Fadil, M. (2014, July 6). On being a foreign correspondent. *Huffington Post*. Retrieved from http://www.huffingtonpost.com/magda-abufadil/on-being-a-foreign-corres_b_5560984. html.

Addario, L. (2015, February 1). What can a pregnant photojournalist cover? Everything. *The New York Times*. Retrieved from http://www.nytimes.com/2015/02/01/magazine/what-can-a-pregnant-photojournalist-cover-everything.html?_r=0.

Ali, S. R. & Fahmy, S. (2013). Gatekeeping and citizen journalism: The use of social media during the recent uprisings in Iran, Egypt, and Libya. *Media, War & Conflict*, 6(1), 55–69.

Al-Saggaf, Y. (2006). The online public sphere in the Arab world: The war in Iraq on the Al Arabiya website. *Journal of Computer-Mediated Communication*, 12, 311–334.

Aslam, R. (2011). From challenge to hope. *Media Development*, 58(2), 3–8.

Blum, W. (2015, January 20). The west's help to Islamic Jihadists. Retrieved from https://consortiumnews.com/2015/01/20/the-wests-help-to-islamic-jihadists/?print=print.

Bradley, M. (June 14, 2010). Anger of the streets of Cairo. *The National*. Retrieved from http://www.thenational.ae/news/world/middle-east/anger-on-the-streets-of-cairo.

Brooks, S. (2006). *As others see us: The causes and consequences of foreign perceptions of America.* University of Toronto Press.

Carr, D. (2012, November 25). Using war as cover to target journalists. *The New York Times*. Retrieved from http://www.nytimes.com/2012/11/26/business/media/using-war-as-cover-to-target-journalists.html.

Chick, K. (2011, October 6). Egypt's 'Facebook girl' eagerly awaits possible Nobel Peace prize. *The Christian Science Monitor*. Retrieved from http://www.csmonitor.com/World/2011/1006/Egypt-s-Facebook-Girl-eagerly-awaits-possible-Nobel-Peace-Prize.

Clayfield, M. (2012). Tweet the press: How social media is changing the way journalists do their jobs. *Metro Magazine: Media & Education Magazine*, 171, 92–97. Retrieved from http://search.informit.com.au/documentSummary;dn=862683231241627;res=IELLCC.

Dawson, W. (2011, January 20). Twitter's reaction to #twitdef—Part 2. Mapping Online Publics. Retrieved from http://mappingonlinepublics.net/2011/01/20/twitters-reaction-to-twitdef-part-2/.

Disler, M. (2014, February 28). Interview: Esraa Abdel Fattah. *Harvard Political Review*. Retrieved from http://harvardpolitics.com/hprgument-posts/interview-esraa-abdel-fattah/.

Ebyline Staff (2011, August 31). How to become a freelance foreign correspondent. Retrieved from http://blog.ebyline.com/2011/08/how-to-become-a-freelance-foreign-correspondent/.

"Editorial: Iran's Twitter revolution" (2009, June 16). *The Washington Times*. Retrieved from http://www.washingtontimes.com/news/2009/jun/16/irans-twitter-revolution/.

EJC (2011). European Journalism Centre. Retrieved from www.ejc.net.

Friedman, U. (2013, November 19). How three decades of news coverage has shaped our view of the world. *The Atlantic*. Retrieved from http://www.theatlantic.com/international/archive/2013/11/how-three-decades-of-news-coverage-has-shaped-our-view-of-the-world/281613/.

Frosh, P. & Pinchevsk, A. (2009). *Media witnessing: Testimony in the age of mass communication.* New York: Palgrave Macmillan.

Gillmor, D. (2004). *We the media: Grassroots journalism by the people, for the people.* Sebastopol, CA: O'Reilly.

Hachten, W. A. & Scotton, J. F. (2007). *The world news prism. Global information in a satellite age* (7th ed.). Malden, MA: Blackwell.

Hamilton, J. M. & Jenner, E. (2003, September/October). The new foreign correspondence. *Foreign Affairs*. Retrieved from http://www.foreignaffairs.com/articles/59194/john-maxwell-hamilton-eric-jenner/the-foreign-correspondence.

Heaven, W. (2011). Egypt and Facebook: Time to update its status. *NATO Review*. Retrieved from http://www.nato.int/docu/review/2011/social_medias/Egypt_Facebook/EN/index.htm.

Hermida, A. (2009). The Blogging BBC: Journalism blogs at "the world's most trusted news organisation." *Journalism Practice*, 3(3), 268–284.

Human Rights Watch. (2010). Iran. Retrieved from http://www.hrw.org/en/node/87713.

Kawamoto, K. (2013). Enhancing citizen journalism with professional journalism education. *Media Development*, 1, 2–6.

Kozlovsky, O. (2010, October 7). Controversial sexy gift for Putin and the future of Russian journalism. *Huffington Post*. Retrieved from http://www.huffingtonpost.com/oleg-kozlovsky/controversial-sexy-gift-f_b_753952.html.

Knight, M. (2012). Journalism as usual: The use of social media as a newsgathering tool in the coverage of the Iranian elections in 2009. *Journal of Media Practice*, 13(1), 61–74.

Kunelius, R. (2001). Conversation: A metaphor and a method for better journalism? *Journalism Studies*, 2(1): 31–54.

Manoff, R. K. (1998, July 3–4). Telling the truth to peoples at risk: Some introductory thoughts on media and conflict. *Global Beat*. Retrieved from http://www.bu.edu/globalbeat/pubs/manoff0798.html.

Mills, J., Egglestone, P., Rashid, O., & Väätäjä, H. (2012, October). Mojo in action: The use of mobiles in conflict, community, and cross-platform journalism. *Continuum: Journal of Media & Cultural Studies*, 26(5), 669–683.

Nguyen, A. (2009). Globalization, citizen journalism, and the nation state: A Vietnamese perspective. In Cottle, S. *et al.* (Eds.), *Citizen Journalism: Global Perspectives*. New York: Peter Lang, pp. 153–162.

Ornebring, H. (2013). Anything you can do, I can do better? Professional journalists on citizen journalism in six European countries. *International Communication Gazette*, 75, pp. 35–53.

Pakistan (2007). Freedom House. Retrieved from https://freedomhouse.org/report/freedom-world/2007/pakistan#.VSkxH5OM6So.

Palmer, L. (2013). iReporting an uprising: CNN and citizen journalism in network culture. Television New Media, 14(5), 367–385.

Phillips, A. (2010). Old sources: New bottles. In Fenton, N. (Ed.), *New media, old news: Journalism & democracy in the digital age*. Los Angeles: SAGE.

Reich, Z. (2008). How citizens create news stories: The "news access" problem reversed. *Journalism Studies*, 9(5), 739–758.

Rehmat, A. & Jan, M. (2006, June). Annual state of media in Pakistan report 2005–06. *Internews Pakistan*. Retrieved from http://www.internews.org.pk/stateofmedia2006.php.

Rhoads, C. & Chao, L. (2009). Iran's web spying aided by western technology. *Wall Street Journal*, June 22, A1. Retrieved from http://www.wsj.com/articles/SB124562668777335653.

Rosen, J. (1999). What are journalists for? *The New York Times Review of Books*. Retrieved from http://www.nytimes.com/books/first/r/rosen-journalist.html.

Samson, J. (2014, November 26). The Chronicle has been desecrated. *Dominica NewsOnline*. Retrieved from http://dominicanewsonline.com/news/homepage/features/commentary/chronicle-desecrated/.

"Scenes of indiscriminate violence in Letpadan as police attack ambulance workers, students, reporter" (2015, March 10). *The Irrawaddy, governing Burma and Southeast Asia*. Retrieved from http://www.irrawaddy.org/photo/scenes-of-indiscriminate-violence-in-letpadan-as-police-attack-abmulance-workers-students-reporter.html.

Singer, J. B. & Ashman, I. (2009). Comment is free, but facts are sacred: User-generated content and ethical constructs at the *Guardian*. *Journal of Mass Media Ethics*, 24(1), 3–21.

Soengas, X. (2013). The role of the Internet and social networks in the Arab uprisings: An alternative to official press censorship. *Scientific Journal of Media Education*, 21(41), 147–155.

Solomon, Z. (1995). Forced intimacy: The Israeli family in the Gulf war. In Solomon, Z., *Coping with War-Induced Stress: The Gulf War and the Israel Response*. NY: Plenum Press.

Squires, J. D. (1993). *Read all about it*. Crown Publishers.

Sullivan, M. (2013, January 5). When reporters get personal. *The New York Times*. Retrieved from http://www.nytimes.com/2013/01/06/public-editor/when-reporters-get-personal.html?_r=2.

Turner, G. (2010). *Ordinary people and the media: The demotic turn*. London: SAGE.

Wahl-Jorgensen, K. (2007). *Journalists and the public*. Cresskill, NJ: Hampton Press.

Williams, A., Wardle, C., & Wahl-Jorgensen, K. (2011). Have they got news for us? Audience revolution or business as usual at the BBC? *Journalism Practice*, 5(1), 85–99.

Yiping, C. (2011). Revisiting peace journalism with a gender lens. Media Development. Toronto, Canada: WACC Publications. Retrieved from http://www.isiswomen.org/index.php?option=com_content&view=article&id=1505:revisiting-peace-journalism-with-a-gender-len&catid=22:movements-within&Itemid=229.

· 7 ·

HOW TO SEARCH FOR TRUTH WHEN THERE ARE LIES, BIAS, AND PROPAGANDA

During a concert in London, Natalie Maines of the Dixie Chicks said she was embarrassed that President George Bush was from her home state of Texas because he sent American troops to war in Iraq. Death threats and protests banned the Dixie Chicks from many radio stations. *I'm Not Ready to Make Nice* was released in 2006 and won three Grammys. Regardless, the Dixie Chicks lost money. The American public did not want to know what Natalie Maines thought and did not want to invest in her music product.

Making a profit is the goal of businesses that compete in the Western marketplace whether they are music or media houses; however, making a profit has limitations and problems. For a media house, one limitation is lack of freedom of expression. Another limitation is to throw out any ethical values or ideals that may reduce profits. James Squires, former editor of *The Chicago Tribune* wrote a memoir: *Read All About It* (1993). The book examined how owners of American newspapers sacrificed journalistic ideals for profit and illustrated how journalism had become the province of large corporations that care more about private profit than about public debate. Squires wrote: "My role models were the editors and publishers who stood up to the government, who told the truth when it was not popular or profitable to do so, the people who had seen journalism as a tool with which to abolish slavery, to stand up to

Fascism and racism. The greater the risks they took, the more consistent and persistent their stands, the taller they stood in my eyes" (Squires, 1993, p. 34).

Today, for a journalist to tell the truth may not always be popular and may sometimes be difficult. The goal of this chapter is to provide journalists with examples of how some media around the world may lie, are biased, or may promote propaganda. These examples may help journalists understand how being transparent with their own work is important. Transparency may be the key to winning back an audience, one who has abandoned traditional media. The bottom line for media houses may be money, but for the journalist it is trust.

What Is a Lie?

NBC news anchor and journalist, Brian Williams, stretched the truth about what happened to him on a US Army helicopter in 2003 in Iraq and was suspended from NBC for six months in 2015 (Steel & Somaiya, 2015, para. 1). Williams had been held up in the media as one who should never lie. Journalists have been taught to tell the truth in whatever form that takes during the reporting, writing, and editing processes.

Is it ever okay for journalists to lie? Most traditional as well as academic journalists would say no. However, there was a journalist covering a conflict who had been stopped by a small boy with a machine gun who demanded to know if the journalist had taken a photograph of him. The journalist lied. Are there times when it is okay to lie? This is when a journalist's values and morals come into play and the journalist must decide. The all or nothing mantra that a journalist should never lie has to be taken incident by incident, but only in times when the safety of the journalist is at risk. Trust is important and once lost, cannot be won back easily. Once a lie has been found, the person lying has a long path to take to gain trust again. Trust is the backbone of media and that loss of trust is where some of the issues plaguing media are happening today.

Don't Believe a Word They Say

Audiences do not trust media. The Pew Research Center conducted a study asking 1,500 people to choose from 36 news organizations they trusted most. The results indicated that the news organizations with the greatest ratio of trust to distrust were the *Economist* at 12 percent trust and 2 percent distrust;

BBC at 36 percent trust and 7 percent distrust; NPR at 29 percent trust and 9 percent distrust; PBS at 38 percent trust and 12 percent distrust and the *Wall Street Journal* with 31 percent trust and 10 percent distrust (Mitchell, 2014, para. 5).

On the other hand, another Pew Research Center study found that the press was widely criticized but was trusted more than other information sources. However, between the years 1985 and 2011, the evaluations of the overall press performance grew more negative. The research indicated that 66 percent of the people polled believed news stories often were inaccurate, 77 percent thought that news organizations tended to favor one side, and 80 percent said powerful people and organizations often influenced news organizations. Other measures used in this study included the press's perceived lack of fairness (77 percent), its unwillingness to admit mistakes (72 percent), inaccurate reporting (66 percent), and political bias (63 percent) ("Press widely criticized," 2011).

Whereas these studies pointed out how media organizations were losing the trust of audiences, trust had been gained by two organizations. Media audiences were trusting Google and Al Jazeera Network. In a 2015 report by Edelman Trust Barometer, a survey of 27,000 people suggested that Google had overtaken traditional media as the most trusted source of news globally (Sterling, 2015). A justifiable rebuttal to this is that Google is an aggregator and not a news provider.

According to Campbell's (2010) survey, Al Jazeera English was also trusted. The Qatar Arabic newspaper, funded by the emir of the richest nation in the Middle East, emerged as a dominant news channel covering the developing world. Al Jazeera Network has 65 bureaus across the globe with the majority located in the southern hemisphere, with 3000 staff members across the world, including 400 journalists from 60 countries. The global footprint of Al Jazeera English continues to grow, broadcasting to 220 million households in 100 countries. Al Jazeera English broadcasts news and current affairs 24-hours a day, seven days a week from Doha headquarters with news centers in London and Washington, DC.

Al Jazeera English replaced BBC World on Yes, Israeli satellite television (Conlan, 2006). Al Jazeera English has received many nominations and awards for news and programming from various organizations, including the International Emmys, The Royal Television Society, The Monte Carlo Film Festival, YouTube, The Foreign Press Association, The Association of International Broadcasters and Amnesty International (see www.pr.aljazeera.com/awards).

However, Al Jazeera was not allowed to be in the United States until 2013 when it purchased Current TV, partially owned by former US Vice President Al Gore. Though Current TV had large distribution throughout the United States, Al Jazeera English averaged only 28,000 viewers, which resulted in Time Warner Cable dropping the network due to its low ratings. After reevaluation, Time Warner Cable began carrying Al Jazeera America in December 2013. Gore and Joel Hyatt have sued Al Jazeera English for non-payment of $65 million due in 2014 (Hagey, 2014). Al Jazeera is countersuing (Gold, 2014).

All has not been positive for Al Jazeera in the Arab world either. An advertising boycott has taken place in Arab counties and the network has been banned in Iraq, Tunisia, and Algeria. Saudi Arabia finally lifted its ban. Egypt claimed that the *State of Al Jazeera* was plotting to overthrow its government, and Sudan's adviser to his president stated that Al Jazeera was too *stupid* to understand the concept of national interest (Campbell, 2010).

How did Google and Al Jazeera become leaders in media information? One reason is the cost-cutting measures by Western media houses of slashing the budgets of foreign bureaus. This opened a window for aggregators like Google and English-language foreign media to step into the void. Another reason is that Western media owners want news coverage based on the distribution of geopolitical power and reader demand (Friedman, 2013). Media owners make decisions based on where the money is rather than on what should be covered. To justify this point, an academic organization, Oxford Internet Institute's Information Geographies, created a blog that showed the results of news coverage of events around the world between 1979 and 2013. Two researchers, Mark Graham and Stefano DeSabbata, used the Global Database of Events, Language, and Tone (GDELT) to isolate 43 million events. The United States emerged as a core geographical focal point. Other most connected countries were Afghanistan and Pakistan. Conflict zones in the Middle East and North Africa received more attention than conflict zones in Africa, like the Democratic Republic of the Congo. More Western news sources were used for the data and that beyond questions of media bias, factors like freedom of the press, Internet penetration and the maturity of media markets played a major role in influencing the geographic scope of international news coverage. The geography of reporting—which is formed as much by human judgment as by the caprice of current events—influenced the way in which the world is perceived (Friedman, 2013, para. 9).

Western world journalists have endorsed the notion that to have a democratic society, the people within that society must be informed on all issues affecting them and the society. The role of a journalist had been to inform people on all issues. If this role changes, or disappears, how will democracies, as we have known them, continue to exist? This situation of allowing reader interest and *follow the money* to guide what is covered in the news creates a bizarre situation: "At the most interconnected time in history, accurate and comprehensive news of the outside world is disappearing—and with it an informed public" (Campbell, 2010, para. 8). In an op-ed article entitled, "Welcome to a World Without Foreign Correspondents," Andrew Stroehlein is quoted: "Too bad Al Jazeera English is not available on most living room screens in the United States, and people there have to choke down the endless rotting fish heads of celebrity news, or the same tiresome group of ignoramuses shouting at each other in a studio" (Campbell, 2010, para. 39).

It's Not Just Us | There Is a Global Issue of Trust

There is a global issue of loss of trust. BBC polled 10 countries to rate people's trust in media. These countries included the United States, the United Kingdom, Brazil, Egypt, Germany, India, Indonesia, Nigeria, Russia, and South Korea. The factors used in the research included the following: reports news accurately, reports all sides of the story, too much foreign influence and lost trust in media. On the last factor, the countries rated their loss of trust in the following way (BBC/Reuters/Media Center Poll, 2006):

Lost Trust in Media:

Brazil	44
Egypt	40
South Korea	39
USA	32
UK	29
India	28
Nigeria	27
Indonesia	17
Germany	15
Russia	10

Audiences who have lost trust in media include people referred to as citizen journalists. These citizens reported that they have lost trust in traditional media and are therefore taking it upon themselves to report on the conflict happening in their own back yards. The traditional media outlets that have lost trust by the people on the street include private and state-owned media.

The reasons why this loss of trust has happened are complex and layered within various cultures and among various events. Most distinctly, the citizen journalists suggested that the lies, bias, and propaganda offered by private and state-owned media justify why media are not to be trusted. This distrust did not just appear out of thin air, this distrust emerged over time. Through journalism studies, trust and credibility have been linked. These studies tried to explain how transitional societies, which have emerged from totalitarian regimes and were heading toward democracy, have given specific meaning to issues of truth, trust, and lies (Tampere, 2007, p. 142). These studies explained that expertise and trustworthiness have been two central attributes of credibility; but, according to a September 2013 Gallup Poll, Americans' trust and confidence in mass media have changed. This Poll demonstrated that when it comes to media reporting fully, accurately, and fairly, only 10 percent of Americans trusted the media a great deal, 30 percent trusted media a fair amount, 36 percent did not trust the media very much, and 24 percent did not trust media at all (Roper Poll, 2014). There also were different levels of trust in relation to certain mediums, such as radio, television, newspapers and magazines; therefore, a scale of trust in news media was created: trust in the selectivity of topics, trust in the selectivity of facts, trust in the accuracy of depictions, and trust in journalistic assessment (Kohring & Matthes, 2007, p. 231). All in all, trust is complex and academics are still trying to sort it out.

Lies, Lies, and More Lies

Lying is also complex because there are many ways to lie. One way media may lie is to lose control of the message. This losing control can happen when governments, during conflict, place constraints on media organizations. These constraints can be as simple as giving media talking points on issues to total message control. An example of how media lose control is through congressional offices in Western countries that are run like campaign operations. Their political consultants demand pre-publication quote approval, a request that leaves the journalist either taking what the congressional office wants them to have or not getting the story. Furthermore, opportunities for jour-nalists to question elected officials are often relegated to conference calls (on which they may or may not get to ask something), gang-bangs in the halls of Congress with 20 other reporters, or the demand for written questions in ad-vance (Rosen, 2013, July/August, p. 53). These situations leave the journalists with few interactive conversations and with only the story, the official wants them to have. The official may not lie, but they may not be telling the entire story, only their version.

Another way for media to lie is through journalism laziness—deciding not to report in a certain way, to leave things out, to not check thoroughly even after deadlines, all because they do not want problems for themselves. At other times, the journalists may have limited access to sources of information or the sources may lie to the reporters. An example of a lie told out of laziness is when the Western world was told that Iraqi soldiers invading Kuwait tossed premature babies out of incubators, according to *The Sunday Telegraph* in Lon-don on September 5, 1990 (Regan, 2002, para. 8). No one checked to see if the story was true. A 15-year-old Kuwaiti girl told the babies' story during the Human Rights Caucus of the US Congress meeting. The congressional com-mittee knew her only as Nayirah. President Bush referred to the story six times in the following weeks as an example of the evil of Saddam's regime. Then the *Los Angeles Times* reported, quoting Reuters, the same story. The public rela-tions firm, Hill & Knowlton, had been hired by Citizens for a Free Kuwait and the firm had arranged the entire thing. Two years later the teen-age witness was discovered to be a fraud; she was the daughter of the Kuwait Ambassador to the United States (Regan, 2002). The story was a lie.

Sometimes journalists promote certain issues without acknowledging that governments, lobbyists, or private interests had paid them. They failed to mention the sources. Anonymous sources are used for a reason, least of all to protect the source; Watergate and the Pentagon Papers are proof. Gov-ernments and individuals contract public relations firms to sell a war. They provide disinformation or partial information as news or fact without attrib-uting sources that might be questionable. Public relations firms feed stories to the press without revealing the nature of the information with the intention of creating a public opinion. The Kuwaiti story of premature babies is one example.

Another example is John Rendon, founder of the Washington, D.C. pub-lic relations firm, The Rendon Group, who shared his story with cadets at the US Air Force Academy in 1996 on the Gulf War in Iraq in 1991. He called himself an information warrior and a perception manager. He told the cadets that when victorious troops rolled into Kuwait City at the end of the war in the Persian Gulf, they were greeted by hundreds of Kuwaitis waving small American flags. The scene sent the message that US Marines were being welcomed in Kuwait as liberating heroes. "Did you ever stop to wonder," Rendon asked, "how the people of Kuwait City, after being held hostage for seven long and painful months, were able to get hand-held American, and for that matter, the flags of other coalition countries?" He paused for effect. "Well, you now know the answer. That was one of my jobs then" (Stein, 2002, para. 5).

Lying can be choosing which sources to quote. Good sourcing is a component of being objective and not being biased; however, cherry-picking sources for a point of view can lead to bias and a lack of objectivity. Examples of how journalists may cherry pick are offered by Workneh (2011). He demonstrates that in the case of Somalia, no local Somali sources were implied or quoted in any of the commentaries given. To be precise, three sources were indicated, identified as "a Western soldier working in Somalia," "an intelligence officer," and "Michael Ranneberger, US ambassador to Kenya" (Workneh, 2011, p. 40). This pattern of sourcing is not uncommon in international reporting, particularly in dealing with conflict/war stories (Lee & Maslog, 2005; Shinar, 2009). Another problem with sourcing is that all the sources have not been checked, even the official sources. An example of not checking could be when the second Bush was president and accused Iraq of having weapons of mass destruction. Media picked it up and reported it as fact. An article in *Mother Jones Magazine* gave a timeline of the Iraq events leading up to war with the statement:

> But the blame for Iraq does not end with Cheney, Bush, or Rumsfeld. Nor is it limited to the intelligence operatives who sat silent as the administration cherry-picked its case for war, or with those, like Colin Powell or Hans Blix, who, in the name of loyalty or statesmanship, did not give full throat to their misgivings. It is also shared by far too many in the Fourth Estate, most notably the *New York Times*' Judith Miller. But let us not forget that it lies, inescapably, with we the American people, who, in our fear and rage over the catastrophic events of September 11, 2001, allowed ourselves to be suckered into the most audacious bait and switch of all time. (Stein & Dickinson, 2006, para. 3)

The lesson should be that any claim made by a government official should be sourced, reported and assessed along with any other and not taken as fact until it has been verified.

To lie, people hide the truth, give partial truths or use frames to accent *us vs. them* mentality. An example of partial truths is what happened in Bosnia. Bosnian Muslim forces had fired a shell at their own people in order to win international sympathy. When Yasuyshi Akashi, former head of the UN mission in Bosnia, finally admitted the existence of this report in June 1996, he said it was no secret since "some journalists already had a copy." Those intrepid reporters had kept the secret to themselves, ensuring that one of the biggest scandals in Bosnia remained effectively buried for more than two years (Hume, 1997b, para. 9).

Further, the international press (Western newspapers in this case) portrayed dominant conflict/war framing as opposed to peace/resolution framing and that, despite claiming to uphold fundamental principles of journalistic reporting, they continued to represent the geo-political interests of the country of publication, albeit in a subtler manner (Workneh, 2011, p. 40).

Bias: Cuts Across the Grain

There was a time in our history when a partisan viewpoint was the norm. However, when Alexis de Tocqueville published *Democracy in America* in 1835, the role of the press had begun to be seen as that of providing *objective* news (Schudson, 1981, p. 4). Objectivity as an ethical value evolved over the next 150 years to become the *supreme deity* of American journalism and a general expectation of the public (Mindich, 2000, p. 1). The Hutchins Commission in 1947 encouraged journalists to reconnect with communities, strengthen civic culture and persuade citizens to play a more active role in politics and self-governance (Friedland, Rosen & Austin, 1994).

As media grew in importance within the American society and gained the responsibility of being a watchdog and the Fourth Estate, the dialogue about objectivity and bias began to change. Academics began to create studies proving that objectivity never can be achieved; there would always be bias. Yet, the concept of remaining objective was still held as sacred in the industry. Arguments shutting down discussions on objectivity included the fear that bias would become the norm and accepted way of distributing information and that journalists who practiced being objective had limited time and resources to make objectivity actually happen. Further discussions had academics agreeing that objectivity may be a pipe dream but anything else would not be acceptable. Then there were suggestions that objectivity may have served as one of the major professional justifications for mass media's contribution to war, that objectivity was a ritual to achieve the image of impartiality before the public and that objectivity was a camouflage technique with which to transmit biased information. The notion of objectivity is complicated.

There are many examples of bias. One was media coverage of the conflict between Russia and Georgia. *Russia Today* described Georgians as the worst villains. CNN, however, expressed empathy toward Georgia. These two prominent media created a confusing atmosphere that included many discrepancies. Even after the war, there were a lot of manipulations and speculations about the causes and the flow of the military conflict published in both media. Because *Russia Today* was directly involved within the conflict, how could they be expected to stay balanced and unbiased? Both the Russian and Georgia media faced significant challenges related to media independence due to the relatively short and fragile democratic development taking place in both countries. It may be naïve to expect an absence of bias from media organizations from either country; instead, it would be more plausible to look to media of third countries to play a neutral observer role (Oganjanyan, 2011). CNN had an opportunity to do this, but did not.

Another example of failed opportunities was revealed in a study by Salla Nazarenko (2008/2009) that concentrated on the depiction of the two breakaway territories of Georgia: Abkhazia and South Ossetia. The conflict was in the media during the first days of the August war in 2008 as well as during the previous escalation of the *frozen conflicts* (the fight has stopped but no settlement has been made and the conflict could resume) in the summers of 2004 and 2006. Through quantitative and qualitative analysis, Nazarenko studied texts of the American *New York Times*, the German *Süddeutsche Zeitung*, Britain's *The Guardian* and the Russian *Novaya Gazeta*. Within these texts, she searched for the frequency of certain historical analogies, terms, and words such as *the return of the Cold war, aggression,* and *democracy.* She looked for whether or not the reporting was balanced or biased (pro-Georgian vs. pro-Russian). Her findings included: articles using mostly official sources, that even the liberally-oriented papers sometimes were patriotic and followed the political agenda, that there was a consensus in naming Russia as aggressor and that the Russian-Georgia war was full of dichotomies: big and small, David and Goliath, democratic and undemocratic, etc. As to the question of balanced reporting, the study concluded that the *New York Times* supported Georgia more than the other newspapers researched; *Süddeutsche Zeitung* was unexpectedly anti-Russian; *The Guardian* showed itself as the most balanced and *Novaya Gazeta* aimed at a multi-faceted and balanced view of that crisis (Nazarenko, 2008/9). This study is an example of how traditional media in a variety of countries can have different approaches to the same conflict.

In addition to objectivity, truthfulness is the second important characteristic that is usually sacrificed in favor of war journalism. Walter Lippman has been quoted, "We must remember that in time of war what is said on the enemy's side of the front is always propaganda, and what is said on our side of the front is truth and righteousness, the cause of humanity and a crusade for peace." By omitting context information (and providing sound bites), the conventional way to depict wars invites untruthfulness and half truths, at times even deliberately misleading information in an effort to polarize publics, demonize the opponent, and glorify one side or a favored party (Neumann & Fahmy, 2012, p. 177). Thus, propaganda becomes the principle means of mass communication, disseminating misinformation and steering public opinion as war progresses (Arsenault & Castells, 2006).

Propaganda Shift from Good to Bad

Propaganda began its lexicon life as simply presenting a point of view; however, the world wars changed propaganda to mean influencing and changing opinions and not always in a good way. What does propaganda imply today in our market savvy, commercial-driven media world? Elements of propaganda provided by Anup Shah on *Global Issues* include the following (Shah, 2005, para. 5):

- Using selective stories that are seen as wide covering and objective
- Including partial facts or just historical context
- Reinforcing reasons and motivations to act due to threats on the security of the individual
- Choosing narrow sources of experts to provide insights to the situation (example, media interview retired military personnel for many conflict-related issues, or treat official government sources as fact, rather than one perspective that needs to be verified and researched)
- Demonizing the enemy
- Using a narrow range of discourse

In the context of peace journalism, Johann Galtung specified tactics used in propaganda (Shah, 2005, para. 14).

- Decontextualizing violence: focusing on the irrational without looking at the reasons for unresolved conflicts and polarization
- Dualism: reducing the number of parties in a conflict to two, when often more are involved
- Manichaeism: portraying one side as good and demonizing the other as evil
- Armageddon: presenting violence as inevitable, omitting alternatives
- Focusing on individual acts of violence while avoiding structural causes, like poverty, government neglect and military or police repression
- Confusion: focusing only on the conflict arena (i.e., the battlefield or location of violent incidents) but not on the forces and factors that influence the violence)
- Excluding and omitting the bereaved, thus never explaining why there are acts of revenge and spirals of violence
- Failure to explore the causes of escalation and the impact of media coverage itself
- Failure to explore the goals of outside interventionists, especially big powers
- Failure to explore peace proposals and offer images of peaceful outcomes
- Confusing cease-fires and negotiations with actual peace
- Omitting reconciliation: conflicts tend to reemerge if attention is not paid to efforts to heal fractured societies. When information about attempts to resolve conflicts is absent, fatalism is reinforced. That can help engender even more violence, when people have not images or information about possible peaceful outcomes and the promise of healing.

To bring these propaganda elements into modern warfare, Miren Guiterrez, editor-in-chief of Inter Press Service, based her list on recent wars such as the *war on terror* and the Iraq crisis. Her propaganda strategies included the following: incompleteness, inaccuracy, driving the agenda, milking the story (maximizing media coverage of a particular issue by the careful use of briefings, leaking pieces of a jigsaw to different outlets, allowing journalists to piece the story together and drive the story up the news agenda), exploiting that people want to believe the best of themselves, perception management (in particular by using public relations firms), reinforcing existing attitudes, and simple, repetitious and emotional phrases (e.g., war on terror, axis of evil, weapons of mass destruction, shock and awe, war of liberation, etc.) (Shah, 2005, para. 6).

Propaganda can be expanded through military control of information during war time. The military manipulates the mainstream media by restricting or managing what information is presented and what the public is told. This is accomplished through organizing media sessions and daily press briefings, or by providing managed access to war zones, and even to planting stories. Over time then, the way that media cover conflicts degrades in quality, critique and objectiveness.

In preparing for or justifying war, additional propaganda techniques are often employed. There are several key stages of a military campaign used to *soften up* public opinion through the media in preparation for an armed intervention. These are: the preliminary stage where the country comes to the news portrayed as a cause for mounting concern because of poverty/dictatorship/anarchy; the justification stage during which big news is produced to lend urgency to the case for armed intervention to bring about a rapid restitution of normality; the implementation stage when pooling and censorship provide control of coverage and the aftermath during which normality is portrayed as returning to the region, before it once again drops down the news agenda (Ottosen, 1997).

Phillip Knightley, an award winning investigative journalist, has his own four stages for preparing a nation for war. First, report the crisis, which negotiations appear unable to resolve. Then quote politicians, who call for diplomacy but warn of military retaliation. Media report this as *we're on the brink of war* or *war is inevitable*. Second, demonize the enemy's leader. By comparing, a leader with Hitler causes the audience to conjure instant images that Hitler's name provokes. Third, demonize the enemy as individuals; for example, suggest that the enemy is insane. And fourth, spell out atrocities, even make up stories to whip up and strengthen emotional reactions (Knightley, 2000).

A government prepares its people for war and media spins the stories. In the United Kingdom, the History Channel produced a documentary on August 21, 2004, *War Spin: Correspondent*. This documentary looked at coalition media management for the Iraq War. The documentary suggested that embedded journalists allowed the military to maximize imagery while providing minimal insight into the real issues. Central command (where all the military press briefings were held) was the main center from which to filter, manage and drip-feed journalists with what they, the military, wanted to provide. At Central command, the military would gloss over setbacks, and dwell on successes, limit the facts, and context and even feed lies to journalists. The military would use spin in various ways, such as making it seem as though reports were coming from troops on the ground, which Central Command would confirm, so as to appear real; then carefully plan the range of topics that could be discussed with reporters, and what to avoid.

Information provided by the government and the military play a significant role in how conflict is covered by traditional journalists. Within the scope of propaganda are definitely the sources but also language. Language plays a dominant role in propaganda techniques. Aaron Delwiche, at the School of Communications at the University of Washington, provides a website discussing propaganda. Here he offers eight basic propaganda devices: name-calling, glittering generalities, euphemisms, transfer (false connections like using symbols and imagery of positive institutions to strengthen acceptance), testimonial, plain folks, band wagon (the everyone else is doing it argument) and fear (Delwiche, 2015). Examples of how language can be used in propaganda is demonstrated in the section on euphemisms: The United States changed the name of the War Department to the Department of Defense in the 1940s; under the Reagan Administration, the MX-Missile was renamed *The Peacekeeper*; and during conflict *civilian casualties* are referred to as *collateral damage* and the word *liquidation* is used as a synonym for *murder* (Delwiche, 2015).

In the 1998 book, *Propaganda Inc.: Selling America's Culture to the World*, Nancy Snow suggests that the reason why a majority of Americans still link Saddam Hussein to 9/11 is because they were repeatedly told by the President and his inner circle that Saddam's evil alone was enough to be linked to 9/11 and that given time, he would have used his weapons against us. The media became caught up in the *rally round the flag* syndrome. They were forced to choose a side, given the choices, whose side did they logically choose but the United States? (Shah, 2005).

Propaganda also enters the discussion when corporate interests are at stake. Dissident viewpoints are variously labeled as biased, ideological, or extreme. Most activists, calling for radical changes in society—whether environmentalists, human-rights activists or opponents of the arms trade—are not consistently and fairly reported by corporate news organizations. Most likely the activists' arguments will be vilified, marginalized or simply ignored (Cromwell, 2002). To learn how to filter through propaganda, Herman and Chomsky have outlined five filters in their propaganda model to be used in society to determine news. These five filters are the following: (1) media owned by large conglomerates are driven by free market ideology; (2) advertising as revenue is market driven; (3) mass media are drawn into a symbiotic relationship with powerful sources of information by economic necessity and reciprocity of interest; (4) flak: letters, telegrams, phone calls, petitions, law-suits, speeches and Bills before Congress, and other modes of complaint, threat and punitive action; and (5) western identification of *the enemy* or an *evil dictator* (Herman & Chomsky, 1988).

Believed to be the enemies of the United States, the United Kingdom, the Middle East, and countries within the European Union in 2015 are groups linked to Al-Qaeda and to ISIS. Both groups use social media for propaganda and for recruitment. A great deal has been written about how successful ISIS has been in inhabiting the online world and disseminating terror and propaganda. ISIS propaganda, consisting of online depictions of mass executions, beheadings, and the inflated hype of triumphalism was solely responsible in many cases for military victories gained without a shot being fired (Wade, 2015). In March 2015, ISIS posted on the Web the names, photos and what supposedly addresses of 100 US military personnel, calling on its supporters to *deal* with them. The group's so-called *hacking division* says the individuals have been part of efforts to defeat ISIS in Syria, Iraq, and Yemen. It says it has decided to release the information about the US servicemen and servicewomen so "brothers in America can deal with you" (Neuman, 2015).

Last Word: How to search for truth is not easy for a journalist. In the twenty-first century, there is no pharmaceutical compound whose proven effect is the consistent or predictable enhancement of truth telling. Just because no truth-inducing drug exists today, doesn't mean there could be one in the future, according to Mark Wheelis, a professor and expert on the history of biological warfare and biological weapons control at the University of California Davis.

"There is a large number of neural circuits that we are on the verge of being able to manipulate—things that govern states like fear, anxiety, terror and depression," said Wheelis. "We don't have recipes yet to control them, but the potential is clearly foreseeable," he said. "It would absolutely astonish me if we didn't identify a range of pharmaceuticals that would be of great utility to interrogators" (Brown, 2006, para. 30).

There has got to be a better way.

Discussion: How has propaganda about the war on terrorism been delivered to the American people via different media platforms?

References

Arsenault, A. & Castells, M. (2006). Conquering the minds, conquering Iraq: The social production of misinformation in the United States: A case study. Information. *Communication & Society, 9*(3), 284–307.

BBC/Reuters/Media Center Poll: Trust in the Media (2006, May 3). Globescan. Retrieved from http://www.globescan.com/news_archives/bbcreut_country.html.

Brown, D. (2006, November 20). Some believe 'truth serums' will come back. *The Washington Post.* Retrieved from http://www.washingtonpost.com/wp-srv/content/article/2006/11/19/truth.html?nav=rss_email/components.

Campbell, D. (2010, January 7). Broadcaster of the year: Documenting an ever-larger swath of the planet. *Adbusters.* Retrieved from https://www.adbusters.org/magazine/87/aljazeera-english.html.

Conlan, T. (2006, December 13). BBC World dropped by Israeli satellite TV. *The Guardian.* Retrieved from http://www.theguardian.com/media/2006/dec/13/bbc.middleeastthemedia.

Cromwell, D. (2002). The propaganda model: An overview. http://www.chomsky.info/onchomsky/2002----.htm.

Delwiche, A. (2015). Propaganda web site. Retrieved from http://www.propagandacritic.com.

Dorothy Thompson (nd). http://www.gwu.edu/~erpapers/teachinger/glossary/thompson-dorothy.cfm.

Friedman, U. (2013, November 19). How three decades of news coverage has shaped our view of the world. *The Atlantic.* Retrieved from http://www.theatlantic.com/international/archive/2013/11/how-three-decades-of-news-coverage-has-shaped-our-view-of-the-world/281613/.

Friedland, L. A., Rosen, J., & Austin, L. (1994). *Civic journalism: A new approach to citizenship.* Waltham, MA: Civic Practices Network.

Gold, H. (2014, September 19). Al Jazeera America sues Al Gore. *Politico.* Retrieved from http://politi.co/1m1W9fk.

Herman, E. & Chomsky, N. (1988). A propaganda model. Excerpted from Manufacturing Consent. Retrieved from https://chomsky.info/consent01/.

Hume, M. (1997, August 25–27). Victim journalism. The peace journalism option. *Global Issues.* Retrieved from http://www.globalissues.org/article/534/the-peace-journalism-option.

Knightley, P. (2000, March 20). Fighting dirty. *The Guardian.* Retrieved from http://www.theguardian.com/media/2000/mar/20/mondaymediasection.pressandpublishing.

Kohring, M. & Matthes, J. (2007). Trust in news media: Development and validation of a multidimensional scale. *Communication Research, 34*(3), 231–252.

Lee, S. T. & Maslog, C.C. (2005). War or peace journalism? Asian newspaper coverage of conflicts. *Journal of Communication, 55*(2), 311–329.

Mindich, D. (2000). *Just the facts: How 'objectivity' came to define American journalism.* New York: New York University Press.

Mitchell, A. (2014, October 30). Which news organization is the most trusted? The answer is complicated. Pew Research Center. Retrieved from http://www.pewresearch.org/fact-tank/2014/10/30/which-news-organization-is-the-most-trusted-the-answer-is-complicated/.

Nazarenko, S. (2008/9). With or without Georgia? Portrayal of Abkhazia and South. Ossetia in *The New York Times, Süddeutsche Zeitung, The Guardian* and *Novaya Gazeta* during the conflicts of 2004, 2006 and 2008. Reuters Institute Fellowship Paper. University of Oxford. Michaelmas, Hilary Trinity Term. Retrieved from https://reutersinstitute.politics. ox.ac.uk/sites/default/files/With%20or%20without%20Georgia%20-%20The%20 Portrayal%20of%20Abkhazia%20and%20South%20Ossetia%20in%20the%20New%20 York%20Times,%20Süddeutsche%20Zeitung,%20the%20Guardian%20%26%20 Novaya%20gazeta.pdf.

Neuman, S. (2015, March 22). ISIS Issues 'Wanted' list of 100 U.S. military personnel. NPR. Retrieved from http://www.npr.org/blogs/thetwo-way/2015/03/22/394644309/isis-issues-wanted-list-of-100-u-s-military-personnel.

Neumann, R. & Fahmy, S. (2012). Analyzing the spell of war: A war-peace framing analysis of the 2009 visual coverage of the Sri Lankan civil war in western newswires. *Mass Communication and Society*, 15, pp. 169–200.

Oganjanyan, A. (2011). Western media on foreign crisis balance and conflict-sensitivity in foreign reporting with an example of the Russia-Georgia war of 08.08.2008. Master's Thesis. Hamburg. Retrieved from http://www.diplomica.de.

Ottosen, R. (1997). The peace journalism option. Conflict and Peace Journalism summer school. Taplow Court, Buckinghamshire, U.K. Retrieved from http://web.archive.org/ web/20000822111932/www.poiesis.org/pjo/pjotext.html.

"Press widely criticized, but trusted more than other information sources" (2011, September 22). Pew Research Center. Retrieved from http://www.people-press.org/2011/09/22/press-widely-criticized-but-trusted-more-than-other-institutions/?src=prc-number.

Regan, T. (2002). When contemplating war, beware of babies in incubators. *The Christian Science Monitor*. Retrieved from http://www.csmonitor.com/2002/0906/p25s02-cogn.html.

Roper Poll (2014). http://www.ropercenter.uconn.edu/.

Rosen, J. (2013, July/August). DC deep-freeze: Pols no longer need us more than we need them. *Columbia Journalism Review*, pp. 53–55. Retrieved from http://www.cjr.org/essay/dc_deep-freeze.php?page=all&print=true.

Schudson, M. & Anderson, C. (2008). Objectivity, professionalism, and truth seeking in journalism. In Wahl-Jorgensen, K. & Hanitzsch, T. (Eds.), *Handbook of journalism studies*, New York: Routledge, pp. 88–101.

Shah, A. (2005, March 31). War, propaganda and the media. Global Issues/Propaganda When Preparing or Justifying War. Retrieved from http://www.globalissues.org/article/157/war-propaganda-and-the-media.

Shinar, D. (2007). Epilogue: Peace journalism—The state of the art. *Conflict and Communication*, 6(1).

Squires, J. D. (1993). *Read all about it*. Crown Publishers.

Steel, E. & Somaiya, R. (2015, February 10). Brian Williams suspended from NBC for 6 months without pay. *The New York Times*. Retrieved from http://www.nytimes.com/2015/02/11/ business/media/brian-williams-suspended-by-nbc-news-for-six-months.html.

Stein, J. (2002, February 27). Propaganda, the Pentagon and the Rendon Group. Retrieved from http://www.alternet.org/story/12514/propaganda%2C_the_pentagon%2C_and_the_rendon_group.

Stein, J. & Dickinson, T. (2006, September/October). Lie by lie: A timeline of how we got into Iraq. *Mother Jones*. Retrieved from http://www.motherjones.com/politics/2011/12/leadup-iraq-war-timeline.

Sterling, G. (2015, January 20). Google overtakes traditional media to become most trusted news source. Search Engine Land. Retrieved from http://searchengineland.com/google-overtakes-traditonal-media-become-trusted-source-news-online-213176.

Tampere, K. (2007). The media's role in a transition society: From public lies to public trust? In Bakire, V. & Barlow, M. (Eds.), *Communication in the age of suspicion. Trust and the media* (pp. 141–154). London: Palgrave.

Wade, D. (2015). Daesh is losing the propaganda war. Retrieved from https://www.academia.edu/9081141/Daesh_is_losing_the_propaganda_war.

Workneh, T. W. (2011). War journalism or peace journalism? A case study of U.S. and British newspapers coverage of the Somali conflict. Paper presented at the annual meeting of the International Communication Association, Boston, MA. Retrieved from http://citation.allacademic.com/meta/p489404_index.html.

· 8 ·

ACTIVISM AND SOCIAL MEDIA

Songs have been used to encourage activism as protests have continued to make headlines around the world. Songs like *The Students Are Back* by Ahmed Fouad Negm and Sheikh Imam, have been used all over the world during protests. Many of these protest songs have been recorded and disseminated to audiences through social media. These songs increase the perceptions by various groups of people that the activists' messages were not being covered adequately through traditional media. To do something about this, one team of activists developed a web site, Conflict Tracker, to attract awareness to armed conflicts and global security concerns. Founded in 2012 in Vancouver, British Columbia, the site had an interactive map with daily events posted to accent the threat of terrorism and the spread of regional ethnic conflicts and uprisings. On the site, the Conflict Tracker Team wrote that the collection of data and events would be non-existent without the submissions of journalists, photographers, and citizens caught up in turbulence. The Team has supported social media's ability to connect people from around the world (Conflict Tracker, nd).

The goal of this chapter is to demonstrate how activism and social media have been used by journalists covering conflict and why. Journalists have used media to promote causes important to them; thus, they too have become activists. There are many examples, such as newspaper editor William Lloyd Garrison, who in 1841 founded the abolitionist newspaper, *The Liberator* ("William Lloyd Garrison," nd). Then Dorothy Thompson (1893–1961), who headed the Berlin bureau of the *New York Post* and the *Public Ledger*, covered the rise of Adolph Hitler and the Nazis. Her negative coverage of Hitler led to her expulsion from Germany in 1934 ("Dorothy Thompson," nd). Besides promoting their own activist causes, journalists also have covered activist groups when these groups did one of the following: created news (e.g., Occupy Wall Street), organized massive demonstrations (e.g., youth demonstrating in Brazil for lower transit fares), staged sensational events to make a point (e.g., Feeding Zaragoza event in Spain where 1000 people ate lunch prepared from thrown away food to protest waste), or were endorsed by a celebrity (e.g., Bono with Irish band U2 advocating for African aid). With their own agenda or covering activists groups, journalists have had the advantage of using traditional media as a platform in which to rally opinion around causes. On the other hand, activists, who were not journalists, have had little access to traditional media. Everything changed when social media emerged and allowed anyone to be a reporter. People, who felt they had been disenfranchised, who did not have access to a media platform, now had a way to communicate activist issues to a broader public.

Activists Use of Social Media

How activists have used media to promote issues is important for journalists to understand for several reasons. First, by understanding the activists' systems, facts can be verified and then endorsed or rejected. Second, the activists want their stories out and have little interest in having their names attached to the information, which can provide journalists with valuable leads on people who may be able to emphasize a peaceful solution rather than violence.

Barriers exist that limit how activists distribute their messages. Governments, traditional journalists, and media owners have constructed these barriers. Government control and surveillance stop many messages that are anti-government. However, with social media, government control and surveillance have been more difficult and activists have found ways to circumvent the government. For example, activists using mobile phones have been able to capture images and videos that could then be communicated through other networks (Khamis & Vaughn, 2011, pp. 11–12).

Then, citizens report that traditional media are not to be trusted, especially when state-owned or censored. On the other hand, traditional media owners say that activists already have access to media through letters to the editor, surveys, and product purchases based on advertisements thus they do not need to create activist media. Some media houses have created ways to use citizen reporters, such as CNN's iReport. However, even this system is imperfect. Any information provided by citizen reporters to traditional media have been subjected to traditional gate keeping practices that filter news content, making it consistent with narratives already found in traditional media (Ali & Fahmy, 2013, p. 55).

Activists who want to promote their causes are using major forms of social media such as Facebook, Twitter, Digg, Instagram, MySpace, YouTube, apps, and blogs (including vblogs). The users of these programs have become technology savvy. Twitter and Instagram users have proven themselves vigilant when it comes to identifying frauds and hoaxes (Adler, 2013, p. 34). Twitter has gained status as an important news driver for activists. Young users are more likely to follow news media outlets on Twitter, suggesting that it serves as a channel for delivering alternative news. Thus, the role of news within social media is especially important because these sites provide users with a different experience than traditional mass media, such as newspapers, television, and radio (Weeks & Holbert, 2013, p. 214). Facebook has become important for activists in several ways. First, people who use Facebook for news and socialization with peers are more likely to participate in protests (Pearce & Kendzior, 2012). Second, using Facebook for entertainment only can drive people away from collective action (Shah, Roihas & Cho, 2009). Also third, digital media used for informational purposes can foster democratic processes and create social capital (Valenzuela, Arriagada, & Scherman, 2012).

Verification of how effective social media may have been in aiding protests and strengthening activists' issues can be described through the technology revolution in the Arab world (Ghareeb, 2000). Social media have gained strength in the Arab region, despite government blockages and intimidation tactics used to curb social media users. In the Arab region, Facebook had 677 million users in 2011 and Twitter exceeded 200 million users with about four billion tweets a month (Salem and Mourtada, 2011b). During the protests in Egypt in 2011, there was a 29 percent growth in Facebook usage in Egypt compared to a 12 percent growth just one year earlier. Calls for protest on Facebook increased 5.5 percent in Egypt on January 25, 2011, during the height of the Egyptian protests, while in Libya they increased by 4.3 percent on February 17, 2011, marking that country's major protests (Salem and Mourtada (2011b).

Do Social Media Meet the Users' Goals?

Stated goals by activists using social media indicated that they wanted to make changes in their government. This goal often has not been achieved. On the other hand, using social media to organize protests during times when disenfranchised people's level of frustration has peaked, then the use of social media has been effective. Social media have not caused the revolutions; they have been a tool. *The Guardian* reported that people in Libya, Tunisia, and Egypt wanted to communicate in moments of historic crisis. The medium that carried the message shaped and defined the message. Timely posts have contributed to the success of social media during these revolutions where publication deadlines and broadcast news formats did not have to be considered. Speed of the posts has been the ultimate success of social media within revolutions since these revolutions have been created based on a loose, nonhierarchical organization similar to the networks of the web (Beaumont, 2011).

Importance of Culture in Social Media Use

Activists are using social media differently from one country to another. So a journalist must investigate how each group may be using media and not assume that each group will be using media the same way. Consistent across the protests and use of social media is the importance culture plays in interpreting the messages. For example, in Libya social media have provided a type of public shield for bloggers since bloggers have the capacity to disseminate new cultural values, to encourage new political practices and to engage the public with support on a large scale (Papaioannou & Olivos, 2013).

Culture plays a dominant role on digital platforms where people are communicating and interacting with one another using cultural codes. In other words, the users' cultural backgrounds define the process of interpreting the information received online. Consequently, culture is central to the entire communication process. To use digital platforms successfully, activists must develop and share a collective identity based on common values, ideas, opinions and visions about the world (Papaioannou & Olivos, 2013). Activists are creating a collective identity by developing new tools. An example is the app created for Syrian refugees fleeing to Turkey. Computer programmer, Mojahid Akil, a Syrian refugee, created the Gherbtna app designed to help exiled Syrians adjust to life in Turkey when they did not understand the culture or the language but must stay and learn to survive. The name of the app is an Arabic word that means exile, loneliness, and the feeling of being foreign ("Mobile Phone Apps," 2015).

The culture in Egypt is different from Libya and from Syria so when the web site Askar Kadhibun (Lying Generals) set out to expose the atrocities of the transitional military rule, the creators of the website did so by digitally documenting the actions of Egypt's Supreme Council of the Armed Forces (SCAF), which directly supervised crimes such as abduction, torture, sexual harassment, rape and random killing (Aboubakr, 2013). The sources Askar Kadhibun used for footages were diverse: anonymous posts on video-archiving sites, activist-members' compilations and eyewitness contributions. Askar Kadhibun's Facebook page had its members referring to themselves as the "internet lie-detector, an alternative—and popular—search engine....We are ordinary youth who are habitually referred to as revolutionary movements but we originated in the Tahrir Square and will remain there. We are sick of the lies of the ruling generals and thieves, and we are out to expose them. We feel it is our duty to shake awake the indifferent and the apathetic and the brainwashed and the deluded and the scared" (Aboubakr, 2013, p. 260). This Facebook page and the activists maintaining its content offer another consistent component of social media in protests: youth.

Youth Activists Dominate Social Media Platforms

Forty-three percent of the world's population was 25 or younger in 2013. Some 70 percent of these young people believed that social media was a force of change (Kumar, 2013, para. 1). The mass media (such as television and music), and in particular the new media (such as the Internet) have been important tools for spreading the global culture to young people around the world; conversely, it can be used as a platform for networking resistance. Researchers from Denmark, France, and Israel found that as a result of the media-induced processes of globalization, young people in those countries have a preference for transnational fiction and movie material (particularly American *soapies*) as well as a new sense of transnational social space provided by the Internet (Gidley, 2002, p. 6).

Young people in Chili have been found to have strong links between their use of online platforms, including news sites and social network sites, with their participation in political and civic issues. These young people's political interest and membership in civic groups were more closely related to actively protesting. Although Facebook use has been a significant tool for youth activism, it is neither the only means nor even the most important one (Valenzuela, Arriagada & Scherman, 2012, p. 309–310).

Social network sites have promoted participation in protests among youth in four ways. One, these social network sites have facilitated access to a large number of contacts, thereby enabling social movements to reach a critical mass (Marwell & Oliver, 1993). Two, these sites have promoted the construction of personal and group identities that are key antecedents of protest behavior through allowing multiple channels for interpersonal feedback, peer acceptance and reinforcement of group norms (Dalton, Sickle & Weldon, 2009). Three, social network sites have functioned as information hubs that allow users to remain in contact and to exchange updates regarding their activities with others who share their interests. Those who belong to social movements and political groups can build relationships with one another, receive mobilizing information that they may not obtain elsewhere, and thereby expand opportunities to engage in political activities (Gil de Zúñiga & Valenzuela, 2011; Kobayashi, Ikeda & Miyata, 2006). Fourth, social media have been an effective means for social interaction. Finding a basis for conversation and social communication, connecting with family, friends, and society, and gaining insight into the circumstances of others are all factors that can instill in young people an interest in collective issues (Valenzuela, Arriagada & Scherman, 2012, p. 302).

Facebook can successfully allow youth to interweave the private world of family, friends and personal life with the public sphere of politics, social movements, and protests, in line with subactivist practices (Bakardjieva, 2010). Subactivism is a term coined by Bakardjieve to mean:

[A] kind of politics that unfolds at the level of subjective experience and is submerged in the flow of everyday life. It is constituted by small-scale, often individual, decisions and actions that have either a political or ethical frame of reference (or both) and are difficult to capture using the traditional tools with which political participation is measured. Subactivism is a refraction of the public political arena in the private and personal world. (Bakardjieva, 2010, p. 92)

Political action movements in emerging democracies have had three elements in common: the dominant role of youth, the absence of political parties as the main organizers and the widespread use of social media as a means of political action (Valenzuela, Arriagada & Scherman, 2012, p. 300).

Criticisms of Activists Using Social Media to Cover Conflict

Though culture and youth have been consistent across the globe for social media users, there have been problems associated with using social media in areas of conflict. These problems include the following:

- Discourse is seldom if ever neutral
- Long-term peaceful resolution has low success
- Eruption of violent extremism
- Creation of fake sites
- Encouragement of users to be slack and not diligent
- Another way of filtering information without really getting at the truth.

Neutrality is when information and facts recorded have transparency with all sides specified. However, if the information appears too one-sided or close-minded, reflecting a more propaganda approach than persuasive approach and hindering acceptance of new or different ideas (Freelon, 2012) then neutrality does not exist. With activists reporting events, they report only the items that are of interest to them. Hardly anyone posts news items because they can, but only because they feel they need to. This suggests that citizen journalists are always deeply involved in the news they report, which puts pressure on its neutrality (Niekerk, 2013, p. 17).

Low success in the long-term for a peaceful resolution has been studied in Brazil, Egypt, and Nigeria. Although the Brazil 2013 protests initially were against the rise in public transport fees, other complaints emerged like the cost of the FIFA World Cup, corruption in government and a lack of investment in education and healthcare. One million people protested with 91 percent of the protesters hearing about the movement through the Internet and 77 percent of them using Facebook. A website created to cover the protests, Midia Ninja, hosted videos. The activists did not want to corroborate with the traditional journalists. During the protests, traditional media were targeted as rioters set fire to a van from a TV channel and reporters were expelled from rallies. "It seems people want to hear their voices reported in a different way" (Pelli, 2013, para. 11). The protests continued two years later with unmet aspirations and the convergence of grievances (Saad-Filho, 2015).

Long-term success has not been evident in Egypt after the social media revolution. Once Mubarak was disposed and the government formed under a new president, Abdel Fattah al-Sisi, new rules were created. Al-Sisi viewed the Egyptian youth as leaders of the protest movement. To reduce the influence of the youth, changes were made within the university system. Al-Sisi appointed the university heads, dismissed faculty members without appeal and forced students to sign documents promising not to participate in political activities. Students had to go through scanners with their belongings searched, and they had to show class schedules to be allowed on campus (Ibrahim, 2014). These changes resulted in additional violent clashes at 20 Egyptian universities, according to Yussof Salhen, 22, at al-Azhar University and spokesperson for the organization, Students Against the Coup (Lynch, 2014).

Although social media covered abuse of women first in Egypt and also in Nigeria, few positive results have remained. Egyptian women protesting abuse created a site called HarassMap, started by American-born Rebecca Chiao in 2012. This tweet site allowed women to report instances of abuse by texting or tweeting using the hashtag #harassmap. This social media tool has not slowed sexual harassment. There are still honor killings, gang rapes, and entrapment of women in the home without a voice; the subjugation of women is unlikely to change any time soon—regardless of social media (McCoy, 2014).

Nigeria's social media protest #bringbackourgirls has not brought back the girls. Hashtags are cathartic. They make a point, but it is unclear if they accomplish anything. Michelle Obama, Hillary Rodman Clinton and former British Prime Minister David Cameron, plus millions of global hashtag activists tweeted #bringbackourgirls. The tweet was in response to the abduction of more than 200 teenage girls on May 7, 2014, by Boko Haram militants who stormed a secondary school in Chibok, Nigeria. After four million tweets, hundreds of the girls had not been rescued (Sam, 2015).

The promulgation of violent extremism online is another criticism of using social media in conflict. Shami Witness on Twitter, an ISIS fanboy and key facilitator of conflict in Syria, was exposed December 11, 2014, by a Channel 4 investigation. He is a West Bengali called Mehdi Masroor Biswas, who worked in Bangalore as a marketing executive for an Indian conglomerate but spent his days and nights prolifically spreading ISIS propaganda online and encouraging Moslem radicals from around the world to travel to Iraq and Syria in order to fight alongside ISIS (Wade, 2014). Biswas acted principally as an information exchange for ISIS, but he also served to validate and normalize fanaticism by publicizing, justifying, and praising acts of rape, genocide, and mass murder. Before the take down of Shami Witness, he was receiving two million visits to his account per month. Though the site has been dismantled, copycat accounts emerged (Wade, 2014). "He was sophisticated enough and understood how to manipulate the English language social media sphere for analyses and attract journalists seeking quick information and snarky posts," according to Phillip Smyth, a researcher at the University Maryland (Karam, 2014, para. 8). Biswas tweeted Abdul Rahman Kassig's beheading video and hailed arrests of Kurdish women fighters in Kobane. He also gave logistical advice about crossing into ISIS territory (Karam, 2014, para. 8).

Using violent extremism in social media can be documented through how ISIS has used social media. The group used Twitter as a tool to spread its propaganda and to recruit new followers (Berger & Morgan, 2015). Estimated number of Twitter accounts used by ISIS supporters was 46,000 but could be as high as 90,000. Determining the exact location of all ISIS supports has been difficult because only a small percentage of users enable location tracking. These users have been all over the world with many clustered mostly in Middle Eastern countries like Saudi Arabia, Syria, and Iraq. The average account of an ISIS supporter had around 1,000 followers though there are 1,500 accounts that have had more than 5,000 followers. These users tweeted 2,000 times over the life of the account (Berger & Morgan, 2015). Twitter suspended 10,000 ISIS accounts between September and December 2014 (Gladstone, 2015). But suspending ISIS Twitter accounts raised ethical questions: would valuable intelligence that could be used to combat ISIS be lost and would the suspensions actually work to radicalize an ostracized community more quickly. Information gathered suggested that many ISIS accounts used follower networks where groups of users follow one another, called swarm accounts. If one of these accounts was shut down, the others could still stay active and the follower base remained intact. ISIS was using an alternative site, Diaspora, a nonprofit, social site that was beyond administrative control (Maniit, 2015). ISIS released the information that James Foley, a freelance journalist working at the time for Agence-France-Presse and GlobalPost in Syria, had been beheaded by ISIS. Tweets with the hashtag of #ISISMediaBlackout attempted to stop information from ISIS being retweeted. As a result, Twitter executives received death threats (Lamothe, 2014; DeMaria, 2014). Some of these threats to Twitter executives have been made by Al-Nusra Al-Maqdisiya, a pro-Islamic State media group ("46,000 Twitter accounts," 2015). In the meantime, an unidentified Internet activist turned over to CNN the information that he had gleaned from Twitter accounts, 26,000 Twitter accounts linked to ISIS. He called himself XRSone and he wanted to show how much questionable and potentially dangerous propaganda there was on Twitter and how easy it was to find them (King, 2015).

Fake accounts are sometimes created by governments to infiltrate specific groups. The US Department of State has had an operation called *Think Again Turn Away*, on Twitter, Facebook, and YouTube, while the CIA had a number of *fake ISIS* accounts, spreading counter-propaganda in English, Arabic, and other languages with varying degrees of co-operation from Middle Eastern governments and none whatsoever from Recep Tayyip Erdoğan, President of Turkey. Not seen as credible voices, these fake sites run the risk of back-firing when exposed or if the message was seen to be too inaccurate or propagandistic (Katz, 2014).

Activism through social media has been said to promote a watered down and nonengaged mode of slacktivism where people were mistaking low-threshold user behaviors similar to that of marketing campaigns for actual commitment and sacrifice (Lindgren, 2013). Studies on slacktivism to see how effective it was resulted in those who *like* and *share* publicly were less likely to be more involved than those who do it privately. The private *doers* actually promoted their values underlying their causes (Seay, 2014).

Filtering also limits the users of social media to a limited set of views and identities often coinciding with their own preexisting positions. Social media have given users the ability to self-select information and to interact with this information by screening out less desirable information (Hahn, Ryu & Park, 2015, p. 56). Therefore, politically active participants in the blogosphere tend to organize into insular, homogeneous communities segregated along partisan lines. This partisan selective exposure can lead to great polarization within societies (Stroud, 2010).

Successes of Activists Using Social Media During Conflict

Regardless of the criticisms, social media have been successful as a tool in a variety of ways. Through organizing action, dictators have resigned. Social media have helped to create collective agency. Through social media, activists have provided a means to alert audiences as to police movement, how to get legal help and how to document excesses and brutality of governments. Along with this documentation, information has been dispersed thereby allowing people to feel they are a part of something, connecting them, giving them courage, making them aware, and offering them sympathy. Social media as a tool has countered misinformation and has provided leads for journalists who take the time to stay connected with the local citizens in areas of conflict.

Dictators have resigned. Mubarak and his close entourage in Egypt were ousted. Though his murder conviction and life sentence have been overturned in the courts, he remained inside a military hospital overlooking the Nile (Kirkpatrick, 2015). The successful overthrow of Gaddafi's regime ended with Gaddafi being captured and killed by the National Transitional Council militants in 2011. It started with a Facebook page, Kollina Kaled Said (We are all Khaled Said), launched on June 10, 2010, after the death of a young man in Alexandria, Egypt, at the hands of policemen. The site attracted 400,000 followers between June and December 2011, and was highly instrumental in coordinating the initial protests (Aboubakr, 2013). Twitter was used as a mobilization tool with activists communicating their images and information via this network. In Egypt, Facebook was used primarily to raise awareness about the ongoing uprising (31 percent), and to organize activists and actions (30 percent) (Frangonikolopoulos & Chapsos, 2012). Accordingly, in the tweets generated during the same period, the hash-tag [#egypt] was the most popular with 1.4 million mentions, while on February 10 alone, when President Mubarak left office, almost 35,000 tweets were generated in Egypt (Frangonikolopoulos & Chapsos, 2012).

Collective agency has been created where people act together through a social movement. Both as a technology and as a space where people mediate their political interests, Facebook has been a resource for creating a collective agency. Furthermore, Facebook has served multiple functions, including surveillance, social integration, and deliberative practice (Valenzuela, Arriagada & Scherman, 2012, p. 311). Social network sites have reduced the costs of collective action, enabling citizens to organize themselves more easily and to voice their concerns more publicly. On the other hand, there has been the risk of furthering inequality if the population of social media users was skewed toward the technologically savvy and those with high human, social and economic capital (Valenzuela, Arriagada & Scherman, 2012, p. 311). Along with documenting events, information has been dispersed through social media that allows people to feel they are a part of something, connecting them, giving them courage, making them aware and offering them sympathy (Mainwaring, 2011). Social media gave the people a sense of solidarity and for some, the *permission* to go further (Beckett, 2011). The activists achieved this in Egypt by establishing a credible mobilization network, communicating, and channeling the rising opposition. Facebook pages such as the *We are all Khaled Said* were not only used as a means to provide information and advice to the protesters, a form of on-line press management tool, but also contributed in raising awareness of civil society on the demands and action taken by the activists. Google maps and gathering points were posted to potential protesters, guiding them and exalting their morale by also posting successful activities from other places and enhancing the feeling of coordinated action (Khamis & Vaughn, 2011, pp. 11–12).

Nevertheless, in the context of today's socially networked society and the rise of social media applications (i.e., Facebook) new perspectives need to be considered. Seeking information via social network sites has been a positive and significant predictor of people's social capital and civic and political participatory behaviors, online and offline (Gil de Zúñiga, Jung & Valenzuela, 2012). Thus, it is relevant to identity and to consider the collective views and goals, which are shared among the participants in order to better understand their use of social media in facilitating social change (Papaioannou & Olivos, 2013, p. 103). New cultural values based on human rights and political freedoms, in particular participation in free elections, are disseminated via Facebook.

Another function of social media used by activists has been to create alerts. These alerts were intended to track police movement, to get legal help and to document police excesses and brutality. The *April 6 Movement* and the *We are all Khalid Said* Facebook group in Egypt used cell phones, blogs, Twitter, Facebook, and YouTube to document police excesses and brutality, organize meetings and protests, track police movements and get legal help for those who had been arrested (Khamis & Vaughn, 2011, p. 9). Images were also posted showing satellite maps marked with arrows indicating where protesters could go to avoid progovernment thugs (Khamis &Vaughn, 2011, pp. 11–12). Other social media apps have been created such as *Where is the Bomb?* a popular feature of Bey2ollak (it will tell you), a traffic notification app launched by five young Egyptians in 2010 to guide the nation's motorists on the status of the roads. The service relied on volunteers on the streets and covered Cairo and Alexandria. The app had more than one million users. The name Bey2ollak is a word in colloquial Egyptian commonly used to start imparting information. Progovernment media countered the app's importance by issuing statements that the explosions were aimed at derailing Egypt's plans for holding a major investment conference and parliamentary elections (Sherbini, 2015).

Countering misinformation, especially in Egypt, was accomplished by the activists documenting what was happening on the street and providing that information to other countries around the world (Mainwaring, 2011). The *Freedom of Expression in Mourning* campaign was an online protest against Tunisia's president, Zine al-Abidine Ben Ali, which was launched when Tunisia hosted the World Summit on the Information Society in 2005. The protest won international coverage with calls for "enough of the dictator's reign" (Radsch, 2011, p. 75).

Providing leads to journalists was another successful way of utilizing social media. Activists and protesters managed to distribute at a global level the images of brutality and state violence, by utilizing the combined performance and interaction between mainstream and social media. Traditional media, such as Al Jazeera and CCNi, distributed worldwide images and news received from the activists. The activists, who acted as a *watchdog* of the state-controlled national media (Cottle, 2011, p. 652) used Twitter as a main broadcaster.

Twitter has been the platform many journalists have visited in order to follow a story and activists have taken advantage of this by pointing journalists to the right place to find video footage. Journalists relied on this network of activists from within and without Egypt, those activists who knew how to download video and how to use Google maps. Tunisian blogger and Global Voices Advocacy Director, Sami Ben Gharbia, who operated the website Nawaat, an independent blog collective that voiced Tunisian dissent, said that much of the content from the Tunisian and Egyptian uprisings that appeared in traditional media was collected from Facebook for translation and posted to open-access sites and Twitter for journalists and others (Ghannam, 2011, p. 16).

These successes were not achieved without problems. The Libyan regime of Gaddafi blocked all communication during the protests in February 2011 and cut off Libya from the rest of the world; however, despite the communication blackout, social media once again came to the forefront. Facebook, Twitter, and YouTube were used by protestors to upload raw footage, photos, and messages of the chaos. The majority of these visuals uploaded by Libyan citizens were shot using camera phones, resulting in images of poor quality. These videos, however, appear to have had the credibility of first-hand accounts, resonating with audiences worldwide (Ali & Fahmy, 2013, p. 64).

Where Is the Future of Activism and Social Media?

The future of covering conflicts may be with social non-movements, documentaries, or circling back to being on the street. Social movements in Arab countries have organized themselves digitally, such as Kifaya (Enough) in Egypt and Gerefna (We are fed-up) in Sudan. Egypt also saw al-Gabha al-Wataniyya lil-Taghir (The National Front for Change), Sitta Ebril (6th of April), and Killina Khalid Said (We are all Khalid Said). These were informal collectives of popular forces that were closer in structure and conduct to social nonmovements as conceived by Asef Bayat in his 2010 book, *Life as Politics*. Bayat defines social movements as "political performances that emerged in Western Europe and North America after 1750," with characteristics of social movements as "an organized and sustained claim-making on target authorities," and a "repertoire of performances, including associations, public meetings, media statements, and street marches" (Bayat, 2010, p. 4). Social nonmovements have not embedded themselves in larger organizations but remain more loosely structured and less ideologically driven like the ones formed in Egypt. They have focused on immediate local demands and have lacked a coherent organizational body (Bayat, 2010, p. 6). Social non-movements have mobilized their activism by going directly to the streets rather than launching their campaigns from a headquarters. This active use of public space, Bayat pointed out, embeds the practices of non-movements in the practices of everyday life of ordinary non-politicized people, as well as opens up more possibilities for imitation of those practices of protests by others, thereby mobilizing more noncollective actors in a nonideological or postideological alliance (Bayat, 2010, pp. 6–21).

Some of the emerging non-movements began to search for a niche for themselves in an expanding public sphere. Though they had started as digital social media, the people in the non-movements began to take digital material back to the street in pre-modern forms of communication, many in their audience were illiterate so non-movements used picture graffiti and street performances. Among these were Askar Kadhibun (Lying generals), La lil-Muhakamat al-Aska-riyya lil-Madaniyyin (Stop Military Trials for civilians), Musirrin (Steadfast), and Salafiyyo Kosta (Salafists of CostaCoffee). Since these non-movements were loosely organized, most of them have gone through several mutations along the short course of their activism. Askar Kadhibun, for example, transformed into several other initiatives such as Kadhibun Bism al-Din (Liars in the name of religion) and simply Kadhibun (Liars), while maintaining almost the same line of activism and similar tactics (Aboubakr, 2013, p. 260).

Kadhibun organizers used low-cost techniques by displaying images on to a white screen with a projector out on the street where the people were. The material had been collected and archived on their Internet site. They staged 300 street showings in several cities and districts around Cairo as well as in rural areas. They called for help on their Facebook page for material and footage of the crimes of the military. Starting during a sit-in that was boring, the organizers set up a screen in the corner of a square and began showing clips from their archives. They did this every night, stealing electricity from any nearby lamppost (Aboubaker, 2013).

The non-movement group, Musirrin, provided training, technical support, equipment and a library to organize screenings, to open discussions and to host events. They expanded how the public could be represented via multiple media platforms (Aboubakr, 2013, p. 261). These nonmovements have collaborated with others. Musirrin collaborated with 11 similar collectives such as the National Front for Justice and Democracy, The Revolutionary Socialists, The Revolutionary Youth Collective and the Youth of Maspero Collective. All were popular youth activism movements (Shukrallah, 2012).

Besides the social media campaigns, nonmovements have been using demonstrations, graffiti art, online statements and fliers with visual material broken down into banners and placards to represent the chains of the revolution. These chains, however, have been actual chains of humans carrying posters and banners for a particular cause. Banners and posters were used in Egypt when the media blackout occurred to tell people where the next meetings would be. These events were filmed and digitally archived on the social media sites, thus the circular movement continued (Aboubakr, 2013).

Skeptics of social media importance in revolutions today have included Linda Herrera, a columnist for a Middle-East online news organization. She argued that Facebook had little to do with the Egyptian revolution. It was the people on the streets calling for action that influenced events; their diligence and hard work was what made the real difference in the Egyptian revolution, not Facebook (2011). While this claim might hold some truth, one must not underestimate the power of social media that allowed information to get out to a wider audience, many of whom were abroad. The photos of Saeed on Facebook were used as a catalyst not only on the Internet but also as protest signs during the uprisings.

Institutions Work with Activists Using Social Media

One institution that created a monitoring project on global media is Google with its GDELT Project. This project monitors the world's broadcast, print and web news in 100 languages and identifies the people, locations, organizations, counts, themes, sources, emotions, quotes and events driving the global society thereby creating a free open platform for computing on the entire world (GDELT website). Google has also released GDELT 2.0 and GDELT Translingual programs. These programs provide the ability to listen to media coverage in 65 languages and have access to information without having to be an expert in data analytics of massive datasets.

Institutions also have worked to assist activists during Internet blackouts by different governments in different countries. Google and Twitter offered the *Speak-2-Tweet*, a service whereby users could call an international telephone number to post and to hear Twitter messages without the Internet (Frangonikolopoulos & Chapsos, 2012, p. 16). NGOs collaborated with the activists to provide infrastructure and training. European social movements advised activists on how to use *ghost servers* in order to confuse the online monitoring of the government (Reissmann & Rosenbach, 2011). Global Voices from Tunisia and the Egyptian Initiative for Personal Rights contributed to the creation of a digital guide that assisted activists in how to use mobile phones and Twitter to share information about arrested activists (Abrougui, 2014).

US NGOs trained a number of activists, focusing on video reporting, media-skills and mapping tools for choosing the best locations for photographing demonstrations. The human rights organization, Witness, taught activists about camera operations and use of audio recording devices. The Kenyan NGO, Ushahidi, built online capabilities for reporting securely with mobile phones and for building online content (Ishani, 2011).

New Paradigm of Where the Public Is Located

By using traditional and digital media with popular culture, the people involved in the non-movements are changing the news and information channels in the Arab region. By taking to the streets and adopting pre-modern means of information dissemination and mobilization, these movements introduce not only a new kind of activism, but also a new direction of media behavior in the Arab region (Aboubakr, 2013, p. 263).

These movements have been influencing media behavior. For example, Lia Tarachansky, filmmaker and correspondent for The Real News Network, based in Jaffa, Israel, has been producing short, documentary-style reports exploring the context behind the news. Instead of adhering to the standard narrative that usually frames Israel and the Israeli-Palestinian conflict, Tarachansky explored the power of denial and raised questions about what Israelis learn, know and sometimes choose not to know, about the 1948 war ("On the Side of the Road"). In a review of her 2013 documentary, the *Daily Beast* noted:

> Tarachansky's method is not to blame or even to teach. It is to examine, narrate and let others speak for themselves. Indeed, rather than attempt to assign blame and assert one's 'greater' right over the other, Tarachansky demonstrates her interest in understanding the dynamics of a conflict which now threatens to implode within Israeli society and destroy what began as one nation's hope for a safer future. (Shakdam, 2015, para. 6)

Through social media, some activists have created an alternative space, which makes up for the limitations of physical public space (Aboubakr, 2013, p. 234). Jürgen Habermas proposed that the public sphere enabled the voicing of diverse views on any issue, and the formation of publicly oriented citizenry actively engaging in meaningful dialogues with one another (Hahn, Ryu, & Park, 2015, p. 56). Here the key debate will be whether any new medium that may contribute to voters' exposure to diverse viewpoints will indeed facilitate chances that those voters will be exposed to differing political views or just heterogeneous contacts. Or, will any new mediums limit open and reflexive online dialogue since much online interaction has been characterized as meeting like-minded individuals, leading to highly fragmented information sharing.

Last Word: Fragmented information sharing has been debated in the Academy for many years. As more technology develops and people are networked through Facebook, Twitter and *smart mobs*, some of these online groups may begin to function as actual political forces. This shift in media production suggests that the relationship between the center and periphery has been dislocated, or dissolved, to the point where one can no longer speak of any one node where the power over symbolic production is concentrated. The public sphere has been located within a community's media distribution area. If that area is global with local issues not impacting the majority of the people within the group, then many issues will be shoved out of sight and the values that have driven media production may no longer exist.

Discussion: How can societal issues be discussed using social media? Give examples of issues discussed in social media and on what platforms.

References

Aboubakr, R. (2013). New directions of internet activism in Egypt. *De Gruyter Mouton*, 38(3), 251–265.

Abrougui, A. (2014, April 14). Tunisian blog launches whistleblowing platform. *Global Voices*. Retrieved from http://globalvoicesonline.org/2014/04/14/tunisia-blog-launches-whistleblowing-platform/.

Adler, B. (2013, May/June). Streams of consciousness: Millennials expect a steady diet of quick-hit, social-media-mediated bits and bytes. What does that mean for journalism? *Columbia Journalism Review*, 25–36. Retrieved from http://www.cjr.org/cover_story/steams_of_consciousness.php?page=all.

Ali, S. R. & Fahmy, S. (2013). Gatekeeping and citizen journalism: The use of social media during the recent uprisings in Iran, Egypt, and Libya. *Media, War & Conflict*, 6(1), 55–69.

Bakardjieva, M. (2010). The internet and subactivism: Cultivating young citizenship in everyday life. In T. Olsson, & P. Dahlgren (Eds.), *Young people, ICTs and democracy: Theories, policies, identities, and websites*, (pp. 129–146). Göteborg: Nordicom, Göteborgs universitet.

Bayat, A. (2010). *Life as politics*. Stanford University Press.

Beaumont, P. (2011, February 25). The truth about Twitter, Facebook and the uprisings in the Arab spring. *The Guardian*. Retrieved from http://www.theguardian.com/world/2011/feb/25/twitter-facebook-uprisings-arab-libya.

Beckett, T. (2011). After Tunisia and Egypt: Towards a new typology of media and networked political change. Retrieved from http://blogs.lse.ac.uk/polis/2011/02/11/after-tunisia-and-egypt-towards-a-new-typology-of-media-and-networked-political-change/.

Berger, J. M. & Morgan, J. (2015). The ISIS Twitter census: Defining and describing the population of ISIS supporters on Twitter. The Brookings Project on US Relations with the Islamic World. Analysis Paper. No. 20. Retrieved from http://www.brookings.edu/~/media/research/files/papers/2015/03/isis-twitter-census-berger-morgan/isis_twitter_census_berger_morgan.pdf.

Conflict Tracker (nd). http://conflict-securitytracker.com/.

Cottle, S. (2011, July). Media and the Arab uprisings of 2011: Research notes. *Journalism*, 12(5), 647–659.

Dalton, R.J., Sickle, A.V., & Weldon, S. (2009). The individual-institutional nexus of protest behavior. *British Journal of Political Science*, 40, 51–73. Doi: 10.1017/S000712340999038.

DeMaria, M. (2014, September 9). ISIS threatens Twitter employees in U.S. and Europe. Theweek.com. Retrieved from http://theweek.com/speedreads/446632/isis-threatens-twitter-employees-europe.

"46,000 Twitter accounts used by ISIS supporters: Report" (2015, March 6). *The Nation*. Retrieved from http://nation.com.pk/international/06-Mar-2015/46000-twitter-accounts-used-by-isis-supporters-report.

Frangonikolopoulos, C. A. & Chapsos, I. (2012, Fall). Explaining the role and the impact of the social media in the Arab spring. *GMJ: Mediterranean Edition*, 8(1), 10–20.

Freelon, D. (2012). Fromthemailbag, 12/14/09. Retrieved from http://dfreelon.org/2009/12/14/from-the-mailbag-121409/.

Ghannam, J. (2011). Social media in the Arab world: Leading up to the uprisings of 2011. Washington, DC: Center for International Media Assistance.

Ghareeb, E. (2000). New media and the information revolution in the Arab world: An assessment. *Middle East Journal*, 54(3), 395–418.

Gidley, J.M. (2002). Global youth culture: A transdisciplinary perspective. In Gidley, J. M. & Inayatullah, S. (Eds.), *Youth futures: Comparative research and transformative visions* (pp. 3–18). Westport, Conn.: Praeger.

Gil de Zúñiga, H., & Valenzuela, S. (2011). The mediating path to a stronger citizenship: Online and offline networks, weak ties and civic engagement. *Communication Research*, 38, 397–421.

Gladstone, R. (2015, April 9). Twitter says it suspended 10,000 ISIS-linked accounts in one day. *The New York Times*. Retrieved from http://www.nytimes.com/2015/04/10/world/middleeast/twitter-says-it-suspended-10000-isis-linked-accounts-in-one-day.html.

Hahn, K., Ryu, S., & Park, S. (2015). Fragmentation in the twitter following news outlets: The representation of South Korean users' ideological and generational cleavage. *Journalism & Mass Communication Quarterly*, 92(1), 56–76.

Herrera, L. (2011, February 12). Egypt's revolution 2.0: The Facebook factor. *Jadaliyya*. Retrieved from http://www.jadaliyya.com/pages/index/612/egypts-revolution-2.0_the-facebook-factor.

Ibrahim, A. (2014, February 13). Egypt student protests continue amid violent crackdown. *Middle East Eye*. Retrieved from http://www.middleeasteye.net.

Ishani, M. (2011, February 8). The hopeful network. Retrieved from http://foreignpolicy.com/2011/02/08/the-hopeful-network/.

Karam, J. (2014, December 14). Shami witness arrest rattles ISIS' cages on Twitter. *Al Arabiya News*.

Katz, R. (2014, September 16). The state department's Twitter war with ISIS is embarrassing. *Time Magazine*. Retrieved from http://time.com/3387065/isis-twitter-war-state-department/.

Khamis, S. & Vaughn, K. (2011). Cyberactivism in the Egyptian revolution: How civic engagement and citizen journalism tilted the balance. *Arab Media and Society*, 13. Retrieved from http://www.arabmediasociety.com/?article=769.

King, H. (2015, March 31). Internet activist publishes 26,000 Twitter accounts he thinks are linked to ISIS. Money.cnn.com.

Kirkpatrick, D. (2015, Jan. 13). Egyptian judge voids Mubarak's last standing conviction and orders retrial. *The New York Times*. Retrieved from http://www.nytimes.com/2015/01/14/world/middleeast/hosni-mubarak-conviction-overturned.html?ref=topics&_r=0.

Kobayashi, T., Ikeda, K. I., & Miyata, K. (2006). Social capital online: Collective use of the Internet and reciprocity as lubricants of democracy. *Information, Communication & Society*, 9, 582–611.

Kumar, R. (2013, January 14). Social media and social change: How young people are tapping into technology. YouThink! The World Bank. Retrieved from http://blogs.worldbank.org/youthink/social-media-and-social-change-how-young-people-are-tapping-technology.

Lamothe, D. (2014, August 19). #ISISMediaBlackout goes viral following purported execution of James Foley. *The Washington Post*. Retrieved from http://www.washingtonpost.com/news/checkpoint/wp/2014/08/19/isismediablackout-goes-viral-following-purported-execution-of-james-foley/.

Lindgren, S. (2013). The potential and limitations of Twitter activism: Mapping the 2011 Libyan uprising. *TripleC (Cognition, Communication, Co-Operation): Open Access Journal for a Global Sustainable Information Society*, 11(1), 207–220. Retrieved from http://www.trip-c.at.

Lynch, S. (2014, April 22). Behind 'students against the coup.' *Al-Fanar Media. News & Opinion about Higher Education*. Retrieved from http://www.al-fanarmedia.org/2014/04/behind-students-coup/.

Mainwaring, S. (2011). Exactly what role did social media play in the Egyptian revolution? Retrieved from http://www.fastcompany.com/node/1727466.

Maniit, A. (2015, August 26). ISIS turns to Diaspora after getting booted by Twitter. *Tech Times*. Retrieved from http://www.techtimes.com.

Marwell, G. & Oliver, P. (1993). *The critical mass in collective action: A micro-social theory*. New York, NY: Cambridge University Press.

McCoy, T. (2014, June 18). Egypt's sexual harassment pandemic—and the powerlessness of hashtags. *The Washington Post*. Retrieved from http://www.washingtonpost.com/news/morning-mix/wp/2014/06/18/egypts-sexual-harassment-pandemic-and-the-powerlessness-of-hashtags/.

"Mobile Phone Apps helps Syrian refuges settle in Turkey" (2015, February 10). *Euro News*. Retrieved from http://www.euronews.com/2015/02/10/mobile-phone-app-helps-syrian-refugees-settle-in-turkey/.

Niekerk, G.V.K. (2013). Citizen journalism: How to encourage critical reading and viewing? *Media Development*, WACC, pp. 15–18.

Papaioannou, T. & Olivos, H. E. (2013). Cultural identity and social media in the Arab spring: Collective goals in the use of Facebook in the Libyan context. *Journal of Arab & Muslim Media Research*, 6(2&3), 99–114.

Pearce, K. E., & Kendzior, S. (2012). Networked authoritarianism and social media in Azerbajan. *Journal of Communication*, 62, 283–298.

Pelli, R. (2013, September). Protesters and poorest create own news media. *Index on Censorship*, 42, 33–36.

Radsch, C. (2011). Blogosphere and social media. In Laipson, E. (Ed.), *Seismic shift: Understanding change in the Middle East*, (pp. 68–81). Washington, DC: The Henry L. Stimson Center.

Reissmann, O. & Rosenbach, M. (2011, October 14). A geek role in the Arab spring: European group helps tackle regime censorship. *Der Spiegel*. Retrieved from http://www.crookedbough.com/?p=3600.

Saad-Filho, A. (2015, March 15). Brazil: Economic policy, the protest movement and the débâcle of the workers' party. *Global Research*. Retrieved from http://www.globalresearch.ca/brazil-economic-policy-the-protest-movement-and-the-debacle-of-the-pt/5439462.

Salem, F. & Mourtada, R. (2011b). Civil movements: The impact of Facebook and Twitter. *Dubai*. Retrieved from http://www.dsg.fohmics.net/ed/Publication/Pdf_En/ASMR_Final_Feb_08Los.pdf.

Sam, O. K. (2015, January 7). Abducted Nigerian girls still missing, a distracted world must remember. *Los Angeles Times*. Retrieved from http://www.latimes.com/opinion/op-ed/la-oe-sam-bring-back-our-girls-20150108-story.html.

Seay, L. (2014, March 12). Does slacktivism work? *The Washington Post*. Retrieved from http://www.washingtonpost.com/blogs/monkey-cage/wp/2014/03/12/does-slacktivism-work/.

Shah, D. V., Roihas, H., & Cho, J. (2009). Media and civic participation on understanding and misunderstanding communication effects. In Bryant, J. & Oliver, M.B. (Eds.), *Media effects: Advances in theory and research* (3rd ed.) (pp. 207–227). New York, NY: Routledge.

Sherbini, R. A. (2015, February 11). Bomb-warning app goes viral in Egypt. *Gulf News*. Retrieved from http://gulnews.com/news/region/egypt/bomb-warning-app-goes-viral...1.1455213?utm_medium_=Social&utm_source=Twitter&utm_campaign=Blog.

Shakdam, C. (2015, February 5). Israeli journalist Lia Rarachansky on Israel, Palestine and the realities of war. *MintPress News*. Retrieved from http://www.mintpressnews.com/Israel-journalist-lia-tarachansky-israel-palestine-realities-war/201765/.

Shukrallah, S. (2012, March 8). 'Revolutionary' movements split over Egypt's looming presidential poll. Ahramonline. Retrieved from http://english.ahram.org.eg/NewsContent/1/64/36160/Egypt/Politics-/Revolutionary-movements-split-over-Egypts-looming-.aspx.

Stroud, N. J. (2010, September). Polarization and partisan selective exposure. *Journal of Communication*, 60(3), 556–576.

Valenzuela, S., Arriagada, A., & Scherman, A. (2012). The social media basis of youth protest behavior: The case of Chile. *Journal of Communication*, 62, 299–314.

Wade, D. (2015). Daesh is losing the propaganda war. Retrieved from https://www.academia.edu/9081141/Daesh_is_losing_the_propaganda_war.

Weeks, B. E. & Holbert, R. L. (2013, April 30). Predicting dissemination of news content in social media: A focus on reception, friending, and partisanship. *Journalism & Mass Communication Quarterly*, 90(2), 212–232.

"William Lloyd Garrison" (nd). http://www.pbs.org/wgbh/aia/part4/4p1561.html.

HOW GOVERNMENTS USE MEDIA DURING CONFLICT

Neutral States as Promoters of Peace

Ultimately, everything can be political. If there is involvement of a government institution in the lives of its citizens, then it is political. A simple demonstration for an issue like protecting grasslands can turn bad if there is not respect between the government institutions and the people. If and when the protests move to violence initiated by either side, peace can be difficult to negotiate. Discussion in the international community on how to solve these problems has been to include neutral states in negotiating peace. Although new ideas in peace building policy have been introduced by NGOs and think tanks, these new ideas ultimately must be supported by the nation state involved (Goetschel, 2009, p. 4). Discussion on neutral states having a role in brokering political ideas centers on the following reasons: (a) neutral states traditionally introduce ideas in international relations, as their own foreign-policy identity is constructed on such an idea; (b) neutral states are experienced and known for being sensitive about sovereignty, since their foreign- and security-policy orientation builds on the assumption of unconditional sovereignty; and (c) neutral states have a track record of trying to shape international relations by soft power and of favoring nonviolent means of conflict resolution (Goetschel, 2009, p. 5).

Typically, neutral states have been small states seen to be weaker compared to their neighboring states. Neutral states have had an idealistic component based on its core commitment to avert war and to promote non-violent means of conflict resolution. These states could have the role of promoting, monitoring, and implementing new ideas thus having an essential role in promoting development of the international order—in particular the peaceful resolution of conflicts. These states could have new types of partnerships with NGOs and would significantly advance the notion of an international society (Goetschel, 2009, p. 9). Finding neutral states, though, has become harder and harder. There seems to always be some hidden reason to remain neutral or to appear to be. A journalist must evaluate each issue separately and each government separately.

The goal of this chapter is to describe how governments have used media in three ways: to restrict, to control, and to demonize the opposition. Governments have used social media as propaganda against other states and as a way to develop international diplomacy. By recognizing how governments use media, journalists can do a better job covering conflict.

How Governments Have Used Media During Conflict

Governments have used media during times of conflict to restrict information, to control information and to demonize the opposition. Though the United Nations Universal Declaration of Human Rights, adopted in 1948, provides, in Article 19, that: "Everyone has the right to freedom of opinion and expression; this right includes freedom to hold opinions without interference and to seek, receive and impart information and ideas through any media and regardless of frontiers" (UN Universal Declaration of Human Rights, 1948), this cannot be enforced easily. Organizations like the Freedom House located in New York City, attempts to monitor press freedoms and evaluates the countries in the world as to degrees of freedom. The 2015 report summarized their findings as follows:

> More aggressive tactics by authoritarian regimes and an upsurge in terrorist attacks contributed to a disturbing decline in global freedom in 2014. Freedom in the World 2015 found an overall drop in freedom for the ninth consecutive year. Nearly twice

as many countries suffered declines as registered gains—61 to 33—and the number of countries with improvements hit its lowest point since the nine-year erosion began. Russia's invasion of Ukraine, a rollback of democratic gains by Egyptian president Abdel Fattah el-Sisi, Turkish President Recep Tayyip Erdoğan's intensified campaign against press freedom and civil society, and further centralization of authority in China were evidence of a growing disdain for democratic standards that was found in nearly all regions of the world. (Freedom House, 2015)

The Freedom House report itemized the changes in the world as follows (Freedom House, 2015):

- Of the 195 countries assessed, 89 (46 percent) were rated Free, 55 (28 percent) Partly Free, and 51 (26 percent) Not Free. All but one region had more countries with declines than with gains. Asia-Pacific had an even split.
- In a new and disquieting development, a number of countries lost ground due to state surveillance, restrictions on internet communications, and curbs on personal autonomy.
- Ratings for the Middle East and North Africa region were the worst in the world, followed by Eurasia. Syria, a dictatorship mired in civil war and ethnic division and facing uncontrolled terrorism, received the lowest Freedom in the World score of any country in over a decade.
- The Worst of the Worst countries were the Central African Republic, Equatorial Guinea, Eritrea, North Korea, Saudi Arabia, Somalia, Sudan, Syria, Turkmenistan, and Uzbekistan.

Outside the UN Article 19, there are several regional media cooperative ventures like the Inter American Press Association with its Chapultepec Agreement where 15 countries in the Americas signed a document to pursue democratic ideals of freedom of speech and of the press (Sipiapa Organization, nd), and the Gulf Cooperation Council (GCC), a confederation of Arab states with the goal of media cooperation.

Although there have been cooperative ventures, there have been many more restrictions on media. Some governments prohibit certain people from being covered in the media, place government personnel in the newsroom, and create strict libel laws with harsh punishments. An example of restrictive policies is when the Saudi Arabian government in March 2015, sentenced Raif Badawi, a blogger, to 10 years imprisonment and 1,000 public lashes (50 a week for 20 weeks). Badawi was guilty of creating a website, Saudi Liberal Network, as a forum for public debate. The government said he had insulted religious authorities. His lawyer was also imprisoned. The irony of Badawi's case is that he was awarded the Geneva Summit's Courage Award for 2015 (Hayden, 2015).

To Restrict

Governments often restrict media during conflict. Restrictions vary from deleting sites, censoring traditional media to actually owning the media thus controlling information. The government may own the servers for social media and can restrict information. A nation state holds a considerable amount of power and influence when it comes to censoring and blocking information from civilians during conflicts (Wall, 2009). In Iran, with regards to the media, the Iranian government increased restrictions on domestic as well as foreign news outlets, making it extremely difficult to get uncensored news (Corn, 2009; Human Rights Watch, Iran, 2010). Also in Iran, members of the authoritarian government were using sites such as Twitter to monitor the protestor's actions, performing a strict gate-keeping role (Loewenstein, 2010).

In Egypt, while many citizens were out on the streets calling for reform and an end to the 30-year-rule of the Egyptian president, others focused on social media to proliferate information about the uprising to a wider audience. In a final attempt to maintain power, Mubarak disrupted social media by blocking the Internet. Blackberry messenger services and cell phone users also experienced problems (Arthur, 2011). Even after mobile phone service was partially resumed, texting was heavily restricted for weeks.

In Nepal, media companies were placed under strict censorship when King Gyanendra took power in 2005, accusing the parliamentary parties of an inability to lead. He banned all news reports and the army arrested political leaders, influential civilians, media people, human rights activists, and others who were considered a threat to the monarchy. Telephone and Internet connections were cut. Ultimately, King Gyanendra imposed rules that kept people in the dark, deprived of the freedom of expression. Despite constitutionally guaranteed press freedom, such restrictive ordinances prevented the media from publishing or broadcasting news and independent analyses (Dahal, 2006, cited in Ghimire and Upreti, 2014, p. 193).

In Nepal, FM radios, which were inexpensive and widely accessible, were first targeted by the royal government. The government seized the technological linkage equipment from independent broadcasting houses—Kanipur

FM, Radio Annapurna and Radio Sagarmatha. The print media companies raised no common objections as they themselves were not targeted at that stage (Ghimire & Upreti, 2014, p. 193). Media began their protest softly with lobbying, memos, negotiations and then asking international media to speak out. When these failed; they went to street protests and judicial solutions. They created a Freedom of Expression Movement fund with 20 media-related associations (Ghimire & Upreti, 2014).

The state-owned media companies in Nepal supported the government takeover and suspension of fundamental rights, including freedom of expression. All the broadsheet dailies adopted a policy of indifference—no support and no opposition to the royal action; they had not been targeted, they would *lay low*. A large number of weekly and other periodicals made a symbolic gesture by keeping editorial and opinion space blank, adopting a more open anti-king posture later. Some defied censorship and printed their opposition to the royal move in black and white (Ghimire & Upreti, 2014, p. 194). Later, the Nepal media did play a role in the anti-monarchist freedom movement in 2006. The media agreed that a concerted action was needed for national unity but also challenged the restrictions of the overambitious and authoritarian regime. This support for national unity heightened public consciousness, which acted as a catalyst for the final overthrow of the monarchy. Headlines encouraged people to turn out on the streets and local media drew attention to events and capitalized on the power of the people, which ultimately raised fear in the monarchy (Ghimire & Upreti, 2014, p. 194). Although the radio stations were the first to raise a voice for freedom, they were the last to actively protest government suppression, due mainly to the fact that they had to renew their licenses annually and feared losing those (Ghimire & Upreti, 2014).

To Remain in Control

Besides restricting information, governments have used many other strong-arm methods to remain in control. The situation is similar in many countries around the world and throughout history. In Haiti, to control the media the military would storm an office, wreck the typesetting equipment, and even confiscate the newsprint. A more recent example is the Maspero Massacre in Egypt in 2011. Military and police forces attacked a peaceful demonstration in front of the state-owned Radio and Television Union building, called Maspero, leaving 28 dead, mostly runover by army vehicles or shot through the head or chest. The Coptic Christians were killed by Muslims and the military (Simon, 2014). Army forces then stormed into the nearby offices of a couple of private satellite stations while the news was aired live and held news crews in custody while the soldiers ran searches for footages of the massacres, which were then confiscated (Aboubakr, 2013, p. 259).

Even if there are press laws within a nation state, which impose boundaries on what can and cannot be said in print, censorship plays a significant role in journalism in a variety of forms including ideology/religious censorship, tribal/family/alliances censorship, and most importantly, government censorship. In addition to censorship, a number of administrative and legal devices have been put into place to restrict freedom of expression.

To control the media is easiest when it is state-owned. Military expansion legitimizes and supports governmental sovereignty not only in facing foreign intervention and threats but also in pursuing authoritarian control over civil society. This political model has suppressed democratic practices in these authoritarian countries; as a result, media have been largely controlled and information provided mostly by governmental agencies (Papaioannou & Olivos, 2013).

Under this arrangement, both state-owned and private media fall subject to huge restrictions by the nation state. National television and journalism come directly under the directives of some type of Ministry of Information, (the office title varies, depending on the country, could be called ministry of communication, ministry of culture and enlightenment, ministry of information policy and variations). The Ministry of National Guidance, an institution equivalent to present-day Ministry of Information in most Arab countries, has oversight on media and guides the media to facilitate the nation state's political agendas and to guarantee the media messages are uniform (AbdulQader, 1986, p. 228, cited in Aboubakr, 2013, p. 69).

The local, private satellite channels can be subjected to soft-to-medium censorship by nation states with the restrictive measures varying between disruptions of service to closure. A nation state can control newspapers that are dependent on state-owned technical facilities such as printing facilities. The control of resources has been a fundamental means of censorship. Socialist regimes have controlled resources such as newsprint, ink, broadcast towers, and studios. In some Latin American countries, the press has been controlled by reducing government advertising and by calling in loans made to newspapers (Evers, 1989).

The media have always been considered a strategic weapon in any conflict, and proof of this is found in the fact that state-sponsored television and radio stations were among the first places to be protected by the regimes when uprisings broke out in Tunisia, Egypt, and Libya (Soengas, 2013, p. 148). Because no free and independent press existed, the information disseminated to the citizens was through media channels contaminated by government propaganda.

To Demonize

Governments are not beyond controlling media especially during times of conflict and war as a way to demonize their opposition. In Bosnia, the governing body in charge of peace implementation, (Office of the High Representative, OHR), found that in 1995, all three sides in the conflict utilized radio and television broadcasting to further their conflict goals and to demonize their opposition (Buric, 2000; Sadkovich, 1998; Thompson, 1999).

During conflict, access to foreign media has been limited, complicated, or obstructed leaving local journalists to work in repressive conditions, with no real way to corroborate their stories. Governments have withheld information from journalists and have kept journalists from reporting information or images about the strength of the rebel/opposition troops or the weaknesses of the regime. Other times governments try to discredit international media outlets, accusing them of bias in order to control the information distributed within their nation state.

Again, Peter Arnett comes to mind. As one of the remaining journalists covering the Gulf War for CNN, his reports on civilian damage caused by the bombing were not received well by the coalition war administration, who by their constant use of terms like *smart bombs* and *surgical precision* had tried to project an image that civilian casualties would be at a minimum. White House sources would later state that Arnett was being used as a tool for Iraqi disinformation and CNN received a letter from 34 members of the United States Congress accusing Arnett of *unpatriotic journalism*. Two weeks into the war, Arnett was able to obtain an uncensored interview with Saddam Hussein. The Gulf War became the first war to be seen truly live on TV.

According to David Bauder writing for the MilitaryCity.Com, the first Bush administration was unhappy with Arnett's reporting on the Gulf War in 1991 for CNN, suggesting he had become a conveyor of propaganda. Arnett was denounced for reporting that the allies had bombed a baby milk factory in Baghdad when the military said it was a biological weapons plant (2003, p. 1).

"I was furious with (CNN founder) Ted Turner and (then-CNN chairman) Tom Johnson when they threw me to the wolves after I made them billions risking my life to cover the first Gulf War," Arnett told TV Guide (Bauder, 2003, p. 1). (The April 5th TV Guide story was taken down from the web shortly after Arnett was fired.)

Journalists have been targets in a majority of conflicts. According to Reporters without Borders, the deadliest countries for journalists have been Syria, Somalia, India, Pakistan, and the Philippines. The countries with the most journalists in prison are Eritrea, China, Turkey, Iran, and Syria. In 2015, there have been 20 journalists killed, 159 journalists imprisoned and 175 netizens imprisoned (Reporters without Borders, 2015).

The laws of a nation state can limit how a journalist works. Licensing has been a major form for controlling media. These licenses are issued by the government. Additionally there have been restrictive press laws, penal codes to suppress journalists and online writers, and during conflict, there have been emergency laws where a government has sweeping legal power to arrest journalists for publishing content deemed to disrupt public order by intimidation, force, violence, fear or terror (Duffy, 2013). One particular group, the Middle East and North Africa countries (MENA)—Morocco, Algeria, Tunisia, Libya, Egypt, Jordan, Saudi Arabia, Syria, Lebanon, Iraq, Iran, Bahrain, Oman, Qatar, and Yemen—have required newspapers and magazines to be licensed in order to publish.

Adding to the licensing and censoring of media by governments, there have been strong differences between how Arab countries and countries with strong press freedoms use media. The Doha Centre for Media Freedom documented these differences by looking at the policies toward media between the Gulf Cooperation Council (GCC) countries: Bahrain, Kuwait, Oman, Qatar, Saudi Arabia, and the United Aram Emirates (UAE) and countries with strong press freedoms: United States, United Kingdom, European countries, Costa Rica, Cape Verde, Ghana, and Japan. The report included how the constitutions, penal codes, media laws, and cybercrime legislation were used in these countries, concluding that there were five areas that represented points of difference between the GCC countries and countries with strong press freedoms. These areas were: defamation, insult to rulers, false news, public order, and licensing of journalists (Duffy, 2013, para. 5).

Pressure by the government on journalists and media institutions has produced false news. During the initial state of the uprising in Egypt, the pressure to falsify events was so huge that two prominent TV anchors both working for the state-owned Nile News Channel resigned their jobs, citing pressures on them and the channel in general to falsify events and incite the audience against protesters (Aboubakr, 2013, p. 254).

Then the Egyptian government used culture to plant fear in the people by publishing local proverbs such as *walk quietly by the wall* (where you cannot be noticed), *mind your own business and focus on your livelihood,* and *whosoever is afraid stays unharmed* (Ghonim, 2012). Proverbs also played a key role in censored media throughout the Caribbean region where the audience would read between the lines for the meaning.

Certain governments used media to block Internet access to impede the free flow of information. Governments often own the servers used to disseminate information on social media and governments can terminate those servers to limit information flow. Governments have been known to infiltrate the Internet to plant false information with the end goal of sabotaging the opposition. For example, during the Kenyan electoral crisis in 2007 technology that was used by citizen journalists was also implemented by government authorities to rig the elections (Zuckerman, 2009). At the time, Kenyan bloggers had more influence than just their online readership, especially if the content was picked up by a traditional media source. The Kenyan government recognized that social media coupled with traditional sources could have a powerful impact on the general citizen population. In Libya, the government used social media as an opportunity to deflect the work of online activists. The Libyan government blocked sites such as YouTube in an effort to control information dissemination. The result, though, was that citizens in Libya created new ways to circumvent these restrictions (O'Neill, 2011) such as sending information to sites out of the country.

Government Social Media Sites Used for Propaganda

Governments have also created their own social media sites to counter the work of protesters, as seen in Iran. In addition, governments have used social media sites against an enemy, such as both Israel and Hamas have done. In November 2012, Israel Defense Forces and Hamas' Alqassam Brigades posted graphic photos of deaths and suffering of civilians as well as more explicit propaganda illustrations through their Twitter accounts (Seo, 2014). These photos and accompanying tweets were widely circulated as they were retweeted by social media users following the event and mainstream media used them in reporting on the conflict (Seo, 2014).

The Israeli government used Twitter, Facebook, Instagram, and YouTube channels to disseminate information about damages and casualties in Israel caused by Hamas. The Israeli sites had more than 200,000 followers and posted information @IDESpokesperson. Twitter hashtags included #PillarOfDefense and #IsraelUnderFire to drum up domestic and international support for their social media campaigns. Benjamin Netanyahu, Prime Minister of Israel, thanked all the citizens of Israel and all over the world who were taking part in the national informational effort. He also posted a photo of an Israeli baby who had been injured in a Hamas attack with the caption: "For Hamas, every time there are civilian casualties, that's an operational success" (Ronen, 2012, para. 3).

Hamas fought back with its own social media-based propaganda campaign. Hamas used the Alqassam Brigades Twitter account, @AlqassamBrigades to post graphic photos of Palestine babies killed by Israeli airstrikes. One tweet asked: "Where is the media coverage of Israel's crimes in Gaza?" (Seo, 2014).

Another example of how governments have created social media to fight their enemies was in Hindi and Urdu news media in India and Pakistan. Both have reported negatively on each other (Chattarji, 2006). News reports and editorials have reflected mistrust whenever a peace process has been initiated between the two countries (Singh, 2007).

The governments posting visuals have also learned that these visuals on social media sites attracted audiences. Studies affirmed this notion to show that visual content generated the most engagements in social media spheres (Seo, 2014). In addition, visuals gained importance when the message needed to be communicated across different cultures and countries.

Media Diplomacy

Governments using media is nothing new; however, governments using online-based communication tools to interact with global publics as part of their efforts to understand, to inform and to influence these global publics is new. Governments, once upon a time, used traditional media to engage with their public, now governments reach foreign publics directly by disseminating information about their countries, launching government-sponsored international broadcasting channels and websites and hosting cultural exchange programs (Lee & Hong, 2012, p. 491). For example, the US State Department has maintained a profile on Facebook and has maintained the department's official blog, Dipnote, with updates posted to Twitter. Some US embassies have created social networking sites on one or more of their host countries' popular websites to interact with publics in that country. Examples include Café USA, operated by the US Embassy in Seoul, and Sweden's 3D-style virtual embassy in Second Life, called the Second House of Sweden (blog existed from 2007 to 2012). Libya took a different route to inform the Libyan population; the government sent all citizens SMS texts warning them about the repercussions of using social media to promote revolts (Papaioannou & Olivos, 2013).

Propaganda used as government diplomacy has included social media. The statecraft agenda of the 21st century was created to accelerate the role social media will play in diplomacy. When a crisis happened, governments have found that it was important to move fast but imperative to be accurate (Esser, 2012). The governments designed to be responsive to people have used social media to provide citizens around the world a more direct voice in policy conversations and a more timely involvement of governments around the world (Esser, 2012). Governments have been bypassing traditional media and have been using social media to reach global audiences, thus providing information, answering questions and sharing ideas with people.

This process of bypassing traditional media, a media that have taken pride in being called the watchdog of the state, means that information provided from government spokespeople may be more biased and more propagandistic. The information issued will definitely be in the interest of the government. To counter this, traditional media have tried to continue their influence in the foreign policy-making process by their coverage of government institutions. These include the BBC, Voice of America, CCTV, Russia Today, and France 24.

Governments of the United States, China, Russia as well as the European Union have allocated increasingly larger budgets to their own global media in order to be fully engaged in a war to win the hearts and minds of people of the world. These governments have suggested that traditional media and social networking sites be combined to create synergy to yield maximum effect (Ma, 2014, para. 5). Government broadcasts were established to promote national interests with information filtered through a nationalistic view. Global media today are expected to play a role in promoting more noble values that are commonly applicable to all people regardless of their nationality. These values include peace, human rights, and general wellbeing. The difficulty lies in that audience reactions cannot all be positive due to differences in culture, customs, religion, history, and mindset (Ma, 2014).

Cognizant of the benefits reaped by using social media, many governments have been active in practicing international public relations to improve their images throughout the world. The foreign news media have mostly become a major target for governments trying to influence news content about international issues and foreign affairs, especially with regard to their own countries. There have been many types of public relations programs, instruments, and media used in public diplomatic activities such as radio, television, newspapers, and news magazines. These were used to convey hard political information (including political advocacy). Academic and artistic exchanges, films, exhibitions, and language instruction have been used for cultural communication (with a view to creating a climate of mutual understanding) (Signitzer & Wamser, 2006, p. 457). An example of an organization used to provide international news to boost the image of the United States is the US-based NGO, the Washington Profile (Molleda, 2011, p. 31).

Young-sam Ma, as the Ambassador for Public Diplomacy of the Republic of Korea, suggested that many governments have competitively engaged in a war of public diplomacy through media to make their countries look attractive and friendly to foreigners while also setting the stage for others to understand their country's positions in the international arena. The success or failure of public diplomacy through media, however, can only be judged by its intended audience. The most critical criterion is the media's credibility, which can be achieved by the independence of media as well as freedom from editorial bias (Ma, 2014).

Under the Radar Media

Media have been created to target special groups of people such as Radio Sawa/Egypt, Al Hurra Television (Middle East) and other broadcasters of special languages (Ma, 2014, para. 3). In a point of being transparent, though, all of these have been funded by governments. The Middle East Broadcasting Networks, Inc. (MBN) has operated radio Sawa and Alhurra with financing through a grant from the Broadcasting Board of Governors (BBG), an independent federal agency funded by the US Congress. The BBG has overseen MBN and has acted as a firewall to protect the professional independence and integrity of the broadcasters. Radio Sawa has maintained an active all-news website (www.radiosawa.com), which provided up-to-the-minute news and information as well as live streaming audio. In addition to the latest headlines, RadioSawa.com also has reported on the latest news in technology, sports, business, and the arts (Radio Sawa, nd).

Al Hurra's mission has been to provide objective, accurate, and relevant news and information to the people of the Middle East about the region, the world and the United States. Al Hurra supports democratic values by expanding the spectrum of ideas, opinions, and perspectives available in the region's media. The name is Arabic for "The Free One" and has broadcasted primarily news and information programming. The network has hosted a number of discussion programs that examined political and social issues of interest to the audience in the Middle East, airing viewpoints not often discussed freely in the region. Through correspondents at the State Department, White House, Congress, and the Pentagon, Al Hurra has illuminated US policies and domestic debates on those policies for Middle Eastern audiences. Guests from American think tanks and interviews with US officials have provided a comprehensive view of US foreign policy as well as a better understanding of the American people and the US system of governance (Al Hurra, nd).

China has joined the media diplomacy movement. During the Olympic Games in 2008, for the first time foreign correspondents were permitted to interview consenting athletes and coaches without seeking official permission. Then during the Urumqi event in 2009, one of the deadliest clashes between Uygurs and Hans, the two largest ethnic groups in the northwestern Chinese region of Xinjiang, instead of an outright ban on foreign media coverage, the Chinese government set up a news center for foreign journalists reporting in Urumqi. Foreign journalists were lodged in a designated hotel and invited to timely press conferences and press tours around the city (Zeng, Zhou & Li, 2015, p. 52). In addition, video footage was released within only a few hours after the event, rather than weeks later, as had been the case in the past (Zeng, Zhou & Li, 2015).

Last Word: Neutrality is offered as a way to broker peace through states that have practiced peace. The challenge of journalists is to find ways to report on conflict through the eyes and ears of the neutral states. How have these neutral states maintained their neutrality in a world so full of conflict?

Discussion: Identify neutral states that have contributed to brokering peace initiatives during conflicts. How have they remained neutral? What techniques did they use? Were they successful or not, and why or why not?

References

Aboubakr, R. (2013). New directions of internet activism in Egypt. *De Gruyter Mouton*, 38(3), 251–265.

Al Hurra (nd). Retrieved from http://www.alhurra.com/info/about-us/112.html.

Arthur, C. (2011, January 26). Egypt blocks social media websites in attempted clampdown on unrest. *The Guardian*. Retrieved from http://www.theguardian.com/world/2011/jan/26/egypt-blocks-social-media-websites.

Bauder, D. (2003, March 31). NBC severs its ties with journalist Peter Arnett after interview with state-run Iraqi TV. *Deseret News*. Retrieved from http://www.deseretnews.com/article/973554/NBC-severs-its-ties-with-journalist-Peter-Arnett-after-interview-with-state-run-Iraqi-TV.html?pg=all.

Buric, A. (2000). The media war and peace in Bosnia. In A. Davis (Ed.), *Regional media in conflict* (pp. 64–100). London: Institute for War and Peace Reporting.

Chattarji, S. (2006). Negative reportage in Indo-Pak media. *The Hoot*. Retrieved from http://www.thehoot.org/web/home/story.php?storyid=1985&pg=1&mod=1&sectionId=38.

Corn, D. (2009, July 8). Torture in Iran. Mother Jones online. Retrieved from http://www.motherjones.com/mojo/2009/07/torture-iran.

Duffy, M. J. (2013, December 17). GCC media regulations lead to timid press. *Muftah*. Retrieved from http://muftah.org/gcc-media-regulations-lead-to-timid-press/#.VUkCMJOM6Sq.

Esser, V. (2012, June 29). The role of social media in diplomacy. *The New York Times*. Retrieved from http://www.nytimes.com/2012/11/26/business/media/using-war-as-cover-to-target-journalists.html?pagewanted=2&_r=0.

Evers, W. M. (1989). Liberty of the press under socialism. *Social Philosophy & Policy*, 2(6), 211–34.

Freedom House (2015). https://freedomhouse.org/.

Ghimire, S. & Upreti, B. R. (2014). Wavering between profit-making and change-making: Private media companies in conflicts in Nepal. *Media, War & Conflict*, 7(2), 187–200.

Goetschel, L. (2009, March 15–18). Neutrals as brokers of peacebuilding. Paper presented at the 2009 Annual Convention of the International Studies Association, New York.

Hayden, S. (2015, February 24). Imprisoned Saudi Arabian blogger Raif Badawi gets Geneva Summit's courage award. *Vice News*. Retrieved from https://news.vice.com/article/imprisoned-saudi-arabian-blogger-raif-badawi-is-awarded-geneva-summits-courage-award.

Human Rights Watch. (2010). Iran. Retrieved from http://www.hrw.org/en/node/87713.

Lee, S. & Hong, H. (2012). International public relations influence on media coverage and public perceptions of foreign countries. *Public Relations Review*, 38(3), 491–493.

Loewenstein, A. (2010, March 24). Viewpoint: Why Iran's Twitter revolution failed. BBC World Service. Retrieved from http://www.bbc.co.uk/worldservice.

Ma, Y. S. (2014, January 11). The role of global media in public diplomacy. *China Daily*. Retrieved from http://www.chinadaily.com.cn/opinion/2014-01/11/content_17230295_3.htm.

Molleda, J-C. (2011, January 10). Global Public Relations. Institute for Public Relations. Retrieved from http://www.instituteforpr.org/global-public-relations.

O'Neill, M. (2011, February 26). How YouTube is aiding the Libyan revolution. *Social Times*. Retrieved from http://www.adweek.com/socialtimes/youtube-libyan-revolution/40683.

Papaioannou, T. & Olivos, H. E. (2013). Cultural identity and social media in the Arab spring: Collective goals in the use of Facebook in the Libyan context. *Journal of Arab & Muslim Media Research*, 6(2&3), 99–114.

Radio Sawa (nd). http://www.radiosawa.com/info/about-us-en/108.html.

Reporters without borders (nd). http://en.rsf.org/.

Ronen, G. (2012, November 15). Netanyahu: Picture of bleeding baby says it all. *Arutz Sheva*. IsraelNationews.com. Retrieved from http://www.israelnationalnews.com/News/News.aspx/162129#.VSvafpOM6So.

Sadkovich, J. (1998). *The US media and Yugoslavia, 1991–1995*. Westport, CT: Praeger.

Seo, H. (2014). Visual propaganda in the age of social media: An empirical analysis of Twitter images during the 2012 Israeli-Hamas conflict. *Visual Communication Quarterly*, 21(3), 150–161.

Signitzer, B., & Wamser, C. (2006). Public diplomacy: A specific governmental public relations function. In Botan, C. H. & Vincent, H. (Eds.), *Public relations theory II*, (pp. 435–464). Mahwah, NJ: Lawrence Erlbaum Associates.

Singh, S. (2007). The Indian media's Pakistan obsession. *The Hoot*. Retrieved from http://www.thehoot.org/web/home/story.php?storyid=2517&pg=1&mod=1&sectionId=38&validtrue.

Sipiapa Organization (nd). http://www.sipiapa.org/en/.

Thompson, M. (1999). *Forging war: The media in Serbia, Croatia and Bosnia-Hercegovina*. Luton: University of Luton Press.

UN Universal Declaration of Human Rights (1948). http://www.un.org/en/documents/udhr/.

Wall, M. (2009). The taming of the warblogs: Citizen journalism and the war in Iraq. In Cottle, S. *et al.* (Eds.), *Citizen Journalism: Global Perspectives*, (pp. 33–42). New York: Peter Lang.

Zeng, L., Zhou, L., & Li, X. (2015). Framing strategies at different stages of a crisis: Coverage of the 'July 5th' Urumqi event by Xinhua, Reuters, and AP. *The International Communication Gazette*, 77(1), 51–73.

Zuckerman, E. (2009). Citizen media and the Kenyan electoral crisis. In Cottle, S. *et al.* (Eds.), *Citizen journalism: Global perspectives* (pp. 187–196). New York: Peter Lang.

· 1 0 ·

ACTION PLAN

Teaching Peace Journalism

Sergeant Kristopher J. Battles is thought to be the last Marine combat artist. His collection of paintings is said to "explore the Marine experience from a disarmingly humanistic perspective" (Kino, 2010, para. 14). He has painted a boy perching in a leafy tree near Carrefour, Haiti; Marines snoozing by piles of body armor in Helmand Province, Afghanistan; and a half-smiling Iraqi woman carrying a toddler.

The Marine Corps museum, which opened in 2006, has in its collection more than 8000 paintings, drawings, and sculptures dating to 1825, long before the corps' first formal program was set up in 1942. According to Kino's article, these combat artists were required to be an artist and a Marine. Company commanders did not worry about protecting the artists, as they needed to do, for example, with embedded journalists, and this has won support for the program throughout the rank and file. "The biggest worry a unit leader has is: 'Oh, my God, who is this guy? How am I going to take care of him?'" said Col. Richard D. Camp, retired, vice president of museum operations for the Marine Corps Heritage Foundation. "But once they find out these guys are fully capable of taking care of themselves, all that is off the table" (Kino, 2010, para. 23).

Kino explained why the Marines have combat artists: "If you and I are in the same fire fight, what you see and what I see are two different things, based on our own background and experience," said Lt. Gen. Ron Christmas, retired, the president and chief executive of the Marine Corps Heritage Foundation. "When a photograph is taken of a battle or any type of scene in combat, you see the image. But what the artist does is he takes that image and interprets it" (2010, para. 35). And, of course, capturing a moment in a painting also serves one of art's most ancient purposes. "It's the pact we make with the warrior: You will live forever and we will remember you," according to Anita Blair, chief strategist at the National Security Professional Development Integration Office. "And to me the best way to do that is through art. We can't give him his life, but we can give him that immortality" (Kino, 2010, para. 36).

Journalists can do the same thing as the combat artist: take an event and interpret it. Journalists can capture a moment through writings, through photographs and through videos to help audiences remember what was happening and to remember the people involved. Unlike the last Marine artist left; however, journalists can retool and find new ways of covering conflict. The goal of this chapter is to make a plan on how to teach peace through media.

How to Create Peace Journalism: In the Classroom and the Newsroom

Reporting the World codified the peace journalism model into a set of questions ("Reporting the world," nd). These questions include asking how violence is explained, what is the shape of the conflict, is there any news of any efforts or ideas to resolve the conflict and what is role of Britain, the West and the international community in this story.

The logic of peace-orientated journalism is to explore the backgrounds and contexts of conflict formation, to present causes and options on each side (not just both sides), to identify the goals of the various parties involved directly or indirectly in a conflict and possible contradictions between them and to offer creative ideas for conflict resolution, development and peacemaking, while respecting all cultures and belief systems.

The use of peace-oriented media in conflict environments has been in practice for the last decade with a variety of projects existing in the field. A missing component has been a comprehensive study of all the projects that would approach the general idea of peace-oriented media rather than a single regional application. Bratić's (2008, p. 493) compiled an extensive set of peace-oriented media projects using the following criteria to identify the positive application of media in conflict regions:

- A recent history or presence of armed conflict/violence in the region—this distinction is made in order to differentiate between media in conflict areas and media projects working toward the democratization of states in transition (e.g., the Czech and Slovak Republics)
- Post-Cold War—only in the last 20 years have mass media equipment and technology become affordable and portable, allowing the establishment of new media sources as an immediate response to a conflict
- Involvement of a third party—the presence of a third party is what distinguishes peace-oriented media from sophisticated propaganda (e.g., American media relations in Iraq)
- Intentional purpose—in order to focus only on specific programs aimed at transforming conflict, the study excludes projects and media channels that are already operating and producing media content in the region of conflict but are not doing anything exceptional in response to the violent conflict.

After providing the criteria whereby projects could be grouped, a next step would be to actually offer examples of how journalists have used the guidelines provided by Galtung, Lynch, McGoldrick and Bratić.

Seventeen Steps to Being a Peace Journalist

Whereas there has been literature focused on promoting instructional guidelines for journalists to use in reporting conflict, the following uses the 17 steps provided by Lynch and McGoldrick (2005, pp. 30–33) to guide a journalist in providing peace initiatives in reporting. Each step is offered here followed by an example of how journalists have covered stories using techniques offered by the scholars familiar with peace journalism, mainly Galtung, Lynch, and McGoldrick. The importance of the 17 steps is as a guide for young journalists to use to cover conflict.

More Than Two Parties Are Involved in Conflict

1. Avoid portraying a conflict as consisting of only two parties, contesting the same goal(s). The logical outcome is for one to win and the other to lose. Instead, a Peace Journalist would *disaggregate* the two parties into many smaller groups, pursuing many goals, opening up more creative potential for a range of outcomes (Lynch & McGoldrick, 2005, pp. 30–33).

To avoid portraying conflict as having only two parties, an article on In-donesia's Papua region, had the authors following peace journalism guidelines. They identified all the parties, approximately nine, and then developed the sources trying to ascertain everyone's goals. They used statistics of violations for the previous four years prior to the conflict to put the long-term impact of the violence in context. They interviewed the local ethnic Malind people who were being most affected by the conflict; organizations such as those fo-cusing on indigenous rights, advocacy for rights, rainforests protection, Pap-uan women's rights and environmental conservationists. They interviewed the other side of the conflict, the developers of the Wilmar plantation who wanted to cut down the rain forest home of the Malind people in order to expand the plantation, the government spokespeople, and people associated with the viewpoint of the World Bank. The authors explained how communi-ty development, land demarcation, and local demarcation were formalized in the area. Then they broadened the discussion to include a global perspective by including information from the 2014 gathering of 10 indigenous groups worldwide ("Conflict in Indonesia's Papua Region," 2014).

Are the People Involved Really Good or Bad?

2. Avoid accepting stark distinctions between *self* and *other*. These can be used to build the sense that another party is a *threat* or *beyond the pale* of civ-ilized behavior—both key justifications for violence. Instead, seek the *other* in the *self* and vice versa. If a party is presenting itself as *the goodies*, ask ques-tions about how different its behavior really is to that it ascribes to *the baddies* (Lynch & McGoldrick, 2005, pp. 30–33).

Colombia's civil war has been seen as being the longest civil war in his-tory spanning 50 years. In an article on the developing peace process in Co-lombia, the journalist used a quote from the Colombian president to blend the people thought to be the *baddies* in a more positive light. President Juan Manuel Santos was quoted in the *Guardian* article:

> The overall goal was not to humiliate the FARC but to persuade the guerrillas to swap their guns for votes—including the FARC's smaller rival, the National Liberation Army (ELN), which has not yet formerly entered into peace talks….They can contin-ue their objectives but through legal democratic channels. I am willing to give them all the guarantees necessary for them to have this chance. It is up to them if they can win or not….I tell them that many former guerrillas in Latin America are now heads of state, so think about it—let's stop the war. (Watts & Broadzinsky, 2014, paras. 24–26)

Broaden the Linkage to the Conflict
to Include Consequences

3. Avoid treating a conflict as if it is only going on in the place and at the time that violence is occurring. Instead, try to trace the links and consequences for people in other places now and in the future (Lynch & McGoldrick, 2005, pp. 30–33).

Rajan Menon with Eugene B. Rumer have co-authored a book on the crisis in the Ukraine, *Conflict in Ukraine*, published by the MIT Press (2015). Menon, in an essay for the *Los Angeles Times*, examined many issues and linked the conflict with the consequences for people in other places now and in the future. Menon posited that sanctions issued by both the European Union and the United States have created problems for Russia's economy causing a 50 percent collapse in the price of oil. Menon also suggested that sending arms to the Ukraine would undermine European security, would raise questions about NATO's future, and would effectively end United States' chances of building any partnership with Russia (Menon, 2015).

Find Invisible Effects of Violence

4. Avoid assessing the merits of a violent action or policy of violence in terms of its visible effects only. Instead, try to find ways of reporting on the invisible effects, for example, the long-term consequences of psychological damage and trauma, perhaps increasing the likelihood that those affected will be violent in future, either against other people or, as a group, against other groups or other countries (Lynch & McGoldrick, 2005, pp. 30–33).

The author, Joseph D'Urso, of the article published in *The World Post* demonstrated the long-term effects of the psychological damage and trauma to the Syrian people through statistics. He stated that there had been 200,000 people killed, 7.6 million people displaced, and 14 million children affected by the conflict. More than 3.9 million refugees had fled to the neighboring countries of Turkey, Lebanon, and Jordon. He provided evidence for how the trauma would continue by the statistics that where there had been 2,500 doctors in the second largest city in Syria, Aleppo, but in 2015 there were only 100. Furthermore, whereas life expectancy had been 75.9 in 2010, it was now 55.7 in 2014 (D'Urso, 2015).

What Are the Goals of the People Who Are Affected by the Conflict?

5. Avoid letting parties define themselves by simply quoting their leaders' restatement of familiar demands or positions. Instead, inquire more deeply into goals:

- How are people on the ground affected by the conflict in everyday life?
- What do they want changed?
- Is the position stated by their leaders the only way or the best way to achieve the changes they want? (Lynch & McGoldrick, 2005, pp. 30–33)

Séverine Autesserre in her book, *Peaceland: Conflict Resolution and the Everyday Politics of International Constructing Knowledge of the Host Country*, published by Cambridge University Press (2014), exposed and analyzed the subculture of expatriates who participated in peace building efforts on behalf of a diverse array of international and nongovernmental organizations. By introducing a subculture of leaders into the conflict resolution process, she suggested that many of the persistent dysfunctions of peace building missions could be traced back to the routine practices, habits and narratives within this subculture (Austessarre, 2014). The argument introduced people on the ground that wanted to effect change their way.

Reveal Common Ground of Parties Involved in Conflict

6. Avoid concentrating always on what divides the parties, the differences between what they say they want. Instead, try asking questions that may reveal areas of common ground and leading your report with answers which suggest some goals maybe shared or at least compatible (Lynch & McGoldrick, 2005, pp. 30–33).

The *Wall Street Journal* article written by Terry Roth (2014) on the reunification of Berlin suggested that the common ground between East and West Germany was that both sides wanted better transportation and then, for easier commerce, both sides wanted the same money (the deutsche mark). To achieve these goals, Germany solicited Russian president, Gorbachev, to support Germany's reunification by securing three million marks in fresh credit and agree to a 12 billion mark grant to pay for the withdrawal of Soviet divisions from East Germany by 1994 (Roth, 2014).

Show How Violence Has Blocked or Deprived Everyday Life

7. Avoid only reporting the violent acts and describing *the horror*. To exclude everything else, the only possible explanation for violence is previous violence (revenge); the only remedy, more violence (coercion/punishment). Instead, show how people have been blocked and frustrated or deprived in everyday life as a way of explaining the violence (Lynch & McGoldrick, 2005, pp. 30–33).

Nick Heath, chief reporter for *Tech Republic UK*, wrote an article on how minerals funded a war that killed millions. In the article about mining in the Democratic Republic of Congo (DRC), Heath told the story of misery that war and mineral wealth have brought to the DRC. In their everyday life, people of the DRC worked in the mines with as many as 15,000 people digging for the mineral cassiterite used in technology, and the minerals coltan and wolframite. These three minerals are referred to as the 3T, a reference to the tin, tantalum and tungsten metals derived from them; with gold, these four materials have been mined in African countries to be used in computers, phones or other electronics. When the armed militia seized control of the mines as a way of funding the armed conflict, the people working in the mines were essentially made into slaves. People worked 24 hours a day in the mines and carried the minerals to the distribution center 50 kilometers away using men, women, and children. The conditions were inhuman and the armed groups saw themselves as outside the law—no one could control them (Heath, 2014, para. 1). The conflicts in the DRC started in 1998 and have killed more than 5.4 million people. Heath used the mining of minerals to demonstrate how violence can permeate the lives of many people when they are not even part of the conflict.

Locate Shared Problems of All Parties

8. Avoid blaming someone for starting it. Instead, try looking at how shared problems and issues are leading to consequences that all the parties say they never intended (Lynch & McGoldrick, 2005, pp. 30–33).

In a research project on water wars and international conflict, Abigail Ofori-Amoah (2004) suggested that war and conflict have been tied to the protection of water resources and though water has not been the main ingredient in international conflicts, it is factored into the problem due to its economic importance (2004, para. 1). Conflicts related to water use can be caused by the military, industry, agriculture, and political figures. Water used as a weapon or as a political goal can also be overused, polluted, and cut off from communities. Waste dumped into the water system can cause illness or displace people who must move to find water to meet their needs. Industrial areas in the midst of conflict may stop maintaining safe practices or may increase pollution or may stop services that will create problems for people, problems never actually intended but became part of the conflict.

Treat All Parties as Equals in Suffering, Fears, and Grievances

9. Avoid focusing exclusively on the suffering, fears, and grievances of only one party. This divides the parties into *villains* and *victims* and suggests that coercing or punishing the villains represents a solution. Instead, treat as equally newsworthy the suffering, fears and grievance of all sides (Lynch & McGoldrick, 2005, pp. 30–33).

Ellen Messer's chapter, "Conflict as a Cause of Hunger," in *Who's Hungry? And How do We Know? Food Shortage, Poverty, and Deprivation*, defined food wars as "the deliberate use of hunger as a weapon or hunger suffered as a consequence of armed conflict" (1998, p. 164). She cited statistics on 32 countries where people suffered malnutrition, poverty-related limitations in their access to food and acute food shortages as a result of armed conflict. She suggested that conflicts have a regional impact on land use, food and commodity markets, livelihoods, and health. Whereas adversaries have starved opponents by seizing or destroying food stocks, livestock, or other assets in rural areas, they also have severed sources of food or livelihood including destroying markets in urban areas. These adversaries have mined or contaminated land and water resources to force people to leave and to discourage their return.

> Food shortage ripples into the larger economy and extends over multiple years when farmers, herders, and others flee attacks, terror, and destruction or suffer reductions in their capacity to produce food because of forced labor recruitment (including conscription) and war-related depletion of assets. Ancillary attacks of disease linked to destruction of health facilities, and hardship and hunger also reduce the human capacity for food production. (Messer, 1998, p. 167)

The author offered examples of many countries: Ethiopia, Eritrea, Cambodia, Myanmar, Afghanistan, Angola, Sudan, Somalia, Rwanda, Burundi, Kenya, Sri Lanka, Iraq, North Korea, Zaire, Colombia, Haiti, Lesotho, Mexico, Guatemala, Nicaragua, El Salvador, former countries of the Soviet Union and Yugoslavia, Nigeria, among others. She suggested that during prolonged warfare, whole generations might be conscripted into the military; with no other schooling, they must later be socialized into peacetime occupations if they were not to revert to violence. In the African conflicts of Mozambique, Liberia, and Sierra Leone, destruction of kinship units was a deliberate military strategy to remove intergenerational ties and community bonds and to create new loyalties—to the military (Messer, 1998, p. 171). Economic sanctions that were meant to forestall or replace military actions and bring about political change could be a source of conflict-related hunger. For example, 500,000 Iraqi children have died in the five years that sanctions were imposed (Messer, 1998, p. 173). These stories illustrated how hunger affects all sides of the conflict.

Moreover, Messer (1998) explained that even allegedly successful multilateral efforts to feed the hungry on both sides of the conflict, such as Operation Life Line in the Sudan in 1980, have been criticized as prolonging the war effort by providing recognition and legitimacy to insurgents and giving everyone time for a respite that encouraged them to fight on (p. 176). She also provided an example of food relief operations by military humanitarianism where an international military force had delivered large-scale food aid where logistics and security concerns made it difficult or impossible for civilian groups to deliver food, as in Iraq, Kurdistan, Somalia, Bosnia, and Rwanda. These efforts were also criticized for prolonging the conflict. "None of these operations have met humanitarian needs very successfully, and the combined military and food dimensions of aid intensify armed aspects of conflict by providing food, employment, income, and opportunities for further pilferage" (Duffield, 1994, p. 55).

How Are All Parties Coping and Do They Have Solutions?

10. Avoid victimizing language such as *destitute*, *devastated*, *defenseless*, *pathetic* and *tragedy*, which only tells what has been done to a group of people. This disempowers them and limits the options for change. Instead, report on what has been done and could be done by the people. Don't just ask them how they feel, also ask them how they are coping and what do they think? Can they suggest any solutions? Remember refugees have surnames as well (Lynch & McGoldrick, 2005, pp. 30–33).

In her chapter on "Forced Intimacy," Zahava Solomon provided a description of how people coped with war stress using two studies, personal testimonies, and clinical reports. Solomon posited that there had been studies on individual groups: elderly, women, children, but nothing on families. The Gulf War forced families to be in the middle of the conflict so many families were forced to be in doors with each other for prolonged periods of time. Schools were closed for weeks. Solomon examined the plight of various groups of families, the nuclear family where the mother and father both still worked, the elderly and adult children returning home, and the separated mates finding a unity to be with children. In addition, due to the missiles and gas, each home had a sealed room and gas masks where the family had to get into in a record time and wait for the all clear. "Moreover, whatever prior tensions were present in the family and whatever emotions the family members harboured—fear, frustration, anger—were inevitably brought into the room and sealed into it with the occupants" (Solomon, 1995, p. 58). This researcher interviewed many families and her results indicated how these families felt through their forced intimacy during conflict.

Reserve Strong Language for the Worst Situations

11. Avoid imprecise use of emotive words to describe what has happened to people.

- Genocide means the wiping out of an entire people.
- Decimated (said of a population) means reducing it to a tenth of its former size.
- Tragedy is a form of drama, originally Greek, in which someone's fault or weakness proves his or her undoing.
- Assassination is the murder of a head of state.
- Massacre is the deliberate killing of people known to be unarmed and defenseless. Are we sure? Or might these people have died in battle?
- Systematic e.g., raping or forcing people from their homes. Has it really been organized in a deliberate pattern or have there been a number of unrelated, albeit extremely nasty incidents?

Instead, always be precise about is known. Do not minimize suffering but reserve the strongest language for the gravest situations or the language will help to justify disproportionate responses that escalate the violence (Lynch & McGoldrick, 2005, pp. 30–33).

Eva Fearn in her BBC News viewpoint article, "Protecting Wildlife in Conflict Zones," stated the obvious, war was a tragedy for humans; but then she used the environment to show how very devastating war was for all living things but in nonscare language, just the facts. "But the environmental destruction it causes has also become a concern. In Afghanistan, the past three decades have seen 50 percent of the country's forests disappear and wildlife hunted out of many areas" (Fearn, 2010, para. 6–7). She cited the journal of *Conservation Biology* that found more than 80 percent of the armed clashes in the past 50 years occurred in countries that contain places of extraordinarily high global species diversity (para. 9). Then Fearn suggested that "because civil unrest can often result for competition for natural resources, there is another powerful reason why conservation is important in conflict settings: it can help build peace" (para. 13). Later in the article, she offered the example of three fishing villages near Lake Edward in the DRC. To address the issue of overfishing, a participatory process began to ascertain why fish stocks were declining and what could be done. The process involved the military, police, fishing community, local security officials, and park managers to agree on plans for managing the stocks. Fearn posited that "[p]eople participating in this effort at good governance are building the foundations of new democratic institutions that will be essential to long-term stability and the future sustainability of fishing, their main resource" (Fearn, 2010, para. 21).

Fearn's article also introduced the reader to how conservation of resources and of economically important species can be discussed with relatively little political, ideological, or military pressure and can serve as a starting point for wider political dialogue (para. 31). She gave examples of creating wilderness buffer areas along contested borders in Peru/Ecuador and a similar *peace park* on the border between Sudan and Uganda. "Conversation 'diplomacy' has become an exciting and critically important outgrowth of the work of conservationists" (Fearn, 2010, para. 35). Fearn's research demonstrated that different viewpoints of how conflict can be covered can be used to encourage a peaceful resolution.

Report the Facts and the Reliability of Other Reports

12. Avoid demonizing adjectives like *vicious, cruel, brutal* and *barbaric*. These always describe one party's view of what another party has done. To use them puts the journalist on that side and helps to justify an escalation of violence. Instead, report what you know about the wrongdoing and give as much information as you can about the reliability of other people's reports or descriptions of it (Lynch & McGoldrick, 2005, pp. 30–33).

The New York Times reporter, Anne Barnard in Gaza City, said she was tired of the hate tweets and sent out her own tweet: "Listen people, if you're going to tweet anti-Arab, anti-Jewish or anti-Muslim tweets, please just take me off your thread. And then that tweet was also re-tweeted many times" (Martin, 2014, para. 19).

Gerard Creces in the *Strathroy Age Dispatch* wrote, "Indeed, the comments sections of the Internet have become the pillory, a place where the general public can throw rotten tomatoes at the wrongdoers of online society. Because the Internet is relatively anonymous (on the surface, anyway) there are no repercussions for attacking what we hate or don't understand. Our user names are different from our given names and we can choose avatars instead of photos of ourselves" (Creces, 2015, para. 6). In addition, "calls of shame, threats, vitriolic rants and even worse can pop up in an instant, sparked by ten second video clips or recorded audio. Somehow, we believe we have ownership of morality—that we have the power to decide who needs to suffer at the public's hands" (Creces, 2015, para. 9).

Use the Names of the People They Give Themselves

13. Avoid demonizing labels like *terrorist*, *extremist*, *fanatic* and *fundamentalist*. These are always given by *us* to *them*. No one ever uses them to describe himself or herself, and so, for a journalist to use them is always to take sides. They mean the person is unreasonable, so it seems to make less sense to reason (negotiate) with them. Instead, try calling people by the names they give themselves. Or be more precise in your descriptions (Lynch & McGoldrick, 2005, pp. 30–33).

There is the new discussion in both the traditional media and social media as to what the people who call themselves the Islamic State should really be called. Language is important. Traditional media refer to them as the Islamic State in Iraq and al-Sham, or ISIS; the Islamic State in Iraq and the Levant, or ISIL; and more recently, the Islamic State or IS. However, French officials declared that France would stop using any of those names and instead refer to the group as "Daesh" (Khan, 2014). The French Foreign Minister Laurent Fabius was quoted as saying: "This is a terrorist group and not a state… the term Islamic State blurs the lines between Islam, Muslims, and Islamists" (Khan, 2014, para. 3). According to people who want to use the term Daesh, it spells out the acronym of the group's full Arabic name, al-Dawla al-Islamiya fi al-Iraq wa al-Sham. It must also be understood that it is a play on words and is considered an insult to mean anything from "to trample down and crush" to "a bigot who imposes his view on others" (Kahn, 2014). The ISIS group has threatened to cut out the tongues of anyone who uses the term, according to Kahn (2014).

Language matters. On the other hand, by using the militants' preferred names, media give them legitimacy. The issue is being decided outside governments and traditional media. Online, between 17 September and 17 October 2014, ISIS was used 4 million times; Daesh was used 1.9 million times. More specifically, online activists and unaffiliated individuals used only, or mostly, Daesh in articles. This reshaping of the discourse online has been the emergence of such phenomena as the trending #daeshbags hashtag on Twitter. Language affects the way people think and behave (Kahn, 2014).

Report on All Wrongdoers

14. Avoid focusing exclusively on the human rights abuses, misdemeanors, and wrongdoings of only one side. Instead, try to name all wrongdoers and treat equally seriously allegations made by all sides in a conflict. Treating seriously does not mean taking at face value, but instead making equal efforts to establish whether any evidence exists to back them up, treating the victims with equal respect and the chances of finding and punishing the wrongdoers as being of equal importance (Lynch & McGoldrick, 2005, pp. 30–33).

Colombia has been attempting to bring the paramilitary rebels back into society through a program run by Agencia Colombiana para la Reintegración (ACR), a government office answering to the president of Colombia. The government has processed 57,000 rebels through the program; whereas, to process them through the criminal justice system would have taken more than 100 years (2014, para. 6). The program has disarmed and demobilized rebels on both sides of the conflict: United Self-Defence Forces of Colombia (AUC), a right-wing paramilitary organization and FARC, the Marxist guerrillas. The rebels have been offered full amnesty from prosecution, provided they agreed to participate in a multiyear reintegration program to adapt to civilian life. They would attend psychosocial, vocational, and educational training sessions and would receive a monthly stipend of $270 (lower than the $444 monthly minimum wage to keep from viewing this as a salary). The program has been successful based on money. It costs $2,500/year to reintegrate a rebel, $7,000/year to imprison, and $125,000 to kill the rebel. According to the program statistics, eight out of ten rebels do not reoffend, whereas, 70 percent of those imprisoned return to prison (Rohrlich, 2014, para. 10). Strong evidence in this research encourages a peaceful resolution to the conflict.

Be Clear as to Who Said What

15. Avoid making an opinion or claim seem like an established fact. Example, "Eurico Guterres, said to be responsible for a massacre in East Timor." Instead, tell who said what. "Eurico Guterres, accused by a top U.N. official of ordering a massacre in East Timor." This avoids having allegations made by one party in the conflict against another (Lynch & McGoldrick, 2005, pp. 30–33).

Calum MacLeod (2013) writing for *USA Today* described a cyber attack that caused computer networks at South Korean banks and television networks to crash. A Chinese Internet address originated the crash, according to South Korea's telecom regulator. Suspicion fell quickly on North Korea. MacLeod reported, however, that South Korean police and government officials declined to blame anyone. "It's too early to assign blame to China or North Korea, since Internet addresses can easily be manipulated" (2013, para. 4). The tension and conflict that existed between North and South Korea would have made it easy for the South Korean officials to *lay blame* on North Korea; however, the reporter used many official sources from China and South Korea to write a more comprehensive and less contentious story.

Cover Issues Still Remaining Even After the Conflict Is Over

16. Avoid greeting the signing of documents by leaders, which bring about military victory or cease fire, as necessarily creating peace. Instead, try to report on the issues which may still remain and which may not create a culture of peace (Lynch & McGoldrick, 2005, pp. 30–33).

One article that sought to report on issues of peace was Peter Gelling's "Former Rebels Turned Forest Rangers in Aceh" published in the *New York Times* (2010). Aceh is located in the northern areas of Indonesia and the conflict was based on a separatist movement wanting to control the revenue from the natural resources in the area. A government program was created called Aceh Green. The program was designed to incorporate sustainable development by integrating former combatants into society and creating jobs that would fulfil the goal of the former separatist movement: ensuring that revenue from natural resources benefited local people. The rebels who knew the Ulu Masen jungle were trained by Fauna and Flora International and recast as forest rangers to protect the forests (Gelling, 2010). This article helped to encourage a peaceful resolution to the conflict.

Look for All Solutions That May Help Stimulate Dialogue

17. Avoid waiting for leaders on *our* side to suggest or offer solutions. Instead, pick up and explore peace initiatives wherever they come from. Ask questions to politicians, for example, about ideas put forward by grassroots organizations. Assess peace perspectives against what you know about the issues the parties are really trying to address, do not simply ignore them because they do not coincide with established positions. Include images of a solution; however partial—they may help to stimulate dialogue (Lynch & McGoldrick, 2005, pp. 30–33).

The Economist published an article on Juan Manuel Santos winning the election in Colombia (S.B./Bogota, 2014). The article stated that the election was widely seen as a referendum on the peace process that Santos's government began with leftist FARC rebels in late 2012. With preliminary agreements on three of five points, the negotiations had gone further than all previous efforts to end the conflict that killed tens of thousands and forced millions from their homes. Just days before the vote Santos revealed that the government had been engaged in preliminary talks with a second rebel group, known as the ELN, to commence a parallel peace process (S.B./Bogota, 2014, para. 3). One comment published on the site with the article, though, suggested that manipulation of the media should have been pointed out since Santos' relatives and personal friends own or direct 80 percent of printed media and radio/TV stations and the manipulation of messages went way too far, not only to discourage voters regarding opponents, but to strongly advertise last-minute announcements intended to bias public opinion and hide public concern in areas as critical as the peace process (S.B./Bogota, 2014, first comment, para. 6). This article stimulated dialogue within the comments for the reporter to dig deeper and look at other issues related to the event.

Coda

This chapter has presented the 17 steps to achieving a peace through media solution to conflict based on the early advice of Johan Galtung, who developed the concept of peace journalism. However, several updates need to be added to the guidelines offered by Lynch and McGoldrick. These include how a journalist must focus on gender, examine the causes of the conflict and learn from the nonviolent revolutions that have taken place around the world.

Focus on Gender

The statistics on how involved women are in conflict from the roles they play in negotiating, in maintaining family structures, in providing food and warmth, in being made victims through rape, hunger, conscription, displacement and illness, cite strong evidence that women must be part of the stories reported on conflict and war. Two Philippine based women organizations—Isis International and Mindanaw Women Writers, In. (Min-WoW)—developed "Engendered Peace Journalism: Keeping Community Whole—A Guide on Gender-sensitive Peace and Conflict Reportage" (2007). These organizations encourage reframing stories through a gender lens. Journalists should consider the following questions when writing a story (Yiping, 2011, p. 18):

- Where are the women/girls in the story?
- How can gender information strengthen the story?
- What are the roles of the male and female subjects and how do these factors inform the issues and story?
- What are the power relationships between men and women, in the leadership of the conflict parties, in the negotiation panels, community structures, family structures? How do these roles and power relations further explain the issue?
- How are the impacts of events and processes written about in a specific story, different for women and for men?
- Where are the points of collaboration between genders? What are the common grounds and shared interests and needs?

These questions were used in programming the community radio station, Radio Purbanchal, in Nepal. The journalists visited women as victims of war and conflict and discussed the issues facing these women and how their rights can be ensured. The discussions initiated by Radio Purbanchal resulted in specific policy recommendations to the state, including the provision of better and qualitative education to women, proper health care and employment opportunities, training, and capacity building programs. Through the radio station, women also organized to advocate for their rights and welfare (Kadel, 2010).

Examine Causes of Conflict

Journalists who report on conflict and war should begin by investigating the reasons that cause the conflict and violence. The causes can provide a more profound understanding of the visible and invisible consequences of violence and guide people in contributing to positive peace. According to Lynch and McGoldrick (2005, p. 18), there are certain criteria that can be taken into account while doing this analysis:

- Violence never completely contradicts with its purpose
- A solution without violence is always possible
- There are more than two sides in every disagreement
- Every side has a rightful claim in their own perspective

Mapping the conflict and identifying all the parties and their goals may be the first steps; but, the process by which some facts are selected and others suppressed should be transparent, especially in a climate wrought with competing information sources. Journalists must continue to seek out truths even when in contrast to official information sources (as in the coverage of Bosnia where US journalists were told to follow US foreign policy but after discovering the rapes in the refugee camps journalists began reporting on those) or the conventional analysis (as in the coverage of South African apartheid that sought media to maintain the status quo). The journalists must also be ready to expose untruths on all sides (where US media failed to do so with the weapons of mass destruction in Iraq).

To do solid reporting, journalists must insist on parity of esteem for *needs and suffering* in place of *worthy and unworthy* victimhood. The shift of emphasis reduces the blame and will more likely lead to an examination of the structural/cultural factors, which perpetuate the conditions for violence. These structural/cultural factors now appear as the problem and can be shared—and contributed to—by all the parties. Because blame cannot therefore be pinned on one, demonized party, suddenly it makes sense to balance and neutralize those factors if the conflict is to be transformed into a nonviolent phase (Lynch, 2002).

Nonviolent Revolutions

There have been many nonviolent revolutions, such as The Prague Spring (1968), The Carnation Revolution in Portugal (1974) and The Las Mariposas Revolution in the Dominican Republic. One revolution that stands out is the Singing Revolution of Estonia (1987–89) where a cycle of singing mass demonstrations, followed by a living chain across the Baltic States (Estonia, Lithuania, and Latvia) resulted in independence from the Soviet Union.

George Lakey in his 1973 book, *Strategy for a Living Revolution,* and in his 1976 "A Manifesto for Nonviolent Revolution," laid out a five-stage strategy for nonviolent revolution (Lakey, 1976).

- Cultural preparation or conscientization: education, training, and consciousness raising of why there is a need for a nonviolent revolution and how to conduct a nonviolent revolution.
- Building organizations: as training, education, and consciousness raising continues, the need to form organizations. Affinity groups or nonviolent revolutionary groups are organized to provide support, maintain nonviolent discipline, organize, and train other people into similar affinity groups and networks.
- Confrontation organized and sustained campaigns of picketing, strikes, sit-ins, marches, boycotts, die-ins, blockades to disrupt business as usual in institutions and government. By putting one's body on the line nonviolently, the rising movement stops the normal gears of government and business.
- Mass Non Cooperation: similar affinity groups and networks of affinity groups around the country and world, engage in similar actions to disrupt business as usual.
- Developing Parallel Institutions to take over functions and services of government and commerce. In order to create a new society without violence, oppression, environmental destruction, discrimination and one that is environmentally sustainable, nonviolent, democratic, equitable tolerant and fair, alternative organizations and structures including businesses must be created to provide the needed services and goods that citizens of a society need.

How does a society create a nonviolent revolution using these five stages? Provide education and training, create nonviolent protests, coordinate with like-minded groups, and build parallel institutions that will bridge the old society into the new one.

Last Word: Storytelling can be an effective tool in transforming the negative energy of trauma into something positive and constructive, both on individual and societal levels. For survivors of armed conflict, for example, including those who go through the cycle of silence in reaction to deep traumatization, the coming out into the open through storytelling is empowering and affirming, enabling them to redefine their sense of identity given their new normalcy.

Discussion: Compare one of the nonviolent revolutions with violent conflict. How could the violent conflicts use strategies from the nonviolent ones?

References

Autesserre, S. (2014). *Peaceland: Conflict resolution and the everyday politics of international constructing knowledge of the host country.* Cambridge University Press.

Bratić, V. (2008). Examining peace-oriented media in areas of violent conflict. *International Communication Gazette, 70*, 487–503.

"Conflict in Indonesia's Papua Region" (2014, March 28). Irinnews.org. Retrieved from http://www.irinnews.org/report/99856/conflict-in-indonesia-s-papua-region.

Creces, G. (2015, April 23). 'Off with their heads' mentality gripping the 'net. *Strathroy Age Dispatch.* Retrieved from http://global-factiva-com.proxy-remote.galib.uga.edu/hp/printsavews.aspx?pp=Print&hc-Publication.

Duffield, M. (1994). The political economy of internal war: Asset transfer, complex emergencies, and international aid. In Macrae, J. & Zwi, A. (Eds.), *War and hunger,* (pp. 50–70). London: Zed Books.

D'Urso, J. (2015, March 12). Millions of children are trapped by war in Syria. *The World Post.* Retrieved from http://www.huffingtonpost.com/2015/03/12/syria-war-children_n_6854612.html.

Fearn, E. (2010, July 20). Protecting wildlife in conflict zones. BBC News. Retrieved from http://news.bbc.co.uk/2/hi/science/nature/8835791.stm.

Gelling, P. (2010, March 4). Former rebels turned forest rangers in Aceh. *The New York Times.* Retrieved from http://www.nytimes.com/2010/03/05/world/asia/05iht-aceh.html?_r=0.

Heath, N. (2014). How conflict minerals funded a war that killed millions and why tech giants are finally cleaning up their act. *TechRepublic.* Retrieved from http://www.techrepublic.com/article/how-conflict-minerals-funded-a-war-that-killed-millions/.

Kadel, K. (2010). A radio by women for community: Radio Purbanchal in Nepal. Retrieved from http://www.isiswomen.org/index.php?option=com_content&view=article&id=1483:a-radio-by-women-for-community-radio-purbanchal-in-nepal&catid=180&Itemid=452.

Khan, Z. (2014, October 9). Words matter in 'ISIS' war, so use 'Daesh.' *The Boston Globe.* Retrieved from http://www.bostonglobe.com/opinion/2014/10/09/words-matter-isis-war-use-daesh/V85GYEuasEEJgrUun0dMUP/story.html.

Kino, C. (2010, July 14). With sketchpads and guns, Semper Fi. *The New York Times.* Retrieved from http://www.nytimes.com/2010/07/18/arts/design/18marines.html?_r=0.

Lakey, G. (1973). *Strategy for a living revolution*. Grossman: New York, NY. Retrieved from http://en.wikipedia.org/wiki/nonviolent_revolution.

Lynch, J. (2002). Can you trust a journalist? *The Guardian*. Retrieved from http://www.the guardian.com/world/2002/jun/09/2.

Lynch, J. & McGoldrick, A. (2005). Peace journalism in the Holy Land. *Media Development*, 52(1), 47–49.

MacLeod, C. (2013, March 21). South Korea: China address source of attack. *USA Today*. Retrieved from http://www.usatoday.com/story/news/world/2013/03/20/south-korean-computer-crash/2001873/.

Martin, M. (2014, July 22). Tweeting from a conflict zone: Does it help or hurt news reporting? NPR. Retrieved from http://www.npr.org/2014/07/22/334035814/tweeting-from-a-conflict-zone-does-it-help-or-hurt-news-reporting.

Menon, R. (2015, February 4). Want to arm Kiev? Better have a plan B. *Los Angeles Times*. Retrieved from http://www.latimes.com/opinion/op-ed/la-oe-menon-arming-ukraine-20150205-story.html.

Messer, E. (1998). Conflict as a cause of hunger. In DeRose, L., Messer, E., & Millman, S. (Eds.), *Who's Hungry? And How Do We Know? Food Shortage, Ppoverty, and Deprivation*. Tokyo, NY, Paris: United Nations University Press. http://unu.edu. Chapter retrieved from http://collections.unu.edu/eserv/UNU:2380/nLib9280809857.pdf.

Ofori-Amoah, A. (2004, Spring). Water wars and international conflict. Water is life web site. Retrieved from http://academic.evergreen.edu/g/grossmaz/oforiaa/.

Rohrlich, J. (2014, December 16). How do you turn 57,000 former militants into model citizens. *Vice News*. Retrieved from https://news.vice.com/article/how-do-you-turn-57000-former-militants-into-model-citizens.

Roth, T. (2014, November 7). After fall of Berlin wall, German reunification came with a big price tag. *The Wall Street Journal*. Retrieved from http://www.wsj.com/articles/after-fall-of-berlin-wall-german-reunification-came-with-a-big-price-tag-1415362635.

S.B./Bogota (2014, June 16). Santos wins. *The Economist*. Retrieved from http://www.economist.com/blogs/americasview/2014/06/colombias-election.

Solomon, Z. (1995). Forced intimacy: The Israeli family in the Gulf war. In Solomon, Z., *Coping with War-Induced Stress: The Gulf War and the Israel Response*. NY: Plenum Press.

Watts, J. & Brodzinsky, S. (2014, March 16). Colombia closes in on a peace deal that could end world's longest civil war. *The Guardian*. Retrieved from http://www.theguardian.com/world/2014/mar/16/colombia-brink-ending-civil-war-farc.

Yiping, C. (2011). Revisiting peace journalism with a gender lens. Media Development. Toronto, Canada: WACC Publications. Retrieved from http://www.isiswomen.org/index.php?option=com_content&view=article&id=1505:revisiting-peace-journalism-with-a-gender-len&catid=22:movements-within&Itemid=229.

· 1 1 ·

THE FUTURE

Dialogue

One of the best and most famous poets of antiquity was a woman, Sappho, who has been called the Tenth Muse, the Pride of Hellas, the Flower of the Graces, the Companion of Apollo, and The Poetess. She was the media maker of the day, born on the island of Lesbos, Greece circa 620 BCE. Her poem, Fragment III or XVI, suggests that the poet would rather see a loved one's face than to fight a battle. What is known about the poet is that she made an impact. Her lyrical poems were memorized and sung, remembered by many, and then poets through the ages have used her poems for inspiration. Sappho left a legacy that has lasted centuries: a simple act of writing poetry can influence many. A simple act of working together, media and international conflict studies, can lessen violence and encourage peace when nation states are in conflict with each other or internally.

Obstacles

There are obstacles to working toward peace when there is conflict. These include language, the media industry, journalists' mindset to include facing the past and audience's mistrust of the media. The goal of this chapter is to describe how these obstacles can be overcome and to assess how the three questions in Chapter 3 have been answered throughout the book.

Language

Language is an obstacle. Though English is the official language of the United States and English is used in many places around the world, it is not the dominant language. The UN has five languages: English, French, Spanish, Russian, and Chinese. Although travelers all around the world can piece together information using English, there is a need to have translation. Rapid translation services have been launched by Facebook as a machine translation service in 2011 and during the 2013 Egyptian uprising, Twitter launched live machine translation of Arabic-language tweets from select political leaders and news outlets. However, the on-demand models translate content only when requested. Although Wikipedia and TED both have translation programs combining machine translation with human correction, their volunteer workflows impose long delays to make material available. Project Lingua, Yeeyan.org, and Meedan.org focus on translating news coverage for citizen consumption. Even the US government's foreign press monitoring agency draws nearly half its material from English-language outlets to minimize translation costs, while the earliest warnings of the Ebola outbreak were missed because they were in French (Leetaru, 2015, para. 3–4).

Media Industry

The media industry is an obstacle when it is consolidated. There are only 10 large media conglomerates that control communications globally (Milord, 2013, para. 1). These are Comcast, The Walt Disney Company, Time Warner, Viacom, News Corp., Liberty Media, British Sky Broadcasting Group Plc, CBS, Gannett, and Bertelsman. This means that one British company, a German company and eight American companies, dominate the news information industries.

Not only are the conglomerates controlling traditional media but electronic media link up with these traditional sources for information as demonstrated in an analysis of Google News and Google Blogs by Nate Silver, a *New York Times* blogger. He found 12 companies with the most links. These are Associated Press, *New York Times*, Reuters, *Wall Street Journal*, Bloomberg News, BBC News, Agence France Presse, CNN, *Washington Post*, TMZ, Al

Jazeera, and the *Guardian* (Silver, 2011). Silver was trying to justify a pay wall for *The New York Times*, instead he verified that through the concentration of media conglomerates as well as their linkages with electronic sources, media are being controlled by fewer and fewer people.

Mindset of the Journalists

An additional obstacle for peace journalism is the mindset of the journalists actually covering conflict, whether they are a foreign correspondent or a local reporter. There are obstacles that arise from a system of media production inherited from authoritarian times, most notably so-called *soft* forms of media control (Cvetković, 2001). Other difficulties lie in the lack of resources and training necessary for quality journalism (Kuspahić, 2003). Yildiz offers the following obstacles that journalists put in the way of using peace journalism techniques (2013, p. 286–287):

- Polarize parties and form categorizations such as us-them, guilty-savior, modern world-cruel State
- Emphasize unquestionable values such as human rights, threats against world peace, the power of the army and alliance, especially in headlines and comment titles
- Use shocking elements instead of asking critical and analytical questions
- Quote experts that will not contradict the dominant ideology thereby legitimizing the existing politics and broadcasting policies
- Highlight fear, threat and violence elements by stimulating the audiences' emotions
- Accuse people who have differing opinions as being against the interest of the State thus exposing them to negative ascriptions
- Accept certain assumptions about the country, made by others, whose truth cannot be examined and then transfer news and comments according to these assumptions
- Include expressions that can create negative associations about a country, that country's regime and its people
- Support the prejudices and insulting expressions created by visual materials like photographs, comics and drawings

Journalists are trained to cover the hard news aspects first. These are timeliness, proximity, impact or consequence, novelty or rarity, conflict, human interest, and prominence. A common motto in journalism education has been: if it bleeds, it leads. Entrenched training is a major obstacle to peace journalism practices.

Facing the past is another obstacle to peace journalism. In addition to the training needed to implement peace journalism, counseling services also are needed to address traumatic experiences of journalists. In a training session conducted by the US Embassy in Kenya, reporters identified only by their media affiliation were debriefed after experiencing violence ("Conflict Sensitive Journalism Initiative," 2008). They shared the following experiences:

- I locked myself in the house for two weeks without stepping outside. It was not easy.
- I witnessed tribal politics in Kisumu, the sending away of neighbors, burning cars, blocking the roads and all manner of things. I miss my friends who left during that time.
- I saw eroded morals when parents were sending their children to loot because they believe police was not shooting children. Some were eventually killed in the mayhem.
- I still hear gunshots at certain locations. I have stopped going to those places.
- As a journalist, I do not think this is my country anymore.
- I lost a lot of friends, I could not go home for some time because I was accused of supporting other people; people were looking for me because I had not done their wish.
- A colleague tried to remove his eyes from the camera to see if it was really real what he was seeing.

Mass media play a decisive role in whether and how a society comes to terms with war crimes committed in the country's name (Bratić, 2008, Howard, 2003); however, little is known about how the mass media actually do contribute to this process of facing the past (Rose, 2005). Any meaningful process of coming to terms with the past does not happen in the courtroom alone. A failure of the general public and national elites to confront openly and publicly their country's violent past can also obstruct efforts of post-conflict democratization (Golčevski, 2013, p. 118).

Journalists interviewed made it clear that they seldom report a conflict when it is already settled and in the phase of reconciliation; the reason: short-term orientation of news, which leads to the fact that coverage ceases at some point in time when it is replaced with something newer and perceived as more interesting. Another reason for mainly covering escalated crises is the supposed interests of the audience. The journalists assume they know what their audiences expect from them. This may explain why there is no coverage of ongoing conflicts, which smolder over decades until something unexpected happens (Zillich *et al.*, 2011, p. 262).

Regaining Audience Trust

Media must win back the trust of the audiences, which can only be overturned with time and patience. Trust cannot be built in a day, but can be destroyed in a moment. How this can be achieved will be through better transparency of the information gathering process, better choices of sources, less emphasis on sensationalism and what sells, and deeper reporting on issues of importance to the public, and how to define that public. Media must change the minds of the people. UNESCO, in its Constitution, states: "Since wars begin in the minds of men, it is in the minds of men that the defense of peace must be constructed" (UNESCO Constitution, 1946). To establish peace journalism as a way to cover conflict, the minds of industry leaders, academics, traditional journalists, and new foreign correspondents must understand the benefits.

Let's Work Together

If communication is to be made across cultures, media technology can be developed so that a single search can reach across all of the world's information in all the world's languages in real time. The players involved in using and teaching media and applying peace journalism are the members of the Academy (journalism and international conflict studies professors), the industry, workers (journalists and citizen journalists), governments, and institutions. Change can happen in the way media cover conflicts in the following ways (Leetaru, 2015):

- Establish dialectic between communication and international conflict studies academics to include research, education, and action. The only way to prevent these incidents from reoccurring is to educate the people, which include the professors. State the urgency to adopt an attitude of peace journalism within the academic curriculum of media studies and how media can work within international conflict studies.

- Rethink notions of hard news values within the media industry and use of the inverted pyramid formula for reporting war and conflict. Introduce peace journalism concepts during the non-violent stage of conflict for better acceptance among the industry owners and the journalists. Adopt peace journalism as an ethical code of conduct in conflict reporting.
- Train journalists to acknowledge and to appreciate different cultures, to negotiate how they process information, to open up multiple meanings and to inspect propaganda and other self-serving representations. Then have the journalists prompt and equip national citizens to do the same thing.
- Be aware, as journalists, of framing within the texts. The stories should include story characteristics such as language, story type, and production. Journalists can also rethink expert sources as well as consider contextual variables such as how a conflict's length and intensity shape the patterns of war/peace journalism framing.

Media intuitions are only a portion of a conflict society. To shape attitudes and opinions in favor of peace, the transformation of violent conflict requires an integrated plan of action. In order to be productive, media need to accompany the other social and political institutions in their pursuit of peace building. The role of media, as Lippmann suggested in the 1920s, is not to be a substitute for inadequate social organization and institutions. Media can be only as strong as social institutions and processes. Legal, political, economic, and other social institutions must assist in transforming the conflict. The media must be understood as an integral and important segment of peace development (Bratić, 2008, p. 501).

How media may work with government institutions is part of the study conducted by Frangonikolopoulos (2010, p. 246), who suggests that on a second level, a move from confrontational to peace journalism should include research on how media can be encouraged to act as a mediator of new foreign policy discourses. It is also necessary to study the ways through which journalists can be encouraged to make constructive contributions in times of (perceived) crisis. In particular, an investigation of the methods through which journalists can develop greater knowledge and empathy is needed as to the position and the problems of the *Other*. This requires more public debate and improved contact and communication between journalists. For example, journalists from Greece, Turkey, and FYROM (Former Yugoslav Republic of

Macedonia) could establish a common Internet site or NGO, through which they could portray the anxieties and positions of their countries, while at the same time facilitating a multi-faceted communication with academics, artists, professionals, and civil society organizations. This would also allow journalists to comprehend and appreciate the subtleties across the involved populations to understand that not all members of the armed forces have *bad* intentions; and different political groups all have significant ideological differences between them, as well as different attitudes toward other involved countries. Journalists participating should learn to distinguish between these differences and, in so doing, inform citizens on resolution-orientated approaches instead of fuelling conflict (Frangonikolopoulos, 2010).

Media could be more involved in conflict resolution. Future studies should pay particular attention to the institutional, social, and psychological legacies from conflict and pre-conflict times, such as the functioning of media systems, the self-identity of journalists, and audience-held notions about representation, truth, and media authority (Golčevski *et al.*, 2013).

Alternative Journalism Models

A plethora of entrepreneurial alternatives to traditional journalistic models has emerged out of the digital shake-up within the last decade. Three models are offered here. First, there are independent journalism projects that can be used as a business model for countries all over the world. Second, an institute/NGO type firm offers long-term programs for peace building and reconciliation that can be duplicated anywhere in the world. Third, the public diplomacy model 21st Century Statecraft is offered as an example of what governments are thinking and doing related to media and conflict resolution.

Independent Journalism Projects

As an example of an independent journalism project, Canada's *The Tyee* (tie-ee) can be used as a model in other areas of the globe. The online magazine started in response to the need for regional information, the reduction of local coverage, and the perceived homogenization by the corporate owners of the media chains that service those areas. *The Tyee* is an independent online Canadian news magazine in British Columbia founded by former reporter for the *Vancouver Sun*, David Beers, who had been fired as features editor during the downsizing by the company and for speaking in opposition to the company on issues affecting British Columbia. The name of the magazine taken from the Tyee salmon—a Chinook or Spring salmon of 30 pounds or more whose name means chief or champion in the Nuu-chah-nulth language. This imagery embodies the magazine's dedication to publishing lively, informative news and views, to roam free and go where they wish as the tyee salmon do. *Tyee* articles focus on politics, culture, and life and features a blog: The Hook. The blog uses short articles and lots of crowd-sourced photography. Long-form articles also are included as features and investigative reporting pieces.

The business model for *Tyee* could easily be used in other countries: focus on local news using crowd-sourcing to cover issues the audience wants covered, sponsor the magazine using interest-group ownership, though Beers attests that editorial judgment is his and his alone, and rents desks in the newsroom to supplement the income of the magazine (space they occupy is too large for their needs but additional entrepreneurs bring a different energy to the workplace) (Beers, nd). The online magazine has celebrated more than a dozen years, garnering awards and increasing its viewers at 77 percent increments.

NGO Projects

Non-governmental organizations (NGOs) offer additional sources for peace journalism to flourish. Many NGOs are developing media projects to foster peace in conflict areas. One such institute offering long-term programs of events and training courses to inform young people about what they can do to promote peace building and reconciliation in Afghanistan is the Institute for War and Peace Reporting (IWPR). Debate moderators host a series of discussions in all 34 provinces of Afghanistan. Specially trained journalists attend all events and produce radio and print stories on the main themes. These events are then followed by a phone-in radio show to reach an even bigger audience ("Helping Afghans work towards peace," 2014). This program can be duplicated in any area where the fighting has stopped and the process of healing begins.

Government Projects

Traditional policy makers are engaging in the use of peace journalism as well. An example is the 21st Century Statecraft created during Hillary Clinton's tenure as US Secretary of State ("21st century statecraft," 2010). The program is designed to respond to shifting social powers and changes in communication flows. It is based on the fact that the majority of the world's more than two billion Internet users will be in developing countries with new markets and new technology policies. The program is intended to address disruptive and transnational forms of social and political activism taking place as well as new forms of decentralized power reflecting fundamental shifts in the structure of information systems in modern societies. Evidence indicates a decentralization of power away from government and large institutions and toward networks of people. Barriers to entry in new markets are far lower. Millions of citizen journalists are documenting life in their countries for the whole world to see. This makes it much more difficult to maintain a large gap between the aspirations of the governed and the actions of the governing. In the era of digital media, governments can no longer control information systems ("21st century statecraft," 2010).

The role of new media in public diplomacy has gone from virtually nonexistent to standard practice. Perhaps the most high profile of these engagements was a question/answer session with Egyptian bloggers on the Arabic social media platform masrawi.com in the spring of 2011, during which more than 6,500 Egyptian youth submitted questions. This, according to the website, is the beginning of a new era in diplomatic engagement that dramatically broadens global participation ("21st century statecraft," 2010). This program does not just mean using the technology—it means listening to what people are saying. Social media affords the opportunity to better understand events on the ground and the perspective of citizens around the world, which bring greater richness to diplomatic engagements ("21st century statecraft," 2010). Though this may be a biased model from a Western perspective, it does offer a synthesis of what other industrialized countries and developing countries are thinking and reacting to with their public diplomacy challenges.

Positive uses of mass communication channels in the reconciliation of post-conflict societies are seldom recorded. In the last 15 years, practitioners from international government agencies and non-profit organizations have conducted such media projects in support of conflict transformation. The Bosnian television network OBN, the Burundian production Studio Ijambo, Cambodian radio UNTAC and the Israeli/Palestinian Sesame Street project are just some examples of this innovative application (Bratić, 2008, p. 487). Programs have been created but more needs to be done if peace is to be realized.

World Peace

Peace journalism faces several challenges—some of them daunting—but not without hope, especially since the call for peace journalism is coming from those who are working in conflict situations and are witnessing crimes against humanity. Second, peace journalism can bring together journalists, peace workers, and academics on one platform thus strengthening their voices. Third, none of the above-mentioned challenges are insurmountable given time, patience and dedication from the journalists, practitioners and academicians who are committed to peace concepts. Ultimately, history teaches us, peace does not come without a price and like all good things; it is worth waiting for (Aslam, 2011, p. 7).

What is peace? Peace is being able to live and work in a safe world—a world where conflict happens but is negotiated and solved without violence. Journalists' role in achieving a more peaceful world is to cover conflict in ways that will foster peace and not ferment conflict. The culture of peace is one where values, attitudes, and behaviors reflect and inspire social interaction and sharing based on the principles of freedom, justice, and democracy, all human rights, tolerance and solidarity, that rejects violence and endeavors to prevent conflicts by tackling the root causes to solve problems through dialogue and negotiation and that guarantees the full exercise of all rights and the means to participate fully in the development process of their society.

Within that culture of peace, journalism values, attitudes, and behaviors referred to as truth, objectivity, and transparency, can reflect and inspire social interaction and sharing because journalists are taught that the principles of freedom, justice, and democracy begin with a free press. To support human rights, tolerance and solidarity, journalists can report on all sides of the conflict, report the root causes of the conflict, encourage dialogue with all the stakeholders and audiences to allow the people to solve their problems through dialogue and negotiation.

Peace journalism is a paradigm through which this can be achieved. Peace journalism is when editors and reporters make choices of what to report and how to report it that create opportunities for society at large to consider and value nonviolent responses to conflict. Though peace journalism has been judged as advocacy journalism, it is not. The roots of peace journalism can be traced to the pacifist debates. Peace journalism today, as used in projects by industry, journalists, governments, and NGOs/institutions, gives evidence that this is an idea for which the time has come. The paradigm shift of who is the *public* supports the theoretical basis to explore how things fit together rather than providing an all-encompassing single explanation of a universal reality. Traditional normative theories look at what media and journalists should be doing to cover conflict; a rethinking of who is the public in light of the proliferation of social media and the advancement of the citizen journalists and what media and journalists should be doing to cover conflict can be defined as *the calling card* of peace journalism.

In chapter 3, the following questions were asked to tie the theoretical concepts into the books' argument of peace through media:

- Can journalists make sense of the issues surrounding conflict and help minimize harm through their reporting?
- Given that cultures vary, should media houses and/or journalists be regulated when covering conflict to adhere to international practices?
- How do governments and institutions impact how conflicts are covered?

To answer question one, evidence was offered as to how journalists make sense of the issues causing conflicts. Journalists need to communicate the differences of cultures and know how journalists work in different cultures. This can be accomplished through language, an analytical approach, and by thinking about the other populations affected by a given conflict: women, children, elderly, disabled, persons identifying as something other than strictly heterosexual, religious affiliation, ethnicity, and internally displaced persons. Journalists can help minimize harm through their reporting by first understanding violence and the nature of contemporary warfare. This includes understanding how media have been covering violence of *them vs. us* to include structural and cultural violence.

To answer question two, should media houses and/or journalists be regulated is a strong *no* but with a codicil: with the growing number of citizen journalists, social media platforms, training, and intentional action are necessary for journalists covering conflict. Laws and regulations may pave the way for authoritarian and dictator regimes to enforce even stricter rules, which will further hinder the work of media workers and not allow societies transitioning into democracies to flourish. Media organizations and journalists need to be free to set their own criteria for reporting conflict. This has worked with the film and record industries; it can work for journalists covering international conflicts. While some societies may not object to strong regulatory efforts (e.g., Rwanda), others believe that regulation should be left to the media market itself (e.g., Northern Ireland) (Bratić, 2011, p. 501). Adhering to values of truth telling and regaining trust of audiences would help when there are so many lies, biases, and propaganda campaigns that have jaded both the journalists and the audiences.

To answer question three, evidence within the book demonstrates that both governments and institutions impact how conflict is covered, but so do activists using social media and traditional journalists. Governments have restricted journalists and media, have encouraged status quo coverage, and have taken over communication corridors through their own websites, Facebook pages, public diplomacy, and bypassing traditional media delivery platforms. Institutions have created their own systems of covering conflict through social media platforms. Activists are becoming savvier in posting coverage of conflict for their advocacy point of view. Traditional journalists are using Twitter to find sources, track conflict, and manage information in areas under conflict.

There is a plan: journalists can retool and find new ways of covering conflict. There can be peace through media.

Last Word: Peace

References

Aslam, R. (2011). From challenge to hope. *Media Development*, 58(2), 3–8.

Beers, D. (nd). About us. Retrieved from http://thetyee.ca/About/Us/.

Bratić, V. (2008). Examining peace-oriented media in areas of violent conflict. *International Communication Gazette*, 70, 487–503.

Conflict Sensitive Journalism Initiative (2008). Activities Report. NPI-Africa. A Peace Resource Organization.

Cvetković, V. N. (2001). Media responsibility of politicians in Serbia. Teme, 25, 145–156.

Frangonikolopoulos, C. A. (2010). Foreign policy and the media in Greece: Marking a shift from "confrontational" to "peace" journalism. *International Journal of Media & Cultural Politics*, 243–249.

Golčevski, N., von Engelhardt, J., & Boomgaarden, H.G. (2013). Facing the past: Media framing of war crimes in post-conflict Serbia. *Media, War & Conflict*, 6(2), 117–133.

"Helping Afghans work towards peace" (2014, October 21). IWPR. Retrieved from https:/// iwpr.net/global-voices/helping-afghans-work-towards-peace.

Howard, R. (2003). Conflict-sensitive journalism. Copenhagen, Denmark: International Media Support & Institute for Media Policy & Civil Society.

Kuspahić, K. (2003). *Prime time crime: Balkan media in war and peace*. Washington, DC: United States Institute of Peace Press.

Leetaru, K. H. (2015, March 27). Looking across languages: Seeing the world through mass translation of local news. Knight Blog. Retrieved from http://www.knightfoundation. org/blogs/knightblog/2015/3/27/looking-across-languages-seeing-world-through-mass-translation-local-news/.

Milord, J. (2013, July 2). The world's 10 largest media conglomerates. *Elite Daily*. Retrieved from http://elitedaily.com/money/the-worlds-10-largest-media-conglomerates/.

Silver, N. (2011). FiveThirtyEight, New York Times Blogger. Retrieved from http:// fivethirtyeight.blogs.nytimes.com/2011/03/24/a-note-to-our-readers-on-the-times-pay-model-and-the-economics-of-reporting/?_r=0.

"21st century statecraft" (2010). U.S. Department of State. Diplomacy in action. Retrieved from http://www.state.gov/statecraft/overview/index.htm.

UNESCO Constitution (1946).Retrieved from http://portal.unesco.org/en/ev.php-URL_ ID=15244&URL_DO=DO_TOPIC&URL_SECTION=201.html.

Yildiz (2013). An attitude analysis of the Turkish media before the Iraq intervention and peace journalism: Examples from Milliyet, Cumhuriyet and Zaman newspapers. Retrieved from http://globalmediajournaltr.yeditepe.edu.tr/makaleler/GMJ_6._sayi_Bahar_2013/pdf/ Yildiz.pdf.

Zillich, A. F., Göbbel, R, Stengel, K., Maier, M., & Ruhrmann, G. (2011). Proactive crisis communication? News coverage of international conflicts in German print and broadcasting media. *Media, War & Conflict*, 4(3), 251–267.

APPENDIX

Exhibit I: Peace Journalism Programs Around the World

- Park University in Parkville, Missouri, Center for Global Peace Journalism, founded by Steven Youngblood (blog: stevenyoungblood.blogspot.com)
- American Council on Education Internationalization Collaborative Advisory County
- Carnegie Corporation of New York, grants to promote international peace and to advance education and knowledge
- Transend Peace University, courses on peace-building media, theory and practice at the University of Sydney, Australia
- Conflict and Peace Forum, established October 2000 to strengthen the knowledge base and analytical capacity of the United Nations in conflict prevention and management, peacemaking, and peace building
- American University in Washington, D.C., international journalism specialty to its graduate curriculum
- The Peace and Conflict Journalism Network (PECOJON)—Philippines, Jeanette C. Patindol

- Peace Projects is a grant program launched by The Journalists and Writers Foundation (JWF) to support innovative conflict resolution and peace building projects focused on preventing, managing and resolving violent conflict and promoting post-conflict peace building. Located in Istanbul, Turkey with offices in Ankara, Turkey and New York, NY
- Reporting the World publication includes a series of occasional papers, articles and booklets, contact editor@peacejournalism.org
- Center for Intercultural Dialogue and Translation (CIDT) builds bridges of understanding between the Arab and Western world through analysis of news from these regions published in the Arab West Report located in Cairo, Egypt
- Afghan Voices, a 6-month program for teens and people in their early 20s from different ethnic backgrounds and provinces across Afghanistan to train in journalism and digital content production in Kabul

Exhibit II: Programs Offered by Studio Ijambo

- Amasanganzira (The Crossroad of Ideas) and Express, which cover the peace process and developments in the transitional government phase
- Iteka n'ijambo (Rights and Dignity), which informs people about their human rights and follows specific cases of abuses around the country
- Wibaza iki? (What Do We Think?), which gives ordinary Burundians often ignored in political processes the chance to express their opinions, hopes, and fears about the pressing issues of the day
- Au dela des faits (Beyond the Event), which takes a step back from the Burundian conflict to examine conflicts and their transformation around the world
- Two programs that educate and spark debate about AIDS: a radio drama (Semerera, or Attention!) and a magazine program (Ndagucire agace, or A Word in Your Ear)
- Two programs that deal with women's rights and the important role that women play in peace and reconciliation (Uko bukeye, Uko bwije [From Dawn to Dusk] and Mukenyezi nturambirwe! [Women Awake!])
- A daily live youth discussion and phone-in program
- Sangwe (Welcome Back), which highlights the positive role musicians can play in the search for peace and reconciliation

- Remesha ibibondo (Give Hope for Life), which allows children to express their hopes and fears for the future
- Programs that allow elders to recount their experiences, incorporating traditional Burundian fables

Exhibit III: Examples of Conflict Sensitivity Training for Journalists

- International Media Support (Denmark) presented a series of conflict-sensitive reporting workshops and seminars for journalists in Sri Lanka in 2002 following declaration of a truce in the country's extended civil war. The program was designed to address highly unreliable and partisan reporting which was rapidly eroding public confidence in the truce, by media narrowly representing single viewpoints in the conflict.
- Search for Common Ground (USA) presented a week-long training course in Burundi in professional and conflict-sensitive reporting for radio producers and reporters from Central and East African countries which have experienced intense conflict, in 2003.
- International Media Support (Denmark) developed, in collaboration with local partner, The Nepal Press Institute, a program of conflict-sensitive training for journalists from traditionally highly politicized and competitive media outlets, who worked as teams to produce major non-partisan reports on significant national issues for simultaneous countrywide distribution in Nepal in 2003–2004.
- Internews (USA) initiated training for more than 200 radio and print journalists in handling conflict issues in their communities—to move beyond "body count" journalism—in recognition of the massively expanded but unprofessional media's opportunity to play a pivotal role in deescalating conflict in Indonesia in 2002–2003.
- International-supported Medios para la Paz (Media for Peace) has operated in Colombia since 1997 to address the difficulties of reliable reporting in the midst of violent conflict. Its activities include media professionals' support and training based on the premise that media coverage can exacerbate a conflict or help reduce it. Much of its work focuses on reporting that can have a positive impact on efforts to achieve peace.
- Search for Common Ground (USA) presented a 10-day workshop in 2005 for senior radio talk show hosts from 20 African countries to con-

sider issues in their communities. A handbook on conflict-sensitive talk-radio was produced for international use.

Exhibit IV: Institutional and NGOs Active in Conflict-Sensitive Journalism

International Media Support, Denmark

Enables local media to reduce conflict, strengthen democracy, and facilitate dialogue by supporting and promoting free and professional media. An international NGO, IMS works in 41 countries. Established in 2001 after Rwanda and the former Yugoslavia, IMS members believe media were manipulated and used as a tool to fuel violent conflict.

For more information: http://www.mediasupport.org

Panos Institute, The Netherlands

Works to insure that information is effectively used to foster public debate, pluralism, and democracy. They focus on amplifying the voices of the poor and the marginalized. Offices have opened in Zambia, Haiti, Nepal, Ethiopia, India, and Paris, with West Africa and Eastern Africa becoming independent institutes. Created by British journalist, John Tinker, in 1974.

For more information: http://www.panosnetwork.org

Press Now, Amsterdam

In the early 1990s, the Balkan wars gave rise to Press Now, an initiative with broad Dutch journalist and government support. Press Now provided both ideological and material aid to the free media in former Yugoslavia. The initiative was adopted and funded by the European Union. Dozens of newspapers, magazines, and radio and television stations in former Yugoslavia were thus able to publicize dissenting opinions during the depressing years of armed conflict and civil war. Following the end of the Balkan wars, Press Now extended its operations to other war zones and is now a professional NGO.

For more information: http://www.iisg.nl/collections/pressnow/index.php

Institute for War and Peace Reporting, London

IWPR supports local reporters, citizen journalists, and civil society activists in three dozen countries in conflict, crisis, and transition around the world. We contribute to peace and good governance by strengthening the ability of media and civil society to speak out. We do this by training, mentoring and providing platforms for professional and citizen reporters; building up the institutional capacity of media and civic groups; and working with independent and official partners to remove barriers to free expression, robust public debate, and citizen engagement.

For more information: https://www.iwpr.net/

Internews Network, Arcate, USA

Internews is an international non-profit organization whose mission is to empower local media worldwide to give people the news and information they need, the ability to connect and the means to make their voices heard.

For more information: http://www.internews.org/

IMPACS (Institute for Media, Policy and Civil Society), Vancouver, BC

To convene the communication and media development, social and behavioral change community for more effective local, national, and international development action. People and organizations are more effective, efficient and work at greater scale when they increasingly:

- access the knowledge (including research data) they need when they need it;
- identify the people and organizations that can help them address their particular issues when they need them;
- develop critical peer review and support relationships with the support network they develop;
- initiate partnerships with other agencies for joint action on common issues; and
- contribute their strategic thinking for critical review by others and critically review the strategic thinking of others.

For more information:
http://www.comminit.com/global/content/overview-communication-initiative

Swisspeace KOFF Centre for Peacebuilding

Swisspeace is a practice-oriented peace research institute. It carries out research on violent conflicts and their peaceful transformation. The institute aims to build the peacebuilding capacities of Swiss and international organizations by providing trainings, space for networking and exchange of experiences. It also shapes political and academic discourse on peace policy issues at the national and international level through publications, workshops, and conferences. Swisspeace, therefore, promotes knowledge transfer between researchers and practitioners. Swisspeace was founded in 1988 as the Swiss Peace Foundation in order to promote independent peace research in Switzerland. Today, the foundation employs about 50 staff members. Its most important donors are the Swiss Federal Department of Foreign Affairs, the Swiss National Science Foundation, the United Nations and since 2015 Swisslos Basel. Swisspeace is an associated institute of the University of Basel, member of the Swiss Academy of Humanities and Social Sciences.

For more information: http://www.swisspeace.ch/

Transcend, London

The Transcend Peace University, TPU is an all-online university, currently headed by Prof. Dr. Johan Galtung, widely recognized as the core founding-figure of the academic discipline of peace-studies. Our interdisciplinary courses are designed to cover issues pertaining to peace and development studies.

For more information: https://www.transcend.org/tpu/

UNESCO, Paris

Institutional media development: UNESCO gives high priority to strengthening the capacities of communication institutions, improving awareness about the necessity of freedom of expression, and raising awareness of the public on the utilization of available communication resources.

For more information: http://www.unesco.org/new/en/communication-and-informaton

Friedrich-Ebert-Stiftung, Bonn, Germany

The Friedrich-Ebert-Stiftung is a nonprofit German political foundation committed to the advancement of public policy issues in the spirit of the basic values of social democracy through education, research, and international cooperation. The foundation, headquartered in Bonn and Berlin, was founded in 1925 and is named after Friedrich Ebert, Germany's first democratically elected president. Today, the Friedrich Ebert Foundation has 6 adult education centers and 13 regional offices throughout Germany, maintains branch offices in over 90 countries, and carries out activities in more than 100 countries. The Friedrich-Ebert-Stiftung is part of the network of German political foundations. Here are some main focal points in Germany and worldwide.

For more information: http://www.fesdc.org/content/aboutus.htm

Exhibit V: Countries with Positive Media Projects

The news is that many countries are beginning projects that include Peace Journalism. The Bosnian television network OBN, the Burundian production Studio Ijambo, Cambodian radio UNTAC and the Israeli/Palestinian "Sesame Street" project are examples of innovative application of practitioners from international government agencies and nonprofit organizations which have conducted media projects in support of conflict transformation (Bratić, 2011, p. 487).

List of countries in conflict and major peace-oriented media projects (Bratić, 2011, p. 495):

African continent	Radio for Peace Building
Angola	SFCG production studio
Burundi	Communicating Justice
	Studio Ijambo, Radio Agatashya, Radio UNMIR, Radio Okapi, Radio Isanganiro, The Hirondelle News Agency, UNHCR information campaign
Cambodia	Radio UNTAC, regulation efforts
Central African Republic	Radio MINURCA, Radio Ndeke Luka
Colombia	Medios par la Paz, organization for journalists
Democratic Republic of Congo	Communicating Justice
	Studio Ijambo, Radio Agatashya, Radio UNMIR, Radio Okapi, Radio Isanganiro, The Hirondelle News Agency, UNHCR information campaign

Indonesia/East Timor	Studio Moris Hamutuk, comic book Geng Bola Gembira
Israel/Palestine	Sesame Street Program, Rechov SumSum/Shara's SimSim, the Common Ground News Service
Liberia	STAR radio, Talking Drum Studio
	Radio talk shows for peace building: A guide/ Liberia Media Project
Northern Ireland	McCann-Erickson's Good Friday Agreement campaign, regulation of commercial press
Rwanda	Studio Ijambo, Radio Agatashya, Radio UNMIR, Radio Okapi, Radio Isanganiro, The Hirondelle News Agency, UNHCR information campaign
Senegal	Radio soap opera in Casamance region
Sierre Leone	Talking Drum Studio, UNHCR campaign, radio talk shows
Sudan	Radio Voice of Hope
Uganda	Radio talk shows
Yugoslavia (former SFRY):	Bosnia, Macedonia, Kosovo TV OBN, Radio FERN, Postujes li Zakon (Respect the Law), Dosta je (It's Enough) and Koliko jos? (How Long?) campaigns, regulation efforts (Bosnia); Nashe Maalo TV series, peace agreement media campaign (Macedonia); Radio Blue Sky Kosovo, Project SPEAR, regulation efforts (Kosovo)
Zimbabwe	Eyes on Zimbabwe

Exhibit VI: Additional Projects and Resources

Soul Beat Africa has published "Communication or conflict prevention and resolution" as reference for African nations in their plans to minimize conflict and opt for peace (Odine, 2013). Another pro peace project is the fostering freedom of expression project through the United Nations. The UNESCO office works to foster free, independent, and pluralistic media in print, broadcast and online. Media development enhances freedom of expression, and it contributes to peace, sustainability, poverty eradication, and human rights. UNESCO offers grants to promote knowledge-driven media development.

Additionally, the Rotary organization offers 50 master's degree fellowships in fields related to peace and conflict prevention and resolution. The programs last 15–24 months and require a practical internship of two to three months. The institutions are:

- Duke University and University of North Carolina at Chapel Hill, USA
- International Christian University, Japan
- University of Bradford, England
- University of Queensland, Australia
- Uppsala University, Sweden

Peace Journalism website: http://captain.park.edu/syoungblood/peace.htm

Peace Journalism resources page: http://captain.park.edu/syoungblood/pjresources.htm

Contains: Case studies, links, handouts, audio/video, etc.

Institute for War and Peace Reporting: www.iwpr.net

International Media Support, Conflict Sensitive Journalism: http://www.i–m-s.dk/

Peace Journalism Facebook group page: http://www.facebook.com/#!/group.php?gid=17063840
    3613

Youngblood's Uganda Peace Journalism Project blog: http://stevenyoungblood.blogspot.com

Journal of Peace Research: http://jpr.sagepub.com/